To: Sheila Anderson

I am proud and honored to call you my friend. You have been very helpful to my wife.

May all success go with you in the future.

Semper Fi

Fenton Baxter Jr.

11-20-2010

MEMOIRS OF A POLITICAL LEGEND

HALF A CENTURY IN KENTUCKY POLITICS 1955 – 2008

Fontaine Banks, Jr.

The Clark Group

Lexington, Kentucky

MEMOIRS OF A POLITICAL LEGEND.

For information, address The Clark Group, 250 East Short Street, Lexington, KY 40507.
800 944 3995 | www.TheClarkGroupInfo.com | info@theclarkgroupinfo.com

ISBN: 978-1-883589-90-5

Design by Kelly Elliott
Capitol photo on back cover by Sid Webb

Contents

Dedication

My memoirs are dedicated with the greatest gratitude and undying love to my family: my parents, Fontaine Banks, Sr. and Annis Crager Banks; my wife, Barbara W. Banks and her parents, James R. and Maude Williamson. And to my children and their wives, Mr. and Mrs. Fontaine Banks III and Mr. and Mrs. Robert Presley Banks. And finally to my wonderful grandchildren, Elizabeth Ann, Patrick Fontaine, Daniel Robert, and Chase Forester.

Acknowledgements

THIS MEMOIR WAS COMPILED through the hard work, long hours and dedication of Kay Hill who attempted so successfully to interpret my scratchy scribbling. I wish to thank my good friends Paul Mauer and Joe Graviss who provided valuable assistance in organizing the manuscript. And I also want to extend my sincere thanks to my friend, Alex Rose, who spent many hours arranging these memoirs and making them more readable.

I would like to acknowledge that my memoir could not have been written without the valuable years of friendship and loyal support of my many wonderful friends who are far too numerous to name. If I did attempt to name all of them, I would be certain to accidentally omit someone. Thus I decided not to attempt to make such a lengthy list. I am comforted by the fact that you know who you are.

Preface

Over the past several years, my family and friends have urged me to write my life story emphasizing those years I served as senior aide (chief of staff) to two of the greatest governors in Kentucky history, Bert T. Combs and Edward T. Breathitt. I approached this task determined to "tell it like it happened" with no hesitation in revealing the secrets of the Combs and Breathitt administrations.

My daily work with Governors Combs and Breathitt provided me with insights into Kentucky politics to which few people have been exposed. I was deeply involved in everything that took place in each of those administrations. Both governors trusted me completely and had great confidence in my ability to do the job.

I am the only Kentuckian to serve as senior aide to two consecutive governors. Governor Combs called me, "Banksie," while Governor Breathitt called me by my military title at that time, "Major."

Foreword

FONTAINE BANKS WAS NEVER one to stand timidly by on the sidelines. He has always known, as Teddy Roosevelt famously put it, that the credit belongs to the man who is actually in the arena. Fontaine has been in many arenas. To quote, he has been "marred by dust and sweat and blood" in both political and military venues (we still owe him a Purple Heart from a particularly harrowing incident in the Korean War), and he has known and truly understood both victory and defeat.

We are fortunate, then, to at last have his memoirs—to enjoy, and perhaps most importantly, to learn from. In these pages, Fontaine has kept alive important aspects of Kentucky's history not often discussed in other works. Many times it's these subtle nuances of history that add texture to the recorded events of times gone by.

As the only Kentuckian to serve two consecutive governors as chief of staff (Governors Combs and Breathitt), Fontaine's applied wisdom has been and continues to be as much a sought after commodity in state politics as are Derby tickets in May. To use another sports analogy, Fontaine Banks is Kentucky's assists leader. You can liken his relationship with past governors to that of a great point guard to great shooters. "Banks to Combs . . . Good!", "Banks to Breathitt . . . Good!" He was always there for them, giving them feeds, helping them become stars while he quietly looked on, no doubt completely at peace with his role in the game.

In addition to Governors Combs and Breathitt, Fontaine has been an invaluable advisor during the course of his astounding more than fifty-year career in government to the likes of Bobby Kennedy, Ted Kennedy, Alben Barkley, Lyndon Johnson, A.B. "Happy" Chandler, Brereton Jones, Ben Chandler, and numerous other state and local officials who have sought his guidance. Still regularly sought after by Democrats and Republicans both in the state and around the nation, this native Pike Countian is also a heavily decorated Marine Colonel, a loving and devoted husband and father, an active grandfather, a devout Methodist, and a successful entrepreneur. But most of all, I would argue, he is a successful human being.

I believe a successful person is one who finds and follows the true meaning and purpose of his life and stays true to that in good times and in bad, enjoys the journey along the way, and who, perhaps above all, helps others to follow their true purpose as well. By this definition, Fontaine Banks is one of the most successful men I've ever met.

But I'll have to take a number if I want to praise him, for there are very few Kentuckians held in as high esteem as he is today. In fact, when Fontaine asked me to write the foreword to his memoirs, my first reaction was "absolutely not." I told him he needed a real heavyweight like those whose pictures I've seen hanging on the walls of his study, his numerous lifelong friends who happen to be past governors, senators, judges—

Fontaine Banks (r) with his close friend Joe Graviss

someone with more experience and tenure with him than I have had. I was deeply moved when he said he'd given it tremendous thought and wanted me to do it. It was like an order.

I recall that Vic Fox, a retired captain in the Navy and J.A.G. Attorney, gave a toast at Fontaine's seventy-seventh birthday party in which he said that Fontaine's men so respected his leadership during his time in the Marines that, if the order was given to attack hell, Fontaine was the only C.O. the men would have followed there to do the job, and they would have won. I realize now that Fontaine gave me the order to write this foreword because every action he takes has a reason, a well thought out reason, a reason that stems from his purpose in life, his inner goodness and desire to help others. In giving me this order, he was giving me a hand, working as usual for the things he believes in – in this case, helping yet another aspiring public servant along the way. If I am able to give just a fraction of what Fontaine Banks has given in life, I will perhaps have deserved his faith in me.

At that same birthday party, given by the wonderful Judge Sara Combs at beautiful Fern Hill in Stanton, Fontaine summed up his feelings very simply—he told his friends that he feels complete because he has his church and relationship with God, his wonderful family, and his devoted friends. With the publication of his memoirs, we can all feel a little more complete knowing we have an account of the extraordinary, yet humble, life of one of Kentucky's preeminent public servants.

Thank you Fontainc, for making Kentucky an even better place to call home.

Joe Graviss
Versailles, Kentucky
June 12, 2008

Special Foreword to the Bert T. Combs Chapters

Two stories are intertwined in the story of Bert Combs as recounted by Fontaine Banks. There is the saga of a reluctant advisor, counselor, and friend to governors—Fontaine Banks, who never wanted to become personally involved in the affairs of politics. There is the odyssey of Bert Combs, a self-described "political accident," who never sought to be governor until he was recruited by the political powers of his day as the least likely to offend. Neither man would have been predicted to make a mark on the history of Kentucky. Both, especially in conjunction with one another, left a history of unparalleled progress, a rare level of integrity, and visionary public administration the likes of which we have yet to see repeated in modern history.

Early into the story, it is apparent that Bert Combs simply would not let Fontaine Banks alone to live a private life with his wife and two children. Fontaine had a promising career already in the making at IBM, seeking to dabble in politics just long enough to help elect the idealistic "little judge" from the mountains upon whom so many Kentuckians were depending to bring this state into modern times. Fontaine saw the promise, gave his utmost to get Bert Combs elected, and then sought to return to his private life as a citizen. But Governor Combs saw that Kentucky's need for Fontaine was truly greater than Fontaine's need to retire from politics. Combs simply would not take "no" for an answer, and when he called Fontaine to come to the governor's office one Monday morning, the governor never let him depart again, naming him chief of staff and considering him a most trusted advisor. Fontaine filled out the rest of his working days serving this Commonwealth with the greatest of energy and devotion in the spirit of the Combs administration. It is impossible to estimate the enormity of the sacrifice to him financially and otherwise.

Fontaine's memoir is a highly personalized insight into the character and personality of the Combs administration. In addition to chronicling the history of this extraordinary period of political ferment and social progress set in motion by an energetic and visionary governor, Fontaine has succeeded in capturing the essence of the man himself: his keen humor, his good heart, his simplicity and complexity all in one, his totally unselfish commitment to the public welfare.

Anyone who ever worked with Bert Combs was stunned by his trenchant intelligence cutting quickly to the essence of every issue as well as an insistent attention to detail. He was making history by establishing a real system of state parks, founding KET, building roads, financing long-neglected or non-existent infrastructure by modern bond issue, passing a sales tax to underwrite a veterans' bonus and to fund education, and bringing mental illness out of the shadows and into the sunshine of competent care for the desperate victims of ignorance and neglect. While tirelessly laboring on this ambitious public agenda, Combs devoted himself as well to beautification of Kentucky by a clean-up campaign and by building a floral clock, balanced off the end of the Capitol by a rose garden. (Unforgettable is Fontaine's chagrin at the political flack caused by the clock). Whether cleaning up political corruption or pigeon droppings at the Capitol, Combs was equally insistent that meticulous care be taken in every endeavor. A perfectionist himself, the governor asked of others only what he demanded of himself—with the result that a highly driven group of staff worked wonders in quietly revolutionizing Kentucky government. The tireless and beloved "Banksie" (Combs invariably had a nickname for his favorites) headed that team.

The loyalty between these two friends runs through every page. I cannot help but be reminded of Tennyson's "Idylls of the King," the poetic epic of good King Arthur, as I read Fontaine's account of the life and times of Bert Combs. The mutuality of talent and devotion is apparent with the turn of every page. He has transported me from gales of laughter to crushing heartache at the inexorable realization that this rare man has left us.

Fontaine's work is a stunning tribute to a partnership that served Kentucky admirably, an administration that neither disappointed nor disillusioned the people. It is truly a vignette of Camelot in Kentucky, paralleling the "Camelot" in Washington, D.C., that was its temporal counterpart. I could not put it down from the moment I picked it up.

I knew the man Fontaine knew. I recognized every detail of his outstanding personality; I know to be true the portrayal that Fontaine has presented for the joy and illumination of all Kentuckians. He has done more than "hold up the mirror to nature." He has resuscitated a true hero.

Sara Combs
Fern Hill
Stanton, Kentucky
June 14, 2008

(l to r) Rep. Richard Henderson; Sara Walter Combs, chief judge of Kentucky Court of Appeals; Fontaine Banks, former chief of staff; Joe Bowen; Joe Graviss; and Dale Allen, mayor of Stanton, at the unveiling of Gov. Bert T. Combs statue in Stanton, Kentucky

1 My Early Life

I WAS BORN ON May 20, 1929, at Hardy, Kentucky, which is located in the coal-mining region of Pond Creek in eastern Pike County. Pike County is the easternmost county in Kentucky. It is bordered by Martin, Floyd, Knott, and Letcher counties; by Virginia on the southeast; and by West Virginia on the northeast. The county seat is Pikeville. Topographically, the county is part of the Central Appalachian Highlands and features alternating steep, narrow ridges and narrow valleys extending in all directions. The settlements in the county are largely restricted to the valleys. The county was named for Gen. Zebulon Pike, the U.S. Army officer and explorer who discovered Pike's Peak in Colorado.

Pike County is located in the heart of the Appalachian coal fields and has been one of the principal coal producing counties in the nation beginning in 1910, almost two decades before I was born there. Mining and quarrying have continued throughout my lifetime to be by far the most important industries in the county. Many Pike Countians have been subsistence farmers, but because of the mountainous terrain and the limited amount of flat land, commercial agriculture was never an important source of income. The vast majority of income to Pike Countians has been from coal mining.

My father was Fontaine Banks. He was twenty-three years of age on the 17th of May, 1929, three days before my birth. My mother was Annis Crager Banks and she was seventeen-years-old when I was born, and did not become eighteen until September of 1929. My grandparents on my father's

Fontaine Banks, Sr., Fontaine's father

Annis Crager Banks, Fontaine's mother

side were H.D. Banks and Maggie Stevens Banks. The "H" stood for Hazador. He had started a construction company in the early 1920s and, one day in 1924, he stepped outside on the third floor of a coal tipple he was building. Frost was heavy and he slipped and fell three stories breaking his back. He lived for one month before passing away.

James Crager, Fontaine's maternal grandfather

The parents of my grandmother, Maggie Stevens, were Zachariah and Cynthia Brown Stevens. My great-grandfather died in 1924, five years before I was born, but I knew my great-grandmother. My mother's father and mother were James and Annie Burkett Crager. His father was James Crager who had been a Civil War soldier in the Confederate Army and who, upon returning to Floyd County in 1865, became a Methodist circuit rider and served in that capacity for the next thirty-five years.

Great grandmother Cynthia Brown Stephens and Great Uncle John

Robert Banks, Fontaine's paternal great grandfather

My grandparents and my great grandparents were farmers and carpenters. In 1930, my brother, Jack, was also born at Hardy. In 1931, my mother's mother, Annie Burkett Crager, died and was buried at Cow Creek in Floyd County.

Grandparents H.D. "Hazador" Banks and his wife Maggie

2 Hardy

THE EASTERN PIKE COUNTY community in which my parents settled when they married was Hardy. Hardy was a coal mining camp of about 300 people. The community was divided into three sections. Two sections, one on each end of the community, consisted of double homes with two rooms downstairs and two bedrooms upstairs. The middle section consisted of individual cottages where the families of management lived. Hardy had a large company store, a post office, another store, filling station and a pool hall. There was a six-room schoolhouse and one church.

During my early years, the most dreaded event was a coal mine accident in which one or more miners were killed. On several occasions, I was present when my father's rescue team brought out dead miners. Usually their children were my playmates. Back then I didn't think much about my father being a hero, but he was. In my estimation, anyone who is a volunteer member of a mine rescue team is a hero. The men who compose such teams are willing to risk their lives for their fellow miners. Indeed, they are willing to lay down their lives for their friends. This is true heroism. No one else can do the job of mine rescue. Not the fire department, the emergency medical services teams, no one but the mine rescue team members. Mine rescue requires special training, great courage and dedica-

Fontaine Banks (l) and his brother Jack Banks

tion to your fellow miners. Today, as I look back, I now appreciate the fact that my father was a true hero.

When I was a boy, we had lots of fun doing many things in the hills. For example, my playmates and I dug out the base of a hillside and created enough room for a tennis court. But mainly it was the mountains surrounding Hardy that were my playground. There were hundreds of large boulders to be used as forts in our games of cowboys and Indians. We loved the trees of the mountain forests especially the Paw-Paw trees. We enjoyed all the wildlife including even the snakes. We were always looking for snakes. We used the Paw Paws as weapons, but when the frost hit them they tasted like bananas—so we ate them instead of threw them. When school started, regardless of the weather, there were classes every day. Neither rain nor snow closed our school because all of us students walked just the short distance from our houses to school.

My father's sister, Boots; her husband, Vern; and her daughter, Verna Lee, also lived in Hardy. The coal mining families were all close friends. Hardy families included the Fains, Apples, Chadwicks, Duffs, Stiltners, Glovers, Vitwalks, Justices, Tacketts, Christians, Liebees, Tecomas, and the Stanleys.

In the early 1930s, during the Great Depression which struck the entire nation, my parents moved to Floyd County and lived with my father's mother for about two years. During that time, my father was caretaker for a golf course near my grandmother's home on Abbott Creek. In the summer of 1934, dad moved back to Hardy when the coal mines reopened. He began to study at the kitchen table under the overhead light. He was studying in an effort to pass the test for foreman. Dad passed the test and became a foreman for Eastern Coal Corporation. I can remember the first time he drew a hundred dollars, and how happy my father was he got to keep that dough.

Our neighbors in Hardy were Mr. and Mrs. George Stanley. They had two sons, George and John, and two daughters, Mary Frances and Josephine. Josephine was a teacher in our elementary school and Frances was a month younger than me; so we began school together at the Hardy Elementary School, a six-room school with pot belly stoves for heat and windows that reached from the floor to ceiling. We were also blessed with an outdoor privy. Two grades of the school had to be taught at the Hardy Methodist Church, which still stands today. My grade school playmates were Chubby Fain, Charles and Ted Chadwick, Fred and Steven Apple, Jimmy Stiltner, Homer Slone, Bobby Grogan, Gerald Fairchild, and a host of others.

My dad's sister, Boots, married Vernon Scott, who was a businessman in Hardy. He had a filling station and later opened a store. In the evenings and in the summer when school was out, I helped him advertise all over the eastern end of Pike County. I had a great uncle, Bill Banks, who was the brother of my grandfather, H. D. Banks. His wife was named "Ossie."

The Hardy Methodist Church was the social and spiritual center of the community. It seated about 200 people and all of those seats were filled every Sunday morning. In fact, even all the standing room was taken. For heat in the winter, the church had a pot-belly stove. Several members had received the call to preach and these lay ministers did a very good job. On Wednesday nights a prayer meeting was held which was always well attended. In the months which contained an "R" in their spelling, the men of the church would put on an oyster stew for everybody. I was eating oysters before I was three years old.

Doe Charles was the superintendent of the Sunday school and I served as his "penny-counter," as he used to call me. Of course, back in those days nobody had much money so anyone who had any put pennies into the offering plate. Sometimes I think that it's not so different today, except its quarters instead of pennies.

At an early age (I can't remember exactly how old I was) in the summer, as soon as school was out, I went to Floyd County to spend time with my grandmother Banks and grandfather Crager. They lived close to each other, only about two miles apart. I tried to help out and, while my grandmother didn't have a lot for me to do, my grandfather had more than enough. For example, I would plow the river bottom land and, if I hit a root or a rock, I would be thrown over three or four rows and the horses would stop and wait for me to get up. All the while, my grandfather would be down at the end of the row laughing at me and calling, "Get up, son, and try it again."

(1) Fontaine Banks' great great grandfather Dr. B.B. Porter

My great-grandmother Stevens had sixteen children so I am related to many people living in Floyd County today—some of whom I don't even know. Floyd County borders Pike County although it was a long way from Hardy to the homes of my grandparents. Floyd County is much like Pike County although not nearly as large, Pike County being Kentucky's largest county. Like Pike, it is located in coal country although the county also had oil and natural gas fields. The county was named in honor of John Floyd, a surveyor and pioneer explorer. Prestonsburg is the county seat, where Governor Combs practiced law.

My mother had two brothers and one sister. The sister was Bonnie and the brothers were Oakie and Woodrow. In 1947, Oakie was killed in a coal mining accident. Woodrow married Marietta Bingham and they had four children (Brenda, Barbara Ann, Bobby Fontaine and Buford) with whom I still stay in touch. My mother's sister, Bonnie, lived with us after her mother died.

I attended the Hardy Elementary School for eight years. The teachers were local folks. I remember well my first grade teacher, Mrs. Obenshain, and my second grade teacher, Josephine Stanley. Some of my other teachers were Mrs. Bevins, Mrs. Albright, Doc Runyon and Carl Ison. My memory fails me when I attempt to remember the others. As a group, they were very good teachers for that day and time. I will always be indebted to them for giving me a strong learning foundation.

My grandfather Crager passed away in 1968, while Grandmother Banks passed on in the early 1970s. My Uncle Vernon had died earlier and my Aunt Boots had cancer and passed away a few years later. My father passed away in 1979, while my mother died in 1990. Six weeks later, in 1991, my wife Barbara's father passed away.

3 Belfry High School

IN 1943, IN THE middle of World War II, after I graduated from Hardy Elementary, I attended Belfry High School. The town of Belfry was a small village that extended for about a mile along US 119 and Pond Creek approximately fourteen miles from Pikeville, but only about two miles from my home at the mining camp community of Hardy. Why the community was named "Belfry" I don't know and I don't think anyone else knows either. I am almost ashamed to say that, even though the school was only two miles from home, I and my buddies rode the bus rather than walk to school as I had done in grade school. Thus, you won't hear any of those stories from me, so frequently heard from old folks, of how I walked to school in the winter through three feet of snow compared to how easy kids have things today. No, I rode the bus and realized that I had it pretty good. Belfry was a large consolidated high school of about 600 students. Since the World War II had been raging for nearly two years, many of the boys had left school to serve in the armed services.

I had some wonderful teachers while attending Belfry. My favorite teachers were P. L. Vines, Odessa Stanley and Clarissa Williams, the librarian. Mr. L. Clyde Farley was the principal. He had a huge vocabulary and every time we did something mischievous (which was quite often), Mr. Farley would get on the public address system and order us to come to his office. While we were there, the librarian, Clarissa Williams, would drag out the "big" dictionary because she knew we bad boys would need it to understand what he had said to us. The same dictionary came out when the principal praised us too. I was one of the leaders of the Student Government Association and served as its first president. This was my first exposure to government of any kind. Little did I know that I would spend almost my whole adult life working in government service.

Mr. Vines taught math and Latin courses and I took all of them. He was a wonderful teacher who could make the dead language of Latin come back to life. For a long time, he had me speaking Latin. The Latin classes were very valuable to me as I learned much about the English language through studying the root Latin words behind so many of our English words. He was also an excellent math teacher. At lunchtime, after he had finished eating, I would go to see him and work the math problems he had assigned so he would know that I could solve them and that he could therefore safely call upon me in class.

After graduating from college and entering the Marine Corps, I came back home on military leave on one occasion and found that Mrs. Stanley was on leave herself—from Belfry High School for one week. I was drafted to teach and so I taught *A Tale of Two Cities* by Charles Dickens in her English classes for one whole week.

During my high school days at Belfry, some of my friends were Bob Vines, Clarence McCoy, Charlie Chadwick, and "Chubby" Fain. We always had girls around. There were Mary Lou O'Brien and her sister, Mae, Ruth Russell, Helen Jean Claghorn, Mary Frances Stanley, and Geraldine Fairchild. The group I grew up with and attended grade school with in Hardy went on with me to Belfry High School.

As I think back about my youth in Hardy, I fondly remember the magnificent playground that the mountains provided. We were literally surrounded by the always beautifully scenic Appalachians with the thick green forests filled with my favorite Paw-Paw trees. We had great fun killing copperhead snakes and hiding out in the mountains while playing cowboys and Indians. We would head up into the hills early in the morning and stay all day, not coming home until the sun had set behind the mountains in the west. It was a wonderful life! Back then there was no television, no drive-in movies or drive-in restaurants. But who needed such things when one had the Eastern Kentucky mountains for his playground. I was indeed a fortunate young boy.

I have been aware over these many years that perceptions of Appalachia generally and of Eastern Kentucky and Pike County in particular differ sharply. One view of it is as a place of poverty, backwardness, societal problems and strange people. Another view of the area is as a place of promise and a preserve of all those virtues and values that are, or should be, at the heart of American life. Some view the region as an economic colony where the people and the natural resources have been exploited for the benefit of other parts of the country. Still others see the area as a borderland—complex, diverse, with a mixed economy, culture, and political life. These varying perceptions are all still in vogue today. In my own personal view, there is some truth in each perception. But I have only one principal perception of Pike County and eastern Kentucky. That perception—no, to me it's more than a perception—it is reality. That reality is best described by one simple word: "home," with all the wonderful feelings that the word, "home," generates.

4 Berea College

MY TEACHER, ODESSA STANLEY, was a graduate of Berea College and her two sisters were still attending Berea when I graduated from Belfry High School. It was Odessa who convinced me to apply for admission to Berea. When it was time for me to take the entrance exams, her two sisters helped me out. It was a great day when I was told that I had been accepted for admission to Berea.

Berea College, located in Berea, Kentucky, was founded to educate former slaves and the children of the Appalachian poor. Its first classes were held in 1866, just after the end of the Civil War. The college was the creation of the Reverend John G. Fee, an evangelical, abolitionist minister from Bracken County, Kentucky. Reverend Fee moved to Madison County in which Berea is located, to land that was given to him by Cassius M. Clay, the famous abolitionist cousin of Henry Clay. Berea College became known as an Appalachian school after it became illegal in Kentucky to educate black and white students together. Berea recruited students from poor families, charged no tuition, and required all students to work in a college industry while attending Berea. The college had become well-known, not only for its excellent academics and student industries, but also as a center for the preservation of mountain crafts and traditions. The school was created as an independent, nonsectarian Christian school. I realized how fortunate I was to have this great opportunity to obtain an excellent college education.

The town of Berea is the second largest city in Madison County, Richmond being the largest, and is located between the foothills of the Cumberland Mountains and the Bluegrass plains. Berea was so named by Reverend Fee, after a town mentioned in the New Testament. When I lived in this beautiful small town, it had a population of about 5,000.

When I arrived, I had one small trunk that contained everything I owned. At 8:00 a.m., I boarded a bus in Williamson, West Virginia and rode it to

Huntington, West Virginia, where I changed for a bus headed for Lexington. Upon arriving in Lexington, I again changed buses for one bound for Knoxville, Tennessee. The bus driver let me off at Berea. It had been a long round-about ride to the college.

When I arrived, Mrs. T. P. Baker, who was the bus agent at Berea and also operated a restaurant, told me I could leave my trunk with her while I found Dean Shutt's office. I was walking across the campus just after my arrival—not knowing where I was going—when a very beautiful young lady stopped me and said, "Do you need help?" Her name was Lucy and later she became Lucy Hodges. She escorted me to the dean's office where I was informed that I had been assigned to live in Blue Ridge Hall. The dorm was on the far side of the campus. Lucy took me back to Mrs. Baker's restaurant where I picked up my trunk and proceeded to haul it all the way back to Blue Ridge Hall. Blue Ridge was a freshman dormitory and, upon arriving there, I was met by three fellow freshmen, Floyd Finch, Jim Pierman, and Arthur Willis who, I learned later, were all pre-ministerial students of the Episcopal Church. They took my trunk to my room and then insisted they show me around the campus. They had arrived early and already knew the campus. After walking me around the campus, they took me to dinner at Kentucky Hall.

I faced an enormous task that first semester of my freshman year. I had been a very good student at Belfry High School, but I had not learned how to study. I almost flunked out that first semester. I was fortunate that I had two professors who took up for me and helped me learn how to study. The second semester I worked my fool head off and made good grades. I breathed a sigh of relief. I had learned to study, made good grades and was able to stay at Berea. Dean Louis Smith, J. O. Van Hook and Elizabeth Peck

Fontaine Banks (front row - far left) with freshman classmates at Berea College

Dr. J. O. Van Hook (r) and Lt. Fontaine Banks (l) on Berea campus in April 1952

were three of my favorite professors. They took a special interest in me and virtually kept me in school in spite of myself. I will always be grateful to them for helping this poor-studying mountain boy.

At Berea, all students worked and, during the first semester, my job was working in the dish/tray room at breakfast. I arose at 5:30 a.m. and worked until 7:30 a.m. Two hours of nothing but washing dirty breakfast trays. But I was thankful for being at Berea and a job in the student industries was an important part of my learning experience there. I must have been a pretty good tray washer because, in my second semester, I received a promotion to food carrier. It was my job to carry food from the kitchen to the cafeteria. A real sharp lady, Mrs. Dick, was in charge of the cafeteria and under her authority everything had to be done perfectly. I felt good that she thought enough of my tray washing to promote me.

During my freshman year, I became active in several campus organizations including student government. In my sophomore year, I was urged by friends to run for the office of president of the Student Council. No sophomore had ever been elected president of that organization. I ran a rather unique campaign with the help of my sophomore friends. For instance, every Saturday night each sophomore male student was assigned a female student to take out on a date and talk up my candidacy. I never knew how many actually talked about my candidacy on their dates, but the result was victory. I won handily on election day. Thus I became the first sophomore ever elected president of the college's student council. It was only after my election that I began to think about what the council should be working on and how to achieve our objectives. I was learning early that getting elected is the easy part. It's governing that's difficult.

While at Berea, I continued to attend church, something many of the students did not do. I attended both the Union Church located on the college campus and the First Methodist Church in downtown Berea where Reverend Sweesy was the pastor. In my sophomore year, I continued to live at Blue Ridge Hall. In my junior year, I lived in Pearson Hall and, in my senior year, I lived in Howard Hall.

In the first few weeks of my first semester at Berea, I made a friend of a girl from Tennessee. We developed a great relationship—she was more like my sister than my girlfriend. She had no brothers and I had no sisters. So we each filled a void in the life of the other. One day she told me that there was going to be a Sadie Hawkins dance and that I was going to be asked by Rena Fern Sexton to take her to the dance. Rena was a very beautiful young lady and I was pleasantly surprised by this unexpected news. Sure enough, Rena invited me to go with her and I readily accepted. After that occasion, Rena and I dated the rest of the time I was at Berea.

When graduation time came, I had no money and was facing the draft as the Korean War had broken out. So Rena and I broke up. During my senior year, I considered becoming a minister. After giving it much thought, I applied to two seminaries and was accepted by both. Thus began one of the most critical periods in my life. I thought of little else for weeks trying to decide what to do. I took long walks across the beautiful Berea campus. When I tried to study, the big decision I had to make interfered to such a degree that I didn't know what I had read. Finally, with God's help, I made my decision. And I do mean with God's help.

One day, I finally felt the answer come to me like a Western Union telegram—a telegram from God. When the message came to me I felt an unbelievable lightness of the soul. It was as if a great weight had been lifted from my shoulders. I was not to become a minister. I quickly returned to my old self. My friends noticed and asked what had made me so happy, so cheerful, so relieved. I would have been just as relieved had the decision been to become a minister. It was the awful weight of uncertainty that had sapped my energy and taken control of my thoughts. I did not accept the appointment to either seminary and instead decided to volunteer in the United States Marine Corps.

5 The United States Marine Corps

GRADUATION FROM BEREA WAS a big occasion for me. Mother, Dad, my Uncle Vernon and Aunt Boots Scott all came down to Berea for the graduation ceremonies. Of course, my immediate future upon graduation had already been determined when I volunteered for the Marine Corps during my senior year. Just two weeks after graduation, I reported to the Parris Island Marine Recruit Depot in South Carolina.

The Marine Corps is part of the Navy, although considered a separate branch, and it provides troops for the Navy trained in land, sea and air operations. The Marine Corps is by far the toughest group of fighting men in America's armed services. The Marines have fought nobly in all American wars all the way back to the American Revolution. When I joined the Marines, the Corps had, only a few years before, played a major role in defeating the Japanese in the Pacific in World War II and was currently engaged in the war in Korea. During wartime the Marine Corps is charged with conducting all land operations essential to the successful prosecution of naval campaigns. Famous for its "*esprit de corps,*" the Marine Corps emphasizes physical fitness and intensive training. The marines are experts in counterinsurgency and guerilla warfare as well as in commando operations and amphibious warfare. I joined the Marines instead of another branch of the armed services because I wanted to see if I measured up to the best.

Fontaine Banks (center) with his Aunt Boots (left) and mom (right) at his Berea College graduation ceremony in 1951

Of course, I realized I was volunteering for the Marine

Corps in a time of war and I knew that, in all probability, I would end up in the thick of the fighting. The Korean War was an effort by the United Nations, led by the United States, to halt the march of Communism, led by Russia and China, across Eastern Europe and Asia. Korea is a peninsula bordered on the north by China and on the west by the Yellow Sea and on the east by the Sea of Japan. During most of the first half of the twentieth century, Korea had been a Japanese protectorate. Korea was finally freed from Japan at the end of World War II in 1945. But after the War, Korea was divided at the 38th parallel into two zones of occupation. A Russian zone in the north and an American zone in the south in which were established respectively, North Korea and South Korea (Republic of Korea). In 1950, North Korea invaded South Korea precipitating the Korean War. The war lasted from 1950 until an armistice was signed in July 1953. Early in the war, South Korean and American forces were nearly driven into the sea, but held on until America could build up its strength in men and supplies. Then we, under the UN flag, drove the North Koreans back across the 38th parallel. With a major victory and an end to the war in sight, the Chinese entered the war on the side of North Korea. The huge numbers of Chinese troops forced our UN forces to retreat. UN forces, under Gen. Matthew Ridgway, recovered and drove the Chinese back to the 38th parallel. Finally, a stalemate resulted and an armistice was declared with each side to remain on its side of the 38th parallel. The fighting in this war was extremely vicious with battles often fought in freezing winter conditions. It was during this conflict that I joined the Marine Corps.

Staff NCO's and officers with Fontaine Banks (third from left in the front row) at Parris Island

Parris Island, where I reported for duty, is one of the chain of the Sea Islands consisting of more than one hundred low islands off the Atlantic Coast of South Carolina, Georgia and Northern Florida. The ocean side of these islands is generally sandy while the side facing the mainland is generally marshy. The islands have a hot, humid, sub-tropical climate. Parris Island is located near Beaufort, South Carolina and has been a Marine Corps training center since 1915.

Life at Parris Island was shockingly different from anything I had experienced growing up back home or at Berea College. We recruits were awakened in the early hours of the morning long before daybreak for running and all types of exercise. By the time we marched to the mess hall for breakfast, we were already soaking wet with sweat and our clothes were wet with salt spots forming on them. The first several weeks were spent getting our bodies up to Marine Corps standards. I got into shape quickly and, in only about three weeks, I could do all the physical activities expected of me. The members of my unit quickly nicknamed me, "Colonel."

A Marine recruit must learn a lot very fast. One of the first things I learned was not to eat much, if any, lunch, but rather to drink all the fluids on the table. Those who ate a big lunch usually lost it during afternoon training. I was at Parris Island during the summer months of June, July and August when it was terribly hot and humid. The hot and humid weather was as tough on us as our drill sergeant.

U.S. Marine Corp - Platoon 18
Fontaine Banks (second row, fourth from left)

Parris Island lived up to its reputation. It was everything I had been told it was and then some. In addition to the terrific heat and humidity, the mosquitoes were everywhere and merciless while the sand fleas were huge. The training was vigorous and I lost at least a pound a day for fifteen consecutive days and my weight dropped down to a mere 150 pounds. Even though conditions were tough, I thoroughly enjoyed learning everything I was taught. While we did not receive leadership training directly, I learned much about leadership by observing the conduct of my sergeants.

After about three weeks of basic training, we were having a battalion formation on the parade field when the order was given for all college graduates to drop out. Of course, I dropped out and then they marched us all to a building where we were sent in one by one. Once inside, I faced a lieutenant colonel. Up to that point in my training, a mere corporal had been "God" to me and now here I was facing a lieutenant colonel. I was scared and awe struck. The lieutenant colonel looked me in the eye and said, "Son, you want a commission, don't you?" Of course I immediately responded, "Yes, sir." The colonel shot back at me, "Then get the hell out of here." The reason this occurred that summer was because so many lieutenants and captains in the Marine Corps had been either killed or wounded in Korea and the Corps found itself terribly short of junior officers.

In my group at Parris Island were 600 college graduates taking special training and being interviewed by psychologists and psychiatrists in order to determine if we were capable of being good Marine officers. In September, when we completed our recruit training, we were commissioned second lieutenants and sent on to Quantico Marine Base in Virginia.

As I mentioned previously, it took me only about fifteen days to become acclimated to the hot, humid weather and the never ending swarms of mosquitoes and sand fleas and other nasty, mean, biting insects. At the end of those first fifteen days, I was as sharp as I could ever be. I had lost fifteen pounds, was in great condition, and was willing and eager to take on anyone including my sergeant which, thankfully, I didn't have to do. Marine training was tough, but I enjoyed it. Four others left Berea to volunteer for the same Marine program of which I was a part. They were Hugo Miller, Stan Shrader, Dan Capps and Ted Smith. Unfortunately, Ted didn't make the grade.

During our training at Parris Island, we knew nothing about what was going on in the outside world. At the end of our training, we were given leave for the weekend. Several of us went to the Hotel De Soto in Savannah,

Georgia. There, one of the members of our group sat at the bar and drank seventeen Moscow Mules, a very strong drink. It appeared that the large number of drinks did not affect him as he continued to act normally as he sat at the bar. One of us finally told him that it was time to go to dinner. When our bar buddy turned and slid off of his barstool, he fell flat on his face and passed out. No dinner for him that night!

Upon our return from leave, on Friday of the first week of September, we all stood in formation as we were each commissioned second lieutenants. It was a proud day for me, but there was little time to celebrate as we were to report to Quantico on the following Monday morning.

Our training at Quantico began in September and extended through February. The first part of our training was conducted at Quantico's main site. Quantico had been a Marine Corps base since 1918. It is located on the Potomac River about eighteen miles northeast of Fredericksburg in Prince William County, Virginia. This place had been used as a naval base for a long time. It was first used for naval operations during the Revolutionary War so it had a long and noble history.

After our training was about half completed, we were sent to Camp Barrett which was way out in the boondocks. While at Camp Barrett, I became good friends with Brad Dillman who later became a famous movie star. I also met a young man named Bob Chambers from New York who became a very good friend of mine.

I completed my Quantico training with a good record. After Quantico I was sent to Cherry Point, South Carolina, for about six weeks of further training. While I was there, the Marine Corps decided that I was a pretty good radar officer and so they trained me in the operational use of radar, which was something completely new to me. After my radar training was successfully completed, I went home to Kentucky on leave. When I was ready to travel to the West Coast for my next assignment, my fellow Marine, Dick Griffith, offered to pick me up in Berea and then we would drive together to the West Coast in his car. While there Dick fell in love with Berea and was especially fond of Boone Tavern Inn and its great Southern food. After that, on many occasions when we talked by telephone, he always wanted to know when the two of us were going to return to Berea for another visit.

As we were driving through an evergreen forest in Arkansas, a tire blew out. As we pulled to the side of the road, three black men came out of the forest and offered to assist us in changing the tire. After helping us, they refused any payment. One of the men said, "My son is a Marine." He also said that, if in the next town we would stop at a certain store, we would receive a reduction in the price of a new tire, "... provided we told the people working there that we were Marines." We did as the men advised and, true to their prediction, the store clerk gave us a very nice discount.

Continuing our trip to the West Coast, we stayed one night in Dallas. The city was hopping as 100,000 soldiers were in town following maneuvers. Traveling across West Texas we ran into a dust storm and then, of all things, it poured down rain. We had to stop in El Paso to clean the mud off of the car. As we were traveling at night in Southern California, we suddenly detected a beautiful aroma, but we had difficulty identifying what it was. Finally, we realized it was the sweet scent of orange blossoms.

Our destination was the Santa Anna Marine Airbase located south of Los Angeles and just north of Laguna Beach. While at the Santa Anna base, it became obvious to me that one of the Marines under my command was having mental problems. As a result, I placed a document in his personnel file stating that he should never be ordered into combat. While serving in Korea about a year later, I became aware of a Marine who was charged with sleeping while on guard duty—a very serious charge. When I was informed of this situation, the name of the Marine sounded vaguely familiar and so I asked for his file. Sure enough, right there in the file was the document I had placed there the year before stating that this Marine should never be assigned to a combat zone. I called this document to the attention of his commanding officer who immediately dropped the charges and transferred the Marine to Japan, out of harm's way. To have continued to serve in Korea would have been to give this Marine the death penalty. He never knew I saved his life and possibly the lives of others who were serving in the Marine's unit.

When I got to El Toro, I immediately went to the building where they process the Marines going to Korea. The Marine officer I went to see was located far down the hallway, but he was in the hall and could see me and my friends coming. My friends stopped and sat down in the waiting room. But I went straight to the officer and told him that I wanted to go to Korea. He looked at me and said, "What's your MOS (Military Occupation Specialty)." I told him and he said, "I need three. What's the MOS of the two guys sitting out there waiting?" I told him that the MOSs of the other two were the same as mine, so he said that the three of us would be slated to go to Korea in June.

Fontaine Banks as a young Marine a week before shipping out to Korea in June 1952

Soon I received orders to go to Hawaii for thirty days of training. My training sessions began at midnight and ended at four o'clock in the morning. I was learning the operational use of radar. All the rest of each day was mine to do with as I pleased. So I slept until about noon, got up and dressed, and traveled the island and did everything I wanted to do and saw everything I wanted to see. Hawaii was an entirely different world to this young man who had spent his entire life in the mountains of eastern Kentucky.

Upon returning from my training in Hawaii, my plane landed at Travis Air Force Base in California and from there we drove to San Francisco arriving at five o'clock in the afternoon. Upon arriving, I drove to Saint Frances Square. I was wearing my summer uniform and it was so cold when I got out of the car that I had to jump back in and turn on the heater. I spent the next two weeks with my two buddies preparing to go overseas to Korea. My two buddies to this day still cuss me out every now and then for getting them assigned to Korea where the bullets were flying.

In mid-June, 1952, I boarded a troop transport in San Diego, which was headed for Korea. We were aboard ship for twelve days crossing the vast Pacific. On board were about 1,500 Marines and sailors. I was the one and only Marine Corps Officer who did not get seasick. The moment the ship pulled away from the dock, my buddy, Dick Griffith, became seasick and, as a result, all he had to eat for twelve days was a few cups of hot tea and some soda crackers. He could barely move—he had to be helped to go anywhere, even to get out of bed.

About halfway through this crossing, we sailed into a bad storm. The noise of the storm and the voices of my men yelling up on deck awakened me. I dressed quickly and hurried up on deck to find out what was happening. The ship was rocking back and forth to an alarming degree. As I climbed up the ladder to the next deck, the ship listed to starboard and I slipped losing my balance. I was staggering and falling toward the railing when, from out of the stormy night, a hand reached out from behind a large ventilator and grabbed my shirt stopping my plunge toward the rail. The saving hand belonged to my first sergeant who, like me, had come up to check on the men. He saved me from falling overboard into the dark, tossing, angry waters of the stormy Pacific. My life would surely have ended in a watery ocean grave. Sadly, my benefactor, the first sergeant, became quite ill about four months later, and was shipped back to the states. I never again heard from the man who saved my life, but I will never forget him.

The storm passed and, after twelve days, our ship landed at Yokuska, Japan, where we Marines disembarked and boarded a troop train headed for Atomi in Southern Japan near Osaka. We traveled all night—the train racing at high speed through tunnel after tunnel. It was a very dirty trip and when we arrived at Atomi the next day, the first thing we all wanted to do was to take a shower.

After spending a couple of days in Atomi, we then flew to K3 (headquarters for the Marine Corps Air Wing) Korea which was Po Hang Don, which is located about eighty miles north of Pusan. Pusan is in southeastern South Korea on the Sea of Japan. It is a major seaport and industrial center that had been the center of a beachhead held by UN forces at the beginning of the war in 1950. It was here in this tiny corner of South Korea that our troops held on for dear life, trying not to be driven into the sea, while General MacArthur made his famous landing at Inchon behind the North Korean lines relieving the pressure on Pusan.

First Lt. Fontaine Banks in Korea

Upon my arrival in K3, I was immediately notified that I would be transferred. My orders assigned me to Marine Ground Control Intercept Squadron Three whose call sign was "Doodlebug." Doodlebug was a radar installation on the Yan Dio Peninsula about ten miles up the bay from the K3 airfield.

When I arrived, I found the unit to be commanded by Lt. Col. "Red" Drew, who I quickly learned was a very fine officer. He had heard that I was coming and that I was an expert on the operational use of radar. Because of that he assigned me to S3, which was the operational office of the unit. This was normally a billet for a major and there were majors there and available, but Colonel Drew wanted me to do the work. So, as a second lieutenant, I became head of the S3 section of the Marine Ground Control Intercept Squadron 3.

My chief duty was to control the air traffic from Japan to South Korea and to direct the bombers north into the bomb line and then on to the 38th Parallel. This job was one of those "24-7" positions. The tour in the Combat Information Center was four hours long as the work was intense requiring a great deal of concentration.

We were stationed on a peninsula, Yong Dil Peninsula to be exact, which is located just north of Pusan. The main Marine Air Wing was stationed at K3 at the foot of the bay while we were at the head of the bay. Normally the staff for the squadron consisted of pilots who had completed their required number of missions and had then been assigned to K3. The commanding officers were Col. "Red" Drew, whom I previously mentioned, followed by Col. Ken Fraser who replaced Colonel Drew and finally Col. J.B. Mass who was my last and favorite commanding officer. Colonel Mass was the commanding officer during most of my time there. He was the skipper of a fighter squadron and we all called him the "Blue Leader."

One of the favorite pranks of the pilots was to take off from K3 and fly up the bay and, as they flew over our base, pull up skyward while turning on the afterburners. The noise would shake us half to death. It was the perfect way to awaken everyone in the early morning before daylight.

Fontaine Banks seated with his wife Barbara and standing behind (l-r) are Vic Fox, Effie Dixon, Don Dixon and Virginia "Ginni" Fox

Before I arrived at Magis 3, the officers had constructed an Officer's Club just off the beach on the Sea of Japan at Yung Dil Bay which was a very beautiful setting. The club had a big fireplace and this is where my friends and I usually relaxed and played chess or checkers or just sat around chatting.

One of the first duties I was assigned was to be the payroll clerk for the Korean national employees. We were about twenty miles from the main base so I would have to take a personnel carrier along with four guards armed with sub-machine guns. The payroll consisted of 1,000 Wan notes. At that time the exchange rate was 5,000 wan to the dollar. We had to fill two sea bags with notes and, when we arrived back at the base, the money smelled like rotten fish.

Security was of paramount importance so we kept guards on watch twenty-four hours a day. After about three weeks every one began to accept me as Operations Officer and they made life easy for me. They realized that I knew my business and treated them fairly.

Over the years, a group of my former Marines has kept in close contact with me. The group includes Victor Fox, Len Sweeny, Stuart Swartz, Byron Watson, Don Dixon, Joe Bailey, Bill Gay, Frank Matthews, Tom Emerson, Bill Hampton, Gary Slone and Larry Wright.

Fontaine Banks (l) receives an award from
General Pate for the best U.S. Marine Corps Reserve unit
with Captain Fuchs (r)

6 Cho-do Island

Cho-do Island is a mountain sticking out of the ocean featuring three tall peaks and one valley. The Air Force had a large radar installation located on one of the peaks. The Marines stationed a company of infantry in the valley to do security work for the Air Force.

The South Koreans had a guerilla unit of several hundred specially trained Marines and infantry stationed on the island. The guerillas used fishing boats that were propelled by Cadillac motors. Almost everywhere they went ashore on the western side of North Korea, they inflicted heavy damage. They returned to Cho-do with young girls they had captured and with the ears of the enemies they had killed. I was reminded of the scalping of pioneers by American Indians during frontier days.

The navy, using a small landing craft, brought supplies to the island on a regular basis. To get to Cho-do by air, a pilot had to cross a ridge line and then quickly descend and land on a short beach. In order to take off, a pilot had to taxi his plane as far back as possible and then, while the plane was being held back by about forty Koreans, he revved up the engine. Then, on signal, the Koreans let go and the plane almost literally jumped over the ridge line.

North Korean pilots, using small observation planes, would regularly fly from the mainland and, when at a reasonable altitude, would cut off their engines and glide over Cho-do Island while dropping small bombs. The pilots would then restart their engines and fly over the island again this time using machine guns to inflict the damage.

Cho-do was never attacked by enemy infantry units because the island was within ten minutes of hundreds of U. S. planes and warships. Before any mainland troops could reach the island, major American naval and air forces would be on the scene.

One night a North Korean plane dropped an incendiary bomb within five feet of where I was standing. Fortunately, I was able to scrape up and toss enough dirt onto the flames to extinguish them. The bomb must have been defective because its ignition rate was thankfully slow. On his second fly over, the enemy pilot dropped a bomb which, when it exploded, threw me backward. I landed on my coccyx. The sharp pain instantly let me know that it was broken. (More than half a century later, I may be awarded a Purple Heart as a result of my injury. As I write this memoir, the records are being reviewed by the Marine Corps.)

The only contact with the outside world that those of us stationed on Cho-do had was either by naval vessel or by a twin engine plane that could land on the beach. During the late summer months, a surplus of supplies was brought to the island in case the coming winter weather would not permit re-supply.

I was stationed at Cho-do twice. The first time was in the late fall of 1952, and the second time was in the late spring of 1953. The island was a very dangerous place. I must say that it was also a very lonely place to be assigned. Cho-do was 125 miles behind enemy lines located only five miles off the coast of North Korea and thirty-five miles from Pun Ying. On the first night of my second tour of duty on Cho-do, I was awakened by the sound of an enemy plane flying over. It was "Bed Check Charlie." He had flown over the island dropping several bombs and firing his machine guns as he flew by. Having been awakened by "Charlie," I ran out of the building and jumped in a hole in the ground. The next morning I found six machine gun bullets in the hole where I had dived. They were only six inches above where my head had been. My knees trembled as I realized how close I came to being shot in the head and killed. This incident reminded me of my almost being hurled overboard during the storm on my crossing of the Pacific bound for Korea. I had been spared twice and was still alive to fight another day. I had been blessed, indeed.

On my last visit to Cho-do, the aircraft I was flying in was about 600 feet above the ocean when, about ten miles out, we were fired upon by artillery. A shell hit the plane knocking out one of the engines. In order to lighten the load and keep the aircraft airborne, we threw overboard everything we could. We diverted to Kimpo where we landed safely, thanks to there being no trees near the runway. We had come in extremely low. If there had been any trees, I could have reached out the window and picked a few leafy branches.

I had two friends who were pilots, John Scarborough and Jim Faulkner. Both John and Jim were from Yazoo City, Mississippi. Jim was a nephew of the great Southern, indeed the great American novelist and short-story writer, William Faulkner who, in 1949, had just been awarded the Nobel Prize for literature. Jim and his buddy, John, flew small aircraft in an observation squadron. Once I visited them in the winter when it was bitter cold. I had to stand in front of the pot-belly stove to keep warm. While doing this, I just couldn't seem to get it right. One side of me was warm and the other cold. When I turned around I would have the same problem in reverse. I just kept turning around until I was dizzy—dizzy, but warm.

Jim Faulkner took me up in his airplane and flew me over Taylock San, a huge mountain right on the front lines. One side of the mountain had been dug out by North Korean forces. The hollowed out portion of the mountain housed an entire regiment of soldiers along with everything the regiment needed, stored right there with them inside the mountain. Across the valley from this fortress, the Marines had placed a fifty caliber machine gun and fitted it with a telescope and set it up in one of the many foxholes the Marines had dug. The machine gunners would sight in on one of the holes on the

Fontaine Banks (r) escorting Lt. Gen. Field Harris at the U.S. Marine Corps Birthday Ball in 1957

North Korean side of the mountain. The gunners would sit patiently waiting for hours at a time and, when an enemy soldier finally stuck his head up out of his hole, he would get immediately blown away with a fifty caliber slug or two imbedded deeply in his brain. You may find this surprising, but I found this gruesome activity interesting to watch.

Another interesting, but tragic incident occurred one day when my colonel and I were having lunch at the Officer's Club. A marine came in and whispered something to the colonel. He looked at me, nodded his head to the messenger and said to me, "We've got to go!" As we left the Officer's Club, he told me that an aircraft had crashed near where our unit was stationed and that a top secret piece of equipment was on board and we had to retrieve it. So when we got back to our unit, several men had formed a guard. We took five of them, each well armed, and traveled far back in the mountains. We were fortunate to locate the airplane. The aircraft had disintegrated upon impact and the pilot was in pieces. While I was retrieving the poor pilot's body parts, the colonel located the top secret equipment. It had begun to rain and we were at the summit of the mountain. We were very wet and cold as we returned down the rugged mountainside. Our troops saw us struggling down the mountain and, when we finally arrived at the Officer's Club, they had a big fire going for us. They sat us down in two chairs and brought us a bottle of tonic. It sure felt good to warm up after having successfully completed our mission. Even so, I was still troubled over the fate of the pilot whose body parts I had collected.

7 The Yalu River

DURING THE KOREAN WAR, fighters and bombers saw a great deal of action. Every day, around the clock, the U.S. Air Force flew hundreds of fighter missions over North Korea. Fighter-bombers were used only in the daylight hours, while medium bombers and B29s were used in the night.

Because of the huge number of air missions over northwest Korea, a great need existed to extend our radar coverage. The long distance involved in these missions caused our land-based radar to be ineffective. The only viable solution was ship-based radar. At this time, the early 1950s, radar was still in its infancy. Radar, however, was being developed and improved.

One day a general sent word to me that I was to travel to Inchon where I would board a destroyer that had radar. Now Inchon is a seaport city in South Korea about ten miles west of Seoul, the capital city of South Korea. Inchon was the city on South Korea's west coast where Gen. Douglas MacArthur had landed UN forces behind enemy lines in a bold and daring stroke of genius, which had changed the course of the war in our favor.

Capt. Fontaine Banks (center) receiving orders with Staff Sgt. Moffett (r)

When I arrived at Inchon, three lieutenant colonels in summer dress uniforms were there to meet me. I was dressed in Marine utilities with a forty-five pistol on my hip, mud all over my shoes, and unshaven. I looked like I had just come from the combat zone. The destroyer entered into Inchon harbor and the four of us were taken out to the ship in a small boat. When we arrived at the ship, it was great fun watching the three colonels attempting to climb up the rope ladders to board the ship. No one offered to help them although there were at least a dozen sailors and the captain watching them struggle with the rope ladders. Since I was only a junior officer, I was the last one to climb up. When my turn came and I began the ascent, immediately four or five sailors climbed down the rope ladder to help me board the ship. The captain began talking to me as soon as I came on board while ignoring the three lieutenant colonels. It was obvious that, because of my dress, the captain and the sailors thought that I was a combat Marine.

The captain told the ensign to take me to a state room, allow time for me to freshen up, and then bring me to him on the bridge of the destroyer. I was able to take a quick shower, get in a shave, and put on some clean dungarees. Then I was taken to the bridge to see the captain. What he wanted with me was to learn all about what was going on ashore. I brought him up to date as best I could.

It seems the captain took a liking to me so he invited me to target shoot with him. This was a very different kind of target shooting. When our jet fighters flew over returning from their missions, the pilots would drop any extra fuel tanks they had into the water prior to landing. The abandoned fuel tanks floated and made good targets. The captain had an M-1 rifle which we used for our target shoot. He was a good shot, and I wasn't bad myself. When hit, those fully loaded fuel tanks really blew up big. It was quite a sight and a lot of fun.

But my purpose for being on board was much more serious than a little target shooting. My purpose was to determine whether we could extend our radar coverage over North Korea. We sailed into the Yalu River three consecutive nights. The Yalu is a large river which runs between northeast China and North Korea. As our UN troops battled toward it in 1950, Chinese troops crossed the river to meet the threat thus entering the Korean War.

We were navigating in enemy waters. Unfortunately, our radar was not advanced enough to erase the land mass so we were unable to accomplish our goal. Each night, as the ship exited the river, the captain fired the ship's cannons that were loaded with white phosphorus shells. The shells were aimed at the islands near shore in order to set the grass and rushes on fire. You could see the glow from the fires for miles.

On our first night out, I was on the bridge when an ensign came and told me that the captain wanted me in the ward room. I went to the ward room and there sat the three Marine colonels with whom I had boarded the ship, along with about ten other Marine officers. They were sitting at a dining table with the captain at the head of the table and an empty seat on his right. "You sit with me," he said. So I sat down at the seat of honor. Next a huge meatloaf about two feet long, ten inches high and nearly a foot wide was brought out—I had never seen a meatloaf that big in my life. Come to think of it, I haven't seen one that big since, either. When the captain cut into it, I could see that it contained whole boiled eggs. The giant meatloaf was a tremendous treat for me. I had been on nothing but C rations for several months.

Two years later, when I returned to the U.S., I was assigned to a reserve unit at Cherry Point, North Carolina. Shortly after I arrived there, I received a message to report to the colonel. I immediately recognized him as one of the three colonels who had been on board the destroyer with me. When I reported to him, he asked, "What the hell was going on on-board that ship?"

I replied, "You guys went on-board in uniform while I went on-board in mud splattered dungarees. They thought I was an infantryman!"

Sure enough, I had received the royal treatment while the three colonels had been snubbed because the captain thought I was fresh from risking my life daily in the front lines while he believed my three companions were a bunch of prima donnas.

When my nine-month tour of duty was almost complete, I extended it by another six months, which would give me fifteen months in Korea. Having served in Korea for fifteen months, I was entitled to fly back to the U.S. rather than having to endure another twelve-day crossing of the Pacific on a troop carrier. While a much better crossing than by ship, my trip home took quite a few days. When I flew back, my plane landed at Midway Island at dawn and we had breakfast there. Midway consisted of two small islands in the central Pacific. In 1941, Midway was an American naval air and submarine base when it was attacked unsuccessfully by the Japanese. The Japanese attacked again in 1942, but again they failed. Then, in June 1942, the Battle of Midway—one of the most decisive naval battles and a turning point in the Pacific War—took place in nearby waters. The invading Japanese forces were defeated and the Japanese Navy lost four air craft carriers. I was on hallowed ground.

From Midway, we flew on to Hawaii where we remained for three days due to bad weather between Hawaii and the U.S. mainland. Finally, we were able to fly to the West Coast.

My experiences in the Korean War were a revelation to me. Before I entered the Marine Corps, this Kentucky mountain boy had seen very little of the world. The old saying is, "Join the Navy and see the world." Well, I joined the Marine Corps and saw a lot more of my country and the rest of the world than I ever expected.

As for the Korean War, it ended in 1953 in a stale mate at the 38th parallel. Many historians contend that the U.S. and the UN did not win the war. But, in my opinion, we did win. The objective of the Communists was to conquer South Korea. That objective was not attained. The forces of freedom had taken a stand against the rapid spread of Communism and halted its march, at least for a time.

I was released from active duty in the United States Marines Corps in October 1953. I returned home to eastern Kentucky to where my parent's lived. Shortly after I arrived home, I purchased a car and headed for Berea. Unfortunately, I arrived too late to enroll in graduate school that fall. So I looked around and found a job working for the Agriculture & Industrial Development Board in Frankfort. I worked there until the following June, 1954, when I entered graduate school.

I enrolled in the Southern Regional Training Program in public administration. The course consisted of completing the equivalent of a semester at each of the Universities of Alabama, Tennessee and Kentucky. My most enjoyable semester was the one I spent at the University of Alabama. The course was excellent and so were the instructors. Next I attended the University of Tennessee. I did not enjoy my stay at Tennessee because I fell ill and was feeling poorly almost the entire semester. I finished

University of Alabama Public Administration graduate students listen to a professor in 1954. Fontaine Banks seated second from right

up with a semester at UK, which I found to be enjoyable as the course was a good one and I was back in good health. When my fellow students and I completed the course at UK, we all had jobs waiting for us in Kentucky state government. Several years later, I completed a summer graduate program in Health Care Management at Cornell University, the ivy league school located in Ithaca, New York.

In December of 1954, I joined the Marine Corps Reserves in which I served for the next thirty-five years. I joined the reserves because I felt a strong duty to aid in the defense of the U.S., the greatest country in the world. I was still strong and healthy and in excellent condition to serve. I took pride in being a United States Marine officer. Although, at times, my service in Korea had placed me in harm's way, I felt it had made a man of me. I believed that I owed a life-long debt to my country and the Marine Corps and I determined to pay that debt as best I could.

I was Commander of the 61st Rifle Company in Lexington for six years and, in the last of those years, I changed from an Infantry Company to a Military Police (MP) Company. We went to summer camp each year, sometimes at the naval base in Philadelphia, sometimes at Camp LeJuene and sometimes at 29 Palms, California. At summer camp, we always had from 150 to 200 men with us and it was always a very enjoyable, but hard working two weeks. I made all of my promotions on schedule. I had made first lieutenant while I was in Korea. In December of 1954, I made captain. When I finally left the Marine Corps Reserves after thirty-five years of service, I held the rank of colonel.

Lt. Col. Fontaine Banks at the microphone with Gen. Field Harris and Captain Fuchs at the U.S. Marine Corps Birthday Ball, November 1956

8 IBM

When I completed my graduate studies, I took a position in state government in Frankfort with the Department of Education in the Division of Vocational Rehabilitation. Superintendent of Education Wendell Butler hired me. Butler had a long, successful career in Kentucky politics and government service. Hickman Baldree was the director of the division and E. P. Hilton was head of the bureau. The agency was far behind in its work and so there was more than enough for me to do. The work proved to be a very good training experience for me.

In December of 1956, however, I resigned from my job and left state government to take a position with IBM (International Business Machines) at its Lexington facility in its Personnel Department. I was the Director of Personnel Processing and Technical Recruitment. IBM had just constructed a huge electric typewriter manufacturing plant in Lexington, and brought thousands of jobs in light industry well suited for Central Kentucky, to Lexington. It was one of the most important events in the economic development of the Bluegrass Region. Prior to the arrival of IBM, the Lexington area was a rural region featuring tobacco farms and the thoroughbred industry typified by the many luxurious horse farms that dotted the Central Kentucky landscape. The only other major employer was the University of Kentucky. Thus, I was excited about being a part of this new venture of "Big Blue," as IBM was nicknamed, which at that was time the world's foremost technology company. It was a wonderful opportunity for me to get in on the "ground floor" of something really big.

After IBM had hired about 3,000 employees, I realized that the company was not hiring the right type of employees for the machine floor where the typewriters were assembled. What IBM needed were some folks who were good at working with machinery. I kept arguing with the foreman of the machine floor that he should hire "country boys" as I called them. "Country boys" were used to working with and repairing machinery. These "city" boys the company had been hiring, for the most part, didn't know where to begin. Because I had so much difficulty convincing the machine floor foreman, I went to the plant's general manager, Clair Vough. He listened attentively as I made my argument. Finally he said, "Fontaine, I'm going to call a meeting of machine floor foremen and managers and let you try to talk them into it."

When the meeting began, I explained to everyone that my "country boys" knew what they were doing when it came to handling machinery. I ended my argument by saying, "If you all will take thirty of my "country boys" and you're not satisfied with them, I'll resign my position with the company." When I said that, General Manager Vough jumped up and said, "Fontaine, you get thirty of your people ready."

I got the thirty right away and two weeks after they started to work, another meeting was called simply for the purpose of informing me that my thirty men were all doing extremely well and that it was the consensus of both the foremen and the managers that my plan was a complete success.

A short time later, I transferred from Personnel to a Methods Group. I immediately faced another major difficulty. It was a logistics problem. The Ordering Department was having a great deal of trouble getting all the necessary parts to the regional office. The first place I tackled was Kansas City. I had our Lexington plant ship a boxcar loaded with typewriters with interchangeable type styles to Kansas City. A Kansas City manager called back a few weeks later and said, "Fontaine, what's your favorite brand of bourbon? I'm going to send you a case. You solved my problem and got me out of trouble. Fontaine, you saved my job." It took awhile, but finally I was able to solve our plant's problems with other IBM locations around the country.

Little did I know, but my days at IBM were numbered and, at the beginning of 1960, I resigned to take a position with Governor Combs and his administration. I enjoyed my employment in the private sector with one of America's greatest companies. The managers at the Lexington plant were very upset at losing me and I was pulled away reluctantly, but that's a story for later chapters.

When I worked for IBM, I lived in Lexington in an apartment on South Limestone Street. My friend, Vic Fox, was one of my roommates.

During the summer of 1954, I applied to become a Mason and was accepted. I joined the Number One Lodge in Lexington as a matter of courtesy to my lodge at Stone, in Pike County. The Masons in the Lexington Fire Department gave me a diamond studded lapel pin. Fifty years later, in March 2004, I received a fifty-year pin. It's hard for me to realize that I have been a Mason for more than half a century.

9 Tying the Knot

DURING THE PERIOD FROM 1952 through 1956, Barbara Williamson from Hardy and then Belfry was attending Eastern Kentucky State College (now Eastern Kentucky University) in Richmond. Occasionally, I would drive to Richmond and drive her back to Lexington and we would have dinner together at some nice restaurant. We dated off and on throughout Barbara's college days, but nothing serious developed.

A few years later, in 1960, we renewed our friendship and fell in love. Then, in late 1960, on a trip back home to Pike County, I asked her to marry me. Thankfully, to the most important question I ever asked, Barbara answered, "Yes." Then, in January 1961, on the day John F. Kennedy was inaugurated president of the United States, I purchased a diamond ring. I then picked up my friend, Vic Fox, for moral support, and we headed for eastern Kentucky. I told Barbara that I would not give the ring to her until I had asked her father for her hand in marriage. Well, he must have known I was coming and what I wanted because he dodged me the entire morning. When I finally got him cornered, I asked him, "Jimmy, how would you like to have me for a son-in-law?"

Fontaine Banks and his wife Barbara

Apparently, this was not the best way to frame the question as his reply was, "I don't need no damned son-in-law."

Barbara was outside the door listening attentively and, when she heard her father's reply, she came running into the room and calmed down her dad. Well, to make a long story short, I gave Barbara the ring that day and, fortunately, it turned out that both families were happy about our forthcoming marriage.

There was, however, one person who was not so happy when I told him I was getting married. In fact, I had more trouble with him than I did with Barbara's father. That person was my employer at that time, Bert T. Combs, governor of the Commonwealth of Kentucky. As his chief of staff, he didn't think he could spare me since much new legislation had to be implemented at the time Barbara and I were to be married and have our honeymoon.

When I told him of my plans, the governor said very emphatically, "No, Fontaine, you can't do that! All the new legislation takes effect on July 1."

I replied, "Governor, I've already taken care of that; I've got it all covered."

Undaunted, Governor Combs said, "Banksie, you just can't do it, you can't do it."

After two weeks of not knowing and getting rather desperate, I got all the ladies in the governor's office to really give the governor a hard time.

Finally, Governor Combs came to me and said, "Get these women off my back and you can have the two weeks providing you give me a telephone number where you can be reached."

I reluctantly gave him the number and, sure enough, he called me several times during our honeymoon. Barbara just couldn't understand intruding on someone's honeymoon—I don't think she ever forgave him.

Barbara picked June 18, 1961, as our wedding date. We were married at the Belfry Methodist Church and had a lawn reception after the ceremony. It rained the whole week prior to the 18th, but Barbara's mother said for us not to worry because Sunday, our wedding day, was going to be beautiful because that's what the *Farmer's Almanac* said. Sure enough, the rainy weather moved out and Sunday was a gorgeous day. The Rev. Charles Elswick married us there in the Belfry Methodist Church.

Unfortunately for me, when it was time for the marriage ceremony to take place, I didn't really care whether or not I got married. I was a little nervous (maybe very nervous), so Barbara's Aunt Stella gave me a pill two hours before the ceremony was to take place. I didn't want to take it, but Aunt Stella was the type of woman you couldn't say "no" to. The pill was supposed to calm me down. Well, Aunt Stella's powerful tranquilizer sure did its job. During the most important ceremony of my life, I was as calm as a zombie and as white as a sheet. I was tranquil alright—I hardly remember a word that the good reverend said. However, I must have managed to answer his questions properly because the next thing I heard was, "I pronounce you man and wife." I figured he must be talking about me so I took Barbara's arm and we marched outside to the reception there on the lawn of the church.

The reception finally over, we left Belfry about 5:00 p.m. on our wedding trip. We drove to the Tennessee mountain cabin owned by Lt. Gov. Wilson Wyatt. Upon our arrival, we found the cabin well stocked with food and drink. After two or three days, the weather suddenly turned cold, so we left the cabin the lieutenant governor had so generously provided for us and headed for Daytona Beach, Florida, where we spent the remaining days of our honeymoon.

After two wonderful weeks with my beautiful bride, we returned to Frankfort. Early the next morning I received a call from the governor to come to the Governor's Mansion at once. Again, it was difficult for Barbara to understand the governor's intrusions, but, in the end, it all worked out.

10 Bert Combs & Me: An Overview of a Reluctant Partnership

THE FAMILIES OF BOTH of my parents were from Floyd County. They were friends of and political supporters of Bert Combs who was practicing law in Prestonsburg, the county seat of Floyd County. From time to time they would bring him up to date with regard to me and my activities. I did not actually meet Bert Combs until early in his 1955 campaign for governor. When I met him I was working in the Kentucky Department of Education having just finished my graduate studies in public administration.

Bert T. Combs was born August 13, 1911, in Clay County. Thus, he was considerably older than me, almost eighteen years older (I having been born May 20, 1929). Combs attended a two-room schoolhouse and later rode a pony to get to high school. A very bright boy, he finished high school at age fifteen. After graduating from the local high school, he attended college and law school intermittently over a ten-year period before receiving his law degree from the University of Kentucky in 1937. He financed his studies by working at odd jobs and by working full time for three years as a Highway Department clerk. Shortly after graduation, he began practicing law in Prestonsburg. He married Mabel Hall in 1937, the year of his law school graduation. After their divorce in 1969, he married Helen Clark Rechtin.

With the advent of World War II, Combs volunteered for the army and rose from private to captain before his discharge in 1946. He returned to Prestonsburg after the war and expanded his law practice. At this time he seemed only moderately interested in politics. He served as city attorney in 1950 and as commonwealth attorney the following year. In April 1951, Gov. Lawrence Wetherby appointed him to fill a vacant seat on the Kentucky Court of Appeals, then Kentucky's highest court. Later that same year, Combs won election to a full eight-year term.

After serving four years on the high court bench, in 1955, leaders of the dominant state Democratic faction chose him from the court's relative obscurity to lead their ticket in the primary against former Gov. A. B. "Happy" Chandler.

I began to visit campaign headquarters and, after several visits, one day Bert Combs asked to meet with me privately. We had a good talk and, after that first meeting, we met many times during the campaign. During these private meetings we discussed many subjects including the momentum of the campaign, issues, political personalities, speech content, and his demeanor on the campaign trail. He requested that I always be open and honest with him in my opinions and never hesitate to tell him my true thoughts—favorable or unfavorable. By the end of the 1955 campaign, we had developed an excellent working relationship. It was a relationship of complete trust and total respect for each other.

Also, by the end of the 1955 primary campaign, I realized that I had a knack for politics. I had not studied politics in school or read books about politics. I had no interest in making a career of politics, but I seemed to take to it right away. I seemed to have a feel for the right and timely thing to do. Bert Combs recognized my aptitude for politics even before I did. He placed a tremendous amount of faith in such a young, inexperienced campaign worker. Combs was an excellent judge of people and their abilities. He also could quickly size up whether you were a person to be trusted. He recognized his need for a few trustworthy and loyal friends and advisors. I was pleased and proud to be counted among them.

After Chandler defeated him in the 1955 primary, Combs and I had little contact during the period 1956-1958. Then, early in Combs' 1959 campaign for governor, he met with me and we renewed our working relationship. By this time, I had already begun to research issues such as the merits of a merit system for state employees, problems with veterans' homes, budget weaknesses, and personnel staffing. We spent a great deal of time together discussing the mistakes of the 1955 campaign and resolving not to repeat them.

As soon as Wilson Wyatt announced his candidacy for governor in 1959, I told Combs that we had to get him out of the campaign. Wyatt, a successful Louisville attorney, would have been a formidable candidate and a tough opponent. Several years later, Combs told me that I had been the first person to suggest to him that he offer Wyatt the lieutenant governor position and that they then run together as a ticket. This may have been the most important single piece of advice I ever gave Combs. In the final analysis it was instrumental in enabling him to become governor.

During the 1959 campaign, Bert Combs and I continued our practice of meeting privately to discuss all aspects of the campaign. We had discussions while walking the streets of Louisville, riding in automobiles and airplanes, or enjoying a drink at the bar of the Seelbach Hotel in Louisville. By general election day in November 1959, Bert Combs and I trusted each other completely, had total respect for each other, and greatly depended upon the opinion of the other.

As a result, Combs fully expected me to take part in his administration. At no time during the campaign, however, did he and I discuss this point. He was completely confident—in fact, he took it for granted—that I would be there working with him. He did not realize that I had no plans to become a state employee. When Governor Combs finally realized my intentions, he was extremely disappointed. On two separate occasions he attempted to convince me to join his administration. He made a third attempt and I grudgingly agreed. I reported to work in Frankfort on April 1, 1960, at the beginning of the fifth month of the Combs administration. They say the "third time is charm."

Governor Combs gave me his absolute, complete authority to do anything necessary to assist him and his administration. I maintained this authority through the final day of his term as governor. In all the years we were together, an ill word was never spoken between us.

Governor Combs loved to tease me in public. He was always playing jokes on me. My fondest memories of him are of the two of us sitting before an open fire, he with a scotch in his hand and me with a martini in my hand, just talking, talking and talking.

11 The 1955 Combs Campaign for Governor

ON JANUARY 10, 1955, Bert T. Combs announced that he would seek the gubernatorial nomination of the Democratic Party. A. B. "Happy" Chandler had already announced his candidacy for the nomination. Combs candidacy came about through circumstances outside of his control. Circumstances provided Combs with an unsolicited opportunity that would change his life, and mine also, more profoundly than either of us would have thought possible.

After the end of World War II, the Kentucky Democratic Party put factionalism behind it and established a unified party. Gov. Earle Clements was in control of the party when, in 1950, he went to the U.S. Senate to fill the seat long held by Alben Barkley. Lt. Gov. Lawrence Wetherby moved up to the governor's seat and assumed command of the state Democratic organization. Then, in 1950, Wetherby won a term in his own right and seemed to confirm Democratic Party unity and solidarity. But post World War II unity was about to come to a crashing end—Happy Chandler was back in Kentucky politics. In 1945 Chandler had resigned his U.S. Senate seat to become Commissioner of Baseball—in mid-1951 he failed to win reappointment by team owners. Chandler then turned his attention to rebuilding his political base back home in Kentucky. The Clements-Wetherby organization, however, was already well organized for 1951, so Chandler decided to focus on winning the governorship in 1955.

Chandler started campaigning immediately after Wetherby's term began. In order to win, Chandler had to break up the existing unified organization. Therefore factional division reasserted itself in Kentucky Democratic Party politics. Everyone knew that the Wetherby Administration would support someone other than Chandler, but no one knew who it would be. Everyone also knew that no matter who the candidate of the Wetherby organization was going to be, he would have a tough time defeating Chandler, a man of incomparable charm, great personality, and tremendous vote-getting power.

That was the situation in late 1954, when Governor Wetherby, Lt. Gov. Emerson "Doc" Beauchamp, and Sen. Earle Clements met at the Governor's Mansion to determine who would be most capable of defeating Chandler's challenge. After a lengthy discussion, they decided upon Bert Combs. Governor Wetherby called Combs at home in Lexington and asked him to come to Frankfort. Combs was flabbergasted at their offer to back him for governor. Combs said, "I just can't see myself as governor."

(l-r) Fontaine Banks with with Henry Ward, Gov. Lawrence Wetherby and Bob Bell

Clements replied, "I'll say to you, my friend, nobody looks like a governor until he becomes a governor." Combs asked for three days to think about it. Combs discussed it with his family and thought carefully about the opportunity. On the third day, he telephoned Governor Wetherby and accepted.

Announcing his candidacy, Combs issued a statement which read, in part, as follows:

> I have decided to seek this office because I have become convinced that a majority of the people is interested in good government and they will support a man dedicated to serving them rather than promoting his own personal political ambitions. I believe that the people of Kentucky are not satisfied with standing still and they certainly do not want to slide backwards. I'm convinced that they desire to be proud of their state and will join in moving progress forward. The opportunity to serve the people in achieving progress appeals to me.

Combs went on to indicate that, in order to be a full-time candidate, he needed to take leave without pay from the Court of Appeals. He said he planned to run a vigorous campaign. He pledged that the Minimum Foundation Program in education would have his complete support. Combs also promised to work diligently with the Kentucky Congressional Delegation to obtain more federal funding for education. He would also support further development of Kentucky's highway system, and he pledged to spare no effort to develop a mental health program and that he would promote full development of the state's economy including bringing new industries to Kentucky.

Within two weeks of announcing his candidacy, Combs decided to resign from the Court of Appeals rather than request a leave of absence without pay. I had thought that, if he lost the primary election, he would have wanted to return to the Court of Appeals. Whether Bert Combs would have been content to remain on the high court and pursue a judicial career for the rest of his working life, is not clear. I don't think he knew, himself. But, from out of the blue, came an opportunity to hold the most powerful position in the commonwealth—the one position in which a person would have an excellent chance to improve the lives of all Kentuckians, especially the less fortunate—especially the people of his native eastern Kentucky. In resigning from the Court of Appeals, Bert Combs retired from the relatively quiet existence of an appeals court judge and began a new career in the rough and tumble, no-holds-barred world of politics. Kentucky politics—politics in the state where they were, as the poet said, "the damndest."

Combs and Chandler each did an efficient job of building a campaign organization prior to the beginning of the campaign. Of course, Combs was less well-known than "Happy" Chandler, who was probably the best known Kentucky politician of the twentieth century. In order to become better known, Combs decided to tour the state making acquaintances. He took his "Get Acquainted" tour to every county west of Louisville where he was not nearly as well known as he was in eastern Kentucky. He held an organizational meeting at the Irvin S. Cobb Hotel in Paducah, where leaders in the counties of the Jackson Purchase Area provided him with an impressive display of enthusiasm.

Combs was beginning to be seen as the champion of reform. Educators and their students especially felt that way. Often, when he arrived in a community to make a campaign appearance, he would be escorted to the meeting place by the local high school band.

In the meantime, Chandler had designated Harry Lee Waterfield as his teammate to run for lieutenant governor. Waterfield had been a long-time member of the general assembly. Henry Ward, who was serving as commissioner of Conservation in the Wetherby administration, unofficially teamed up with Bert Combs. Governor Wetherby had repeatedly praised Ward for having developed the finest state parks system in the U.S.

Now that Combs was a candidate, the state Democratic Party Chairman Rumsey Taylor announced that the formal opening of the campaign would take place on June 2, in Shelbyville. Combs' Shelby County Campaign Chairman, Judge Ralph Mitchell, called attention to the fact that both Keen Johnson and Alben Barkley had opened successful statewide campaigns in Shelbyville.

At the campaign opening, an overflow crowd of about 9,000 jammed the Shelby County Fairgrounds to hear Combs speak from the bandstand. Delegations came from all over the state. On the platform with Bert Combs were many dignitaries including Sen. Earle Clements, Gov. Lawrence Wetherby, Lt. Gov. Emerson Beauchamp, Campaign Chairman Rumsey Taylor, Congressmen John Watts and Carl Perkins and Jefferson County Judge Bert VanArsdale. In his speech, Combs had the honesty and integrity to announce that an increase in taxes would be necessary in order to fund educational programs. Taking that position on taxes and standing firmly on it throughout the campaign, may have cost Combs the primary.

On the other hand, throughout the entire campaign, Chandler stated that he could finance educational programs without increasing taxes. Chandler declared that the Wetherby administration had forgotten education. In January 1955, as Chandler voiced his indignation, Combs said that the campaign should not be about the election of Bert Combs, but rather about what was good for Kentucky. He invited his listeners and supporters to call it "The Peoples' Campaign—a campaign for progress and integrity." He said state government was going to display the kind of courage and vision that would provide the answers to the problems of the unemployed and would also create new opportunities for Kentucky's boys and girls through improved educational funding. Throughout the campaign, Combs stuck closely to the proposals he had announced in his opening speech.

In the campaign, Combs major supporters included Governor Wetherby, Lieutenant Governor Beauchamp, Congressmen John Watts, Carl Perkins and William Natcher, virtually all of the elected officials of the City of Louisville and Jefferson County, state Superintendent of Public Instruction Wendell Butler and State Senator John Young Brown, Sr. Several members of the judiciary endorsed him, including all of the members of the Court of Appeals. The campaign got a tremendous boost when Senator and former Vice President Alben Barkley gave Combs a rousing endorsement while strongly attacking Chandler. Things were looking good in the Combs' camp.

Well, in the final analysis, things weren't so good after all. Happy Chandler won the primary by 18,000 votes out of more than 400,000 cast. Only eleven counties had voting machines, hence the final total would not be known for several days. However, Combs could see "the handwriting on the wall" and sent Chandler a message which said, "Congratulations and best wishes. You and the other democratic nominees have my full support in the General Election." Combs had won the First, Third, Seventh and Eighth Congressional Districts. He carried 424 precincts by a majority of 11,743, and he carried his home county by an overwhelming majority.

Combs put on a real good front during the campaign especially toward the end. I think he felt like I did. We were hopeful, but deep down we suspected we were going to have some tough problems. But anytime you spend that much time and effort campaigning for the high office of governor, you have doubts. I am sure that Combs had his, but he did a great job of keeping the rest of us up and feeling optimistic about the race.

Chandler's victory seemed to most Democratic leaders to eliminate Combs, the eastern Kentuckian, from future consideration for public office, especially the governor's office. The pundits said that the experienced Chandler had outclassed the inexperienced Combs. This was true to some extent—while Chandler was eloquent, colorful and entertaining, Combs campaigned like a judge in court, reeling off the points of his program without humor or emotion. While it was true that Combs was not the best speaker in the world, he told the voters clearly where he stood. He was probably too candid about where he stood. His early campaign statement that the state needed $25 million more than existing revenues could provide hurt him. It was a mistake and Chandler seized on it and never let go.

While much of the after-election analysis was true, I thought that in the 1955 campaign, Bert Combs laid the foundation for later success. He ran an intelligent, honest campaign and ran it with integrity. He had run against a much more experienced and better known candidate and had fallen just 18,000 votes short. While most disagreed with me, I thought the 1955 campaign experience boded well for the future. In fact, on election night itself, I felt Bert Combs was the right candidate for the 1959 race for governor. He had developed a feel for the pulse of the people. While time would prove me right, in that moment of defeat, another governor's race was the last thing Bert Combs wanted to hear about.

12 Teaming up Against "Chandlerism": The 1959 Democratic Party

On primary election night in 1955, I was with Bert Combs at the Seelbach Hotel in Louisville. As I walked down the hall fairly early in the evening, I could hear three different radio interviews: one with Governor Wetherby, one with Lieutenant Governor Beauchamp, and one with Senator Clements. Each was telling a different story and each seemed to be making excuses. I knew then that Combs was beaten. But, as I said earlier, I felt he would be in great position to win the 1959 governor's race. Even though my belief was in the distinct minority, I was confident of Combs winning the Democratic nomination in 1959.

After his defeat by Chandler in 1955, Combs returned to practicing law in Prestonsburg. He continued, however, to closely observe how state government was being operated under Governor Chandler. He supported former Governor Wetherby in his unsuccessful race for the Senate in 1956. He shared with many others the conviction that Wetherby's defeat by Republican John Sherman Cooper rested firmly on Chandler's shoulders. Combs could see Chandler's growing ambition to win the Democratic nomination for president. He noted the widening breach between Chandler and members of the General Assembly. There were very few days, however, when Combs thought of seeking the Democratic nomination for governor in 1959. Early in 1958, however, Bert Combs began to talk publicly about the failures of the Chandler Administration. He attacked Chandler for raising taxes by $3 million when he had promised no new taxes.

After attacking Chandler for violating his no-tax-increase pledge, Combs said, "... Now you are probably wondering what I'm going to do about all this. We are going to mobilize the forces of those who believe in morality, integrity, and honesty in government. We are going to gird our mettle for battle and are not going to stop fighting until the money changers are driven out of state government."

Combs made a few other similar speeches, but, on March 19, 1958, he stated that he was not ready to say whether he would once again seek the Democratic nomination for governor. Instead he said he would go to Frankfort to talk informally with anti-Chandler legislators. Combs said there was a job to do and that job was to take control of state government away from Chandler and give it back to the people who could manage it in the most efficient manner. Speculation immediately arose that Combs was coming to Frankfort to announce his intention to seek the gubernatorial nomination. After all, he had said in February that he would make a statement before the end of the current session of the General Assembly. A week later, during the final days of the session, after numerous chats and conferences with various legislators, Combs announced his candidacy for the 1959 Democratic nomination for governor.

Besides Bert Combs, Wilson Wyatt had expressed an interest in running. He announced his candidacy on April 9th. Wyatt was a popular Louisville attorney who had been mayor of Louisville during World War II. After the war, Pres. Harry Truman appointed him housing expediter in the Office of War Mobilization and Reconversion. More recently, he had managed the unsuccessful presidential campaign of Adali Stevenson (who lost to Dwight Eisenhower). Wyatt had also played a prominent role in Stevenson's unsuccessful 1956 campaign for president when Eisenhower won a second term. He had powerful supporters, for example, he was the principal counsel for Robert Worth Bingham's *Louisville Courier-Journal* and *Louisville Times,* as well as for the other Bingham family enterprises including the WHAS radio and television stations. It appeared that Wyatt would be a very formidable opponent for Combs.

As soon as Wyatt announced his candidacy for governor, I told Bert Combs that we had to get him out of the race. It was apparent to me that, if both Combs and Wyatt ran, the Chandler-backed candidate, Harry Lee Waterfield, would win the nomination. I suggested to Combs that he offer the lieutenant governor spot on the ticket to Wyatt. While in those days there was no official ticket with governor and lieutenant governor candidates combined on the ballot, a kind of unofficial ticketing of governor and lieutenant governor candidates often took place. This is what I suggested to Combs—an unofficial Combs-Wyatt ticket in the 1959 Democratic Primary.

An independent poll was soon published which showed 35 percent for Combs, 30 percent for Harry Lee Waterfield, the Chandler-backed candidate and only 15 percent for Wilson Wyatt. While that left 20 percent still undecided, I argued that the undecided voters would vote for either Combs or Waterfield, not Wyatt. We were attempting to convince Wyatt that "the handwriting was on the wall" for him as a gubernatorial candidate. Still, skillful negotiations would be required in order to get Wyatt to withdraw from the governor's race and, instead, run for lieutenant governor. After a short while, the negotiations proved successful and a pact was made creating a Combs-Wyatt unofficial ticket. The Combs-Wyatt agreement was unanimously welcomed by the anti-Chandler Democrats. The Kentucky Democratic Party also gave its approval.

As the campaigned progressed, Combs repeatedly stressed that he and Wilson Wyatt were such a great team that the election and the inauguration would not disturb their planning for improvements in state government. They would hit the ground running. Combs planned that Wyatt be a full-time lieutenant governor particularly utilizing his skills in connection with the administration's economic development plans.

The following is a joint statement of principles and promises issued by Combs and Wyatt:

1. Enactment of a merit system for state employees;
2. Putting an end to the Chandler assessment of city employees for campaign contributions (the so-called "two percent for Happy");
3. Enactment of election law reform;
4. Abolition of the unit rules of the Kentucky delegates to the Presidential Nominating Convention and allowing each delegate to vote according to his preference;
5. Judicial reform;
6. Interstate cooperation in the form of a Rico compact;
7. Development of close, cooperative ties with the state's Congressional Delegation;
8. Establishment of an Industrial Research Bureau;
9. Abolition of the Court of Claims;
10. Abolition of the Highway Advisory Board;
11. Increased support for education;
12. Highway construction on an "as needed" basis only;
13. Development of adequate programs for bringing new businesses to Kentucky;

14. Support for the State Fair; and
15. Improvements in agriculture.

The Chandler-backed candidate, Harry Lee Waterfield, was a western Kentucky politician, newspaper publisher, and farmer. He had lived most of his life in the Purchase region. He published five western Kentucky newspapers and had served as president of the Kentucky Press Association. Wyatt was a noted shorthorn cattle breeder and was well known for practicing modern conservation methods in his farming operation. He had entered politics in 1937, winning election to the Kentucky House, and then he was Speaker of the House in 1944 and 1946. He led the drive to create the Legislative Research Commission to serve as the monitor of government activities between General Assembly sessions.

In 1947, Waterfield was unsuccessful in an attempt to become governor. He lost to Earle Clements by 32,000 votes in the primary. In 1955, he ran successfully for lieutenant governor on the ticket with "Happy" Chandler. So, in 1959, he entered the governor's race while he was the sitting lieutenant governor and with Chandler's backing. Waterfield was a popular and dangerous opponent.

During the campaign, both Combs and Wyatt, now teamed, and other anti-Chandler Democrats, denounced "Chandlerism" at every opportunity. The term, "Chandlerism," meant corruption in state government. What the term meant specifically was, at least partially, spelled out in Combs-Wyatt campaign literature. One piece of such literature was titled, "A Team You Can Trust," and contained the following statement:

> "'Chandlerism' is wringing 2% a month from state employees to finance Chandler candidates in Kentucky and "Happy for President." 'Chandlerism' is kicking Doris Owens out of office. 'Chandlerism' is ripping Henry Carter. 'Chandlerism' is moving the State Health Department from Louisville to Frankfort only because Louisville voted against Chandler. 'Chandlerism' is forcing recipients of welfare funds to attend meetings to hear Chandler speak. 'Chandlerism' is changing highway commissioners to further the political ambitions of Happy and Harry Lee. 'Chandlerism' is the degrading of our legislative branch of government by the Governor and his henchmen. 'Chandlerism' is destroying the child welfare program to serve the whims of Vego Barnes

> instead of the needs of Kentucky's children. These are just a few of the endless examples of 'Chandlerism.' In short, 'Chandlerism' is revenge, vindictiveness, hate, tyranny, hypocrisy and greed. Together we can put a stop to it."

Here's an example of "Chandlerism. Happy's political henchmen would deliver the paychecks of the state employees every payday, but before a check reached an employee's hands, Happy's 2 percent had to be forked over in cash. This accumulated quickly as a nice slush fund for a possible future run for president. Looking back, I think it may have been poetic justice that, in 1959, when Fidel Castro came to power in Cuba, he froze all the assets of Americans in Cuban banks including Happy's "2 percent fund." When Happy went to Florida to attempt to recover the funds, needless to say, he was unsuccessful. His trip, however, became a campaign issue. When Bert Combs was speaking at Keeneland, he proclaimed that Happy was heard yelling across the water in the direction of Cuba, "Castro, Castro, give me back my 2 percent." This brought the cheering crowd to its feet. I remember it well—I nearly fell out of the stands I was laughing so hard.

In Paris, at the end of the campaign, Combs said, "If I could say but one thing on my behalf to you in the closing days of this campaign, it is that I have never lied to the people of my state, never broken a promise to them, even though the course of truth has once cost me the governorship of this state."

This brings us to primary election day—May 27, 1959. I felt confident of victory that day. Bert T. Combs won the primary over Harry Lee Waterfield by 33,001 votes. That one on the end of the 33,000 was my vote. The election had not been a runaway. Voting in all the Congressional Districts had been close except in the Third District, which Combs carried by almost 30,000 votes and the First District (Waterfield's home District), which he carried by almost 6,000 votes. Combs carried his home District by almost 11,000 votes. Combs carried his own county by 3,317 out of a total of 12,973 votes cast.

In analyzing the primary election, Chandler's record as governor undermined his own credibility and hurt his candidate, Harry Lee Waterfield. Chandler had imposed various new excise taxes and imposed a sizeable increase in the state income tax in spite of his 1955 campaign promise not to raise taxes. Thus, Chandler undermined his own credibility allowing Combs to emerge as a symbol of courageous honesty for having told the voters in the 1955 primary that he needed to raise taxes.

Combs was still not a polished speaker, but his mountain twang proved pleasing to the voters, partly because they had become accustomed to it and partly because they equated it with truthfulness and forthrightness. Also, while Waterfield had a pleasing personality, he couldn't shake off his association with Chandler. Primary election night was a grand occasion at Combs headquarters—"Happy Days Were Here Again!"

13 Anti-Climax: The 1959 General Election

THE FALL CAMPAIGN WAS an anti-climax. Combs overwhelmed his Republican opponent, John Robsion, Jr., by a record margin of 180,093 votes. The final tally was Combs 516,549, Robsion 336,456. Robsion was the son of John Marshall Robsion, a former Congressman and U.S. Senator from Barbourville who had passed away in 1948.

The only real concern that we had in the fall general election was making sure that there was not supreme overconfidence. We believed that, if we got the vote out, we would win by a record majority, which is exactly what occurred. But, even so, the fall campaign wasn't as easy as the result makes the election appear. There were some rough spots.

For example, both Governor Chandler and Lieutenant Governor Waterfield dragged their feet in supporting Combs. In August, Chandler warned state employees that they would lose their jobs if they were active in the gubernatorial race. Then, in October, according to the *Cynthiana Democrat*, he said, "I'm not mad at anybody, but I am saying that Combs is the biggest liar I've seen in thirty years of politics."

Also, in October, U.S. Sen. John Sherman Cooper announced that he would campaign full time for Robsion. Senators Cooper and Thruston Morton, Congressman Eugene Siler and Robsion, himself, seemed to be banking heavily on a Democratic schism to produce a Republican victory. Undoubtedly, the so-called schism between the Combs and Chandler forces did have an effect on the results, but not enough of an effect to produce a Republican victory. The effect of the schism was that approximately 100,000 Democrats who voted in the May primary, did not go to the polls in the November election.

Even so, it was a great win for Bert Combs and the rest of the Democratic ticket. As stated above, it was a record victory margin of just over 180,000 votes. Wilson Wyatt's margin of victory over Republican Cleve Mobley

(l-r) Phillip and Phyllis Swift, Barbara and Fontaine Banks and Lt. Gov. Wilson Wyatt at a dinner in the Governor's Mansion

was even greater than Combs margin. Wyatt won the lieutenant governor's race by 191,746 votes. Like the victory margin of Combs, Wyatt's margin was a record for a lieutenant governor's election.

During the 1959 general election campaign, Combs elaborated more fully on his program for progress he had introduced earlier. Essentially, Bert Combs believed that Kentucky needed to become a progressive state. Kentucky had always been "too proud to whitewash and too poor to paint." It was time now, said Combs, for some painting to begin. He was most insistent on the issue of funding for education, stating that funding had to be increased dramatically.

Combs also said that the state must have better highways and more and better state parks. The commonwealth must recruit new industry to the state and build additional airports. Finally, a merit system should be enacted for state employees. Combs strongly felt that educational, economic and social conditions must improve to the point that no longer would Kentucky's youthful citizens leave their homes to seek better opportunities in other states. As Combs prepared to take office, the unanswered question was how to finance his program.

14 Inauguration Day

INAUGURATION DAY 1959, THE Tuesday following the first Monday in December, dawned bright and clear. The old timers would have said that the elements were smiling on the inauguration of Bert T. Combs as the Commonwealth of Kentucky's forty-eighth governor. Combs and Lt. Gov. Wilson Wyatt were inaugurated as a team just as they had campaigned as a team since the formation of their coalition. After all, it was the merger of the two men that had defeated the Chandler machine.

The many weeks of preparation involved the hard work of seventy-two committees consisting mainly of volunteer workers. James H. Nutter, assisted by Dolly Nichol, headed the inaugural activities. James Gray drew the important assignment of coordinator. By Inauguration Day the stage had been set for this quadrennial event which, at the time, was considered to be Kentucky's outstanding pageant.

The Kentucky State Police estimated the crowd watching the parade at 40,000. An estimated 10,000 watched from near the inaugural platform. The platform had been erected upon the steps in front of the Capitol. There were about 800 chairs for the seating of persons prominent in the political affairs of Kentucky and their guests. In attendance were five former governors. They were Flem D. Sampson (1927-1931), Keen Johnson (1939-1943), Simeon Willis (1943-1947), Lawrence W. Wetherby (1950-1955) and Albert Benjamin "Happy" Chandler (1935-1939; 1955-1959), the outgoing governor. Six of the commonwealth's eight congressmen were in attendance—Burt, Natcher, Perkins, Shelf, Thoroughfield, and Watts.

Frankfort Mayor, John Gerard, introduced outgoing Governor Chandler who reminded the audience of the accomplishments of his first term in office (1935-1939) and told the crowd that, in 1942, newly-elected Lt. Gov. Wilson Wyatt had praised his administration. Chandler's reference to praise from Wilson Wyatt, one of his present day critics, elicited from the crowd a mixture of laughter, cheers, boos and cackles. Then Happy declared, "There has not been during my time here a single dishonorable act in connection with the management of your affairs committed by me or any of my associates to my knowledge." This statement drew more boos and cat calls whereupon Chandler admonished the crowd for their shameful manners. Happy also said that he had left the state's budget in balance. In his inaugural address, by way of rebuttal, Combs challenged Chandler's statement about the General Fund balance saying, "Happy and I have not been talking to the same auditors." This rejoinder implied Combs' doubt about the state's financial condition as Chandler had characterized it.

Following Chandler to the podium was incoming Lt. Gov. Wilson Wyatt. This was the first inauguration that featured a speech by the new lieutenant governor. This unprecedented distinction was given in recognition of Wyatt's key role in the election of the Combs-Wyatt team—it was Combs' idea to provide time for a Wilson Wyatt speech. It was simply another of Combs' many generous acts. He was no egotist. He was more than willing to share this moment of triumph with Wyatt.

Raising their right hands and with their left hands resting on a Bible held by Combs' daughter, Lois, Bert Combs and Wilson Wyatt took the oath of office together. Immediately after the oath was administered, a field battery of the 623rd Field Artillery Battalion fired a nineteen-gun salute.

Combs opened his inaugural address by expressing felicitations to the audience and to Governor and Mrs. Chandler. Combs then quoted a few lines from a poem:

"The tumult and the shouting dies
The Captains and Kings depart,
Still stands the ancient sacrifice,
A humble and contrite heart.
Lord God our Host be with us yet,
Lest we forget,
Lest we forget."

Shortly after the inauguration ceremonies ended, Combs and Wyatt held their first press conference in the Capitol. They were met there by approximately seventy-five representatives of the media. They handled the press conference as if they were old hands at this business. As expected, most of the questions were addressed to the new governor. During the press conference, only two cabinet appointments were announced. Combs' announced that his choice to serve as adjutant general was Arthur Young Lloyd. He also stated that W. E. Bruce Kennedy was his choice to serve as the commissioner of the Department of Economic Development.

Combs also quickly let it be known that he would discard the so called Highway Advisory Commission. Combs said he would ask the 1960 General Assembly to devise a sound budget plan that could not be set aside by some future governor. He said he would keep what was good that Chandler had set up, but useless jobs would be eliminated and, of course, he would employ some in whom he had faith. On the second day of his term as governor, Combs announced about a dozen important appointments. The appointments were as follows:

- Robert Matthews of Shelbyville as his chief administrative assistant;
- Wendell Ford of Owensboro as his administrative assistant;
- Cattie Lou Miller of Horse Cave as his executive assistant;
- Dr. Robert L. Martin of Frankfort as commissioner of Finance;
- Ted Gilbert of Frankfort as superintendent of Public Instruction;
- H. E. Jones of Buechel as acting commissioner of Economic Security;
- Earle C. Clements of Morganfield as commissioner of Highways;
- E. Foster Ockerman of Lexington as commissioner of Motor Vehicle Transportation;
- Harold T. Bennett, Jr. of Hopkinsville as commissioner of Personnel;
- William E. Scent of Louisville as commissioner of Revenue (temporarily); and
- Carlos Oakley of Morgantown as commissioner of Welfare.

This was an excellent group of appointments.

Within twenty-four hours of taking the oath of office, Combs issued an Executive Order, which took the first steps toward an effective merit system for state employees. Thus, he was quickly on the way to fulfilling one of his major campaign pledges. The merit system would require legislation to fully enact it.

On December 10, Combs announced two more appointments. The first was Owen Glenn Kerr of Paducah as commissioner of Industrial Relations and, secondly, Phillip Swift of Frankfort as commissioner of Aeronautics. The Combs Cabinet was in place and his administration was ready for action—ready to make every effort to bring a lagging Commonwealth of Kentucky into the twentieth century.

And where was I? No mention had been made of an appointment for Fontaine Banks. Where was I? I'm going to save that bit of information for the next chapter.

15 Beginnings: The Combs Administration & My Unexpected Role

In December, 1959, at the time of the inauguration of Bert T. Combs as governor of the Commonwealth of Kentucky, I was very happily employed by IBM in Lexington. I held a good position with the company and I had a bright future with Big Blue. I had absolutely no plans to become a member of the Combs administration. I had played a very active and influential role in both of the Combs' campaigns and I was satisfied with that.

About two weeks after his inauguration, I received a telephone call from Governor Combs. He said he was going to be at the Phoenix Hotel in Lexington later that day and requested that I join him there. I agreed and when I joined him, I found him very upset because I had not come to work for him in Frankfort. For about half an hour the governor attempted to persuade me to come to Frankfort and work for him and be an important part of his administration. He was very insistent and used all of his lawyer persuasiveness on me, but I held my ground and told him that I could not. I told him that my plans did not call for working in his administration. Governor Combs was not used to losing an argument. He left the hotel both deeply disappointed and quite angry with me.

About a month later, the governor again called me and asked me to join his administration. He seemed to desperately want me as a member of his team. Once again, I held my ground and turned him down.

Then, in late March of 1960, Governor Combs once again called me and said, "Banksie, I want you in my office at nine o'clock tomorrow morning." Before I even had time for a single word, he hung up. He wasn't going to give me a chance to say "no." Well, on the drive from Lexington to Frankfort the next morning, I decided that, if Governor Combs asked me again to join his administration, I would go ahead and do it.

When I was ushered into the governor's office, we hadn't talked for more than a minute when he asked me again to join his administration. When I agreed, Combs looked a little surprised, but very pleased. A big smile came across his face and he said, "Banksie, thank you."

I promised to turn in my resignation at IBM the next day, but that I was required to give two weeks notice. He was willing to compromise on that point because, after all, he had gotten his way with me. He smiled again and said, "I understand."

When I resigned my job at IBM the next morning, nothing happened immediately. Then, about noon, I met with the director of personnel who said, "Fontaine, don't you know what's going on?"

I said that I didn't know anything was going on.

He said, "You mean, you don't know?"

I replied, "I don't know what?"

The director then said, "Well, all hell has broken loose over your resigning! Mr. Vough is very upset because you were his fair-haired boy."

I said, "What? I didn't know that!"

The director then said, "Mr. Vough had picked you out as being one of the future stars in this company and he wanted you to stay at IBM and work with him."

Surprised, I replied, "I didn't know that!"

He then said, "Fontaine, everybody in the plant knew that except you." He paused and then continued, "Fontaine, he's not going to take this easily."

He was right. Mr. Vough, the plant manager, was very agitated over my resignation. In fact, I had to spend my final two weeks at IBM explaining to everybody why I was leaving. Finally, after a long two weeks, I left IBM and joined the Combs administration as director of Recruitment, Placement and Training in the Department of Personnel.

Fontaine Banks and Gov. Bert Combs at the opening of the Kentucky State Fair, 1962

About two weeks after I had settled into

my new position, the phone rang and a voice said, "Banksie, come here," and then the phone went dead. I didn't know whose voice it was at first and then I thought to myself, "There's only one voice like that and it belongs to Governor Combs. He's hung up on me again."

I walked over to the governor's office where I was met at the door by Wendell Ford. He was obviously very nervous as he escorted me in to meet with the governor. Governor Combs took one look at me and said, "Banksie, they tell me that you can solve problems."

I replied, "I've solved a few in my life and I've failed to solve a few also."

The governor handed a piece of paper to me and said, "Take this list and when you get all these problems done, come back and tell me."

I looked at my watch—it was 9:00 a.m. At 2:30 that afternoon I was back at the governor's office and Wendell asked, "What are you doing back here?"

I said, "I'm here to tell the governor that I've solved those problems he gave me." He looked at me almost unbelievingly and took me into the governor's office. Combs was extremely pleased and, true to the saying, "no good deed goes unpunished," the governor gave me another list.

This continued for about two months. I would report to the governor and he would hand me a new list of problems to be solved. By mid-summer I was spending more and more time in the governor's office and less and less time in my own office in the Department of Personnel. Then one day, my phone rang and a voice just said, "Banksie, come here."

By now I was used to receiving these extremely short phone calls from Governor Combs and I hurried to his office where I was again met by Wendell Ford. Once again Wendell looked nervous and a bit upset. He then told me that the governor was in a bad mood. As I walked into the governor's office, Governor Combs jumped up from behind his desk and pointed a finger at me and said, "Banksie, why aren't you back there?"

I said, "Governor, back where? I don't know what you're talking about."

Combs glared at Wendell and Ford said haltingly, "I haven't had a chance to tell him."

Governor Combs was exasperated and almost shouting said, "Do I have to do everything around here?"

As he said this the governor grabbed me by the arm and marched me through the back door of the governor's office, through the cabinet meeting room, and straight into the office that today is used by the secretary of the cabinet. As he did this, the governor said excitedly, "Banksie, this is your office; from now on you work for me and you don't report to anybody but me."

He then turned around quickly and walked off.

I said, "Wendell, what's going on?"

He sunk down in a chair, sighed, and said, "We've had all kinds of problems and you've been the only one that's been able to solve any of them. The governor is very fond of you and wants you to be a member of his staff here in the governor's office."

Well, from that day forward I found myself in charge of all legislative affairs, in charge of personnel decisions, and in charge of all contacts with the counties and cities. I had a full plate on my desk. Shortly thereafter, I found myself with even more duties when Wendell's mother passed away and he had to return home to Owensboro.

One morning, when Governor Combs was on his way to his office, he stopped and said, "Banksie, you're my senior advisor." Nothing was ever said about that to any of his staff; I just very quietly assumed the role and didn't discuss it with anyone.

The 1960 Regular Session of the General Assembly convened in January and the Democratic and Republican legislators met in caucus on Monday, January 4, to choose their floor leaders and caucus chairmen and to select a slate of nominees for the officer positions in each house. House Democrats chose Tom Wathen of Morganfield as Caucus Secretary, R. P. Maloney of Lexington as House Caucus Chairman, and Thomas L. Ray of Louisville as House Floor Leader. The Republicans chose Paul Cornett of Merchons as Caucus Chairman and Leonard Hislope of Somerset as Floor Leader. The Democratic Caucus nominated Harry King Lohman of Ashland for Speaker of the House. His election was assured since, in the House, Democrats outnumbered Republicans by eighty to twenty.

The Senate Democrats nominated Alvin Kidwell of Sparta as their candidate for president pro tem and chose James C. Ware of Covington as their senate floor leader. Cabell Frances of Stanford was chosen as Democratic senate caucus chairman.

Governor Combs addressed the opening session of the 1960 General Assembly and carefully explained that his Administration's recommendations about specific appropriations would have to await the outcome of judicial processes then underway involving the clarification and constitutionality of the Veterans' Bonus Referendum. Then, after having enumerated some of the worthy and encouraging achievements of the 1950s, the Governor emphasized the importance of the tasks that remained to be done. He referred to the 1960s as the "decade of decision." Then Governor Combs set out his recommendations which were as follows:

1. The paying of a Veterans' Bonus because it was a moral obligation imposed on state government by the passage of a popular referendum;
2. The funding of immediate and substantial salary increases for teachers;
3. The establishment of a Central School Building Authority and an appropriation sufficient in amount to establish as adequate agricultural research program at the University of Kentucky;
4. The establishment in every department of state government of a permanent merit system for state employees;
5. The outlawing of the practice of exacting political contributions from state government employees;
6. The enactment of a law requiring the installation of voting machines in every precinct;
7. The enactment of laws correcting and ending voter registration abuses and providing for fair and efficient purgation of the voting rolls;
8. The enactment of laws to close the glaring loopholes in the absentee voting statutes;
9. The amendment of existing laws governing the state and its political subdivisions in order to provide a greater degree of freedom for Kentucky cities and towns;
10. Approval of the Act passed by the 1950 Extraordinary Session of the General Assembly providing for the taking of a census of the people on the question of calling a convention for limited review of the Constitution of Kentucky;
11. The abolition of the Court of Claims and the Highway Advisory Commission;
12. The initiation of programs designed to protect those Kentuckians who did not have and could not afford adequate medical attention;

13. The serious consideration of enacting laws to prevent conflicts of interest and to provide the sternest of penalties for any member of government who uses his or her office for unscrupulous advantage;
14. The review of the laws governing allowable weight limits of trucks with a view toward possible further revision of such laws as the condition of the highways justifies and also including a study of motor vehicle transportation in general to insure that each form of transportation pays its equitable share of highway costs;
15. Enactment of laws to accomplish the purpose of the Rural Finance Act if it should be invalidated by the courts or approval of an adequate appropriation to implement the Act if it should be found constitutional and the enactment of additional laws in support of the lieutenant governor in return for his promise to devote part of his time in office to foster Kentucky's economic development;
16. The enactment of legislation providing for broad and improved forestry programs with emphasis on the prevention and control of forest fires and expanded nursery programs together with the luring into the state of the burgeoning timber industry;
17. A study of the possibility of broadening soil conservation and small watershed programs, giving special consideration to the creation of small lakes and other watershed in Kentucky to serve multiple purposes such as recreation, conservation, new industry, and flood control;
18. The enactment of regulations to provide more protection especially from oil and gas wells in order to protect the public interest, the interest of farmers and sportsmen, as well as to afford assistance and encouragement to the mining industry; and
19. The promotion of the Division of Parks to Department status.

On January 6, the *Louisville Courier Journal* carried an editorial under the caption, "A Sound Beginning for Combs." It began as follows:

"Governor Bert Combs, in his address to the opening session of the General Assembly, has proposed a legislative program unprecedented in scope and quality and in its daring and foresight and approach to the basic problems facing our state. Not in recent times has a Governor made a more inspiring beginning of his administration."

On January 12, Senator Ware introduced Senate Bill (SB) 31 which abolished the state Highway Advisory Commission. [On December 14, 1959, Governor Combs had abolished the commission in one of his first Executive Orders. Senator Ware's bill was for the purpose of making the provisions of the Governor's Executive Order permanent.] On January 21, just nine days after its introduction, the bill passed the Senate by a vote of 36-0. A week later the House passed the bill by an 88-0 count. Thus, SB 31 became the first of the Combs administration's bills to reach the new governor's desk. On February 1, he signed it and the Highway Advisory Commission became history. Combs had speedily delivered on one of his campaign promises.

The governor's recommendation to abolish the board of claims was soon accomplished through the passage of SB 32. By approving Combs' Executive Order abolishing Chandler's board of claims, the General Assembly quickly had made good on a second Combs' campaign promise. SB 32, while abolishing the old Board of Claims, established a new one with the members composed of existing state government personnel who served on the Board with no additional compensation. On February 25, the governor signed SB 32 into law. The new administration's legislative program was off to a fast start.

In the meantime, another important administration bill made its way through the General Assembly and onto the governor's desk for signature. This was House Bill (HB) 62 by the provisions of which the General Assembly was authorized to call a constitutional convention. The Governor signed the bill on February 4, HB 62 thus becoming the second administration bill to reach Combs' desk.

HB 168, introduced February 1, also related to constitutional matters. This administration bill created a Constitution Revision Commission as an agency of the Legislative Research Commission (LRC). The purpose of the commission was to study, review, and examine the Constitution of Kentucky in order to recommend any changes found necessary.

In January two critically important administration bills were introduced. One was HB 85 known as the "Veterans Bonus Bill" and the other was HB 75 known as the "Sales Tax Bill." The Veterans Bonus Bill provided for the payment of a bonus to all residents of Kentucky who had been members of the armed forces of the United States and who had been on active duty for at least ninety days during the Spanish-American War, World War I, World War II, or the Korean Conflict. The veterans had to have been residents of Kentucky at least six months prior to enlistment and resided in Kentucky on November 3, 1959, the day the referendum received the majority of the vote.

The maximum amount of the bonus for domestic service was $300 while the maximum for those veterans who had served overseas was $500. Dependents or heirs of deceased veterans were also to receive the bonus.

None of the twenty-eight Republicans in the House of Representatives voted for this measure. They said that they boycotted the bill because its terms denied a bonus to Kentucky veterans who did not reside in the state on November 3, 1959, the date the referendum passed in the general election. The House passed the bill 78-0, but the twenty-eight Republican members of the House made certain they were in caucus when the bill came up for a vote. Apparently, they thought this was a smart move and would enhance Republican chances in the next election. The bill passed the Senate also and, with the signature of Governor Combs, became law.

HB 75, the Sales Tax Bill, recognized the commonwealth's obligation to finance the payment of the bonus to Kentucky's veterans since payment had been approved by the voters. The Sales Tax Bill was the means of raising the funds necessary to pay the bonus. The bill provided a levy of 3 percent on retail sales made in the state. It should be remembered that the Sales Tax Bill was also, to some extent, an income tax reduction measure. The bill provided for repeal of the surtax and increased the personal exemption to twenty dollars for the filer and each of his dependents. The Sales Tax Bill also provided for a reduction in the cigarette tax. On January 29, the House passed the bill by a vote of 84 to 9. The Senate quickly followed the action of the House passing the bill by a 28-8 count. Governor Combs signed the bill early in February.

The passage of the Sales Tax Bill was absolutely critical to the success of the Combs administration. How to finance his progressive agenda for the commonwealth had been a problem during the campaign. However, the public's acceptance of the referendum authorizing payment of a bonus to veterans offered a solution to the funding problem. The referendum provided for a sales tax to finance the payments. During the campaign, however, Combs did not come out in favor of the Veterans Bonus and its sales tax funding mechanism. Instead, he took the neutral position that, if the people wanted it that was fine and, if they didn't want it, that was also fine with him. He would simply comply with whatever the majority of voters wanted. Several campaign staff members thought it was very important to remain neutral, but to quietly attempt to arouse interest in passage of the referendum. Combs remembered how his forthrightness about the need for additional funding had hurt him in the 1955 primary campaign. Happy Chandler had pounded him on that position throughout the entire campaign. It was best to stay neutral, but help quietly where possible. Thus, candidate Combs stayed aloof.

The Veterans Bonus passed, however, laying in the new governor's lap the solution to funding his program to move Kentucky forward into the twentieth century. Knowing full well that a tax of only one cent would cover bonus costs, Combs obtained from the General Assembly a three percent sales tax that provided ample funding for every facet of his program. Combs realized, however, that enactment of the sales tax was only the first step. He understood that he needed visible results to secure long-term acceptance of the tax. Thus, during the four years of his administration, he not only made more money available for education, highway construction, state parks, industrial development, and human resources, but he also ensured that a full-scale public relations campaign accompanied every endeavor. The dedication of new schools, classrooms, highways, parkways, state parks, and industrial complexes always found the governor on hand to tell the public that it was the sales tax that made it possible. He realized, long before anyone else, that perpetuation of the sales tax would ensure continued improvements while its repeal would signal retrenchment and stagnation for his beloved Kentucky.

Yes, the Veterans Bonus Referendum with its provision for a sales tax was, indeed, a fortunate occurrence for the Combs administration. It meant the difference between scaling back the programs proposed by the governor during the campaign and being able to proceed without the worry of where the funding would come from. I doubt that a sales tax could have been enacted in any other way besides being tied to a bonus for veterans. That was something almost everybody supported. Even those not particularly in favor of the bonus did not feel compelled to oppose it with so many Kentucky families benefiting from its passage. Of course the veterans and their families were very much in favor of it. They did the campaigning for its passage. For a long time afterward, many, many veterans told me that they had moved away to work in Ohio, Michigan and other states, but in the summer of 1959, they returned to Kentucky and registered to vote and cast their ballots in the November general election in favor of the bonus. With this wonderful source of funding suddenly becoming available just when we needed it, I was beginning to think that "Somebody Up There" liked the Combs administration.

On February 3, 1960, Representative Ray introduced HB 199, which contained the provisions for a statutory merit system for state employees. The bill sailed through the House, passing by a vote of 86 to 7 on February 24. The Senate followed with passage on March 6, by a count of 26 to 6. On March 17, Governor Combs signed the bill into law. While some of the remarks of Combs during the campaign could be construed as embracing all state employees, it is safe to say that he was well enough acquainted with the realities of Kentucky politics to know not to expect that every state employee would be protected. In the end there were a considerable number of categories of employees to which the merit system did not apply. These categories included employees of the governor and lieutenant governor, members of boards and commissions and most of the heads of departments and their principal assistants and division directors, secretaries to those high-ranking officials, and officers and members of the staffs of state institutions of higher learning and also, generally, to employees in unskilled labor positions. The reason the merit system did not apply to most high-ranking officials and their staffs was that it was believed that a governor should have the opportunity to appoint persons whom he believed he needed to implement his program. Otherwise, he might be faced with the difficult problem of having persons who opposed him and his programs serving in key positions in his administration.

The Department of Personnel, the Department of Health and Economic Security, and the Department of Fish and Wildlife Resources were immediately brought under the provisions of the act. The final date for the bill's application to the other departments was July 1, 1961. The legislation providing for the merit system not only fulfilled a campaign promise, but it also greatly improved state government. With protection now in place, many well qualified individuals flocked to state government realizing they no longer had to serve merely at the pleasure of their supervisors. The merit system was one of the most important pieces of legislation enacted during the Combs administration. Its effect is felt just as much today in state government as it was back in 1960.

Success followed success for the Combs administration in the 1960 regular session of the General Assembly. A bill establishing the Business Development Corporation of Kentucky was signed by the governor on March 21. Next was HB 273 which provided for the establishment of the Kentucky Public School Authority. The purpose of the Authority was to lend assistance to local boards of education. This administration bill encountered little opposition and it quickly passed and was signed by Governor Combs on March 25.

HB 274, which authorized the purchase of voting machines, had no opposition and passed in both houses without receiving a single vote against it. HB 275, a companion bill to HB 274, making the installation of voting machines in the counties mandatory no later than the date of the 1961 primary election, was passed with some small opposition. Both HB 274 and HB 275 were signed by the governor on March 25.

HB 277, authorized any state college or university or state government, itself, on the particular institution's behalf, to obtain federal aid and also authorized such institutions to utilize current appropriations to meet the matching requirements of federal grants. The bill passed each House without a dissenting vote and the governor signed it into law on March 25.

16 The Billion Dollar Budget

LEGISLATORS AND THE PUBLIC had been eagerly awaiting the new governor's first budget message. This was to be the highlight of the session. Governor Combs had been waiting for the Sales Tax Bill to be enacted before submitting his first budget to the General Assembly. Now that HB 75 had been passed and signed into law by the governor, the stage was set.

On February 17, 1960, Governor Combs delivered his historic budget message. Having received a standing ovation from the members of the legislature gathered in the House of Representatives in a joint session, Combs began his message as follows:

> Some of you I know have waited for the budget with impatience. So, to tell the truth, have I. In a very real sense, this is a budget which Kentucky has needed for the past half century. Today, with this budget, Kentucky leaves her old, depressing place at the bottom of the ladder and the day is coming when Kentucky will go forward. This, of course, is not solely because of my budget. Your courage in enacting tax legislation, your wisdom in keeping communities within bounds has made this budget possible. I am fully aware that you have been under tremendous pressures during recent weeks. The nature of the pressures and the sources from which they came have made your conduct all the more admirable.

Throughout the budget message, the governor pointed out the increases in funding for particular programs as compared with appropriations provided in the 1958-1960 biennial-budget for those same programs. For example, the $16 million appropriation for the University of Kentucky and the five other state colleges was a substantial increase enabling administrators to increase salaries, employ 160 additional instructors, accommodate 4,000 additional students and invest millions more in planning, expansion and improvements. Specifically, the University of Kentucky could proceed with construction of a $6 million Chemistry and Physics building, a $2 million expansion of the University's library, a $1.5 million commerce facility, an enlargement of the Student Union building, and a number of additional dormitories.

This was Kentucky's first billion dollar budget. It included $109,825,000 for the road program and provided additional millions through the sale of bonds and federal subsidies. The budget proposal included $38,900,000 for the Department of Economic Security, an increase of $9,167,000 above the Department's appropriation in the 1958-1960 biennial-budget. Of this increased amount of funding, $1,636,000 was to be used to begin a program of medical aid to the indigent and $5,400,000 was to be utilized to increase public assistance.

Governor Combs concluded his budget message with these words:

> So unless Bonus costs exceed current estimates, the expenditures recommended are within the revenues expected. Let me say that I am sincerely happy and grateful to be able to present to you a budget that meets so many of Kentucky's old and heavy needs, a budget made possible by your cooperation. I deeply believe that this is a day Kentucky will have reason to applaud for this budget and program of improvements and the progress that it makes possible, makes a drastic break with the distressing patterns of the past and departs for a new and better day.

The budget bill introduced by Representative Ray on February 17, was passed by the House on February 29 by the vote of 96-0. On March 7, the Senate followed approving the budget by the unanimous vote of 38-0. On March 10, a very pleased Governor Combs signed the bill.

The enactment of the Budget Bill implemented a number of recommendations that Combs had made in his State of the Commonwealth address. Included were substantial and immediate increases in teachers' salaries, appropriations sufficient to establish an adequate agricultural research facility at the University of Kentucky, and the beginnings of a program designed to help those Kentuckians who could not afford proper and adequate medical attention. The budget increased appropriations for the Department of Conservation thus facilitating a greatly improved forestry program together with a broad soil conservation program.

The fact that not a single vote was cast against the administration's budget in either house was widely publicized by the media. The consensus was that a courageous and dynamic leader had at last arrived to head state government. That leader was Gov. Bert T. Combs. As for Happy Chandler and his faction, at least for now, he was lying low, hiding out under a log and keeping his powder dry. Keeping Happy quiet was, in itself, quite an achievement.—an unprecedented and previously thought to be impossible accomplishment. Although this had not been the aim of the Combs budget, it was a welcome by-product.

Between February 26 and March 2, five bills were introduced that were regarded as Combs' administration bills since each was a recommendation made by the governor in his State of the Commonwealth speech. The first of these bills was HB 401 which directed the establishment of a Strip Mining and Reclamation Commission to be attached to the Department of Conservation. As I expected, the bill met with strong opposition. No smooth sailing here. On March 14, the House passed it by a vote of 69-12, but the bill was amended in the Senate and the House declined to concur in the amendment. On March 18, however, the Senate, after much haggling, rescinded from its amendment and passed the bill by the count of 24-5. This was an important victory for the Combs administration that created much needed law to finally begin to protect eastern Kentucky citizens from the worst of coal mining abuses.

SB 235, providing for the regulation of oil and gas production, was passed and signed by Governor Combs. With the passage of SB 235, together with the passage of HB 401, the strip mining and reclamation bill, environmentalism was born in the Commonwealth of Kentucky and none too soon.

Another important bill, HB 437, revising the Minimum Foundation law, was passed by both houses and signed by Governor Combs. This bill was designed to give effect to several financial improvements which had been provided in the Governor's budget. The bill also changed the minimum school term from nine months to 185 days and revised the transportation formula in recognition of changes in population.

HB 438 was a provision to regulate absentee voting. HB 439, the General Reorganization Act, implemented the governor's recommendation that the Division of Parks be raised to the status of a full department. Among the Reorganization Act's many provisions was the creation of the Department of Child Welfare, the first such department in the United States. The General

Assembly, at Governor Combs' request, also established the Division of Mental Retardation in the Welfare Department.

HB 444, the Conflicts of Interest Bill, implemented another of Combs' recommendations. This bill, which became effective on July 1, forbade any member of the General Assembly or any employee of the legislature or other state agency from knowingly receiving compensation from an outside employer for any services or negotiations with the state. It also forbade such persons from purchasing any interest in real property in which the state had an interest, and forbade such persons from appearing as an expert witness or from acting as an agent for the state in business dealings with himself or his interests.

HB 497, the Truck Law, did not fully meet the expectations of Governor Combs. The original bill, which applied to all coal haul trucks, was amended in the House to exempt trucks hauling coal within a fifty mile radius of the mine site from paying any additional fee in excess of $300. This weakened the Truck Bill tremendously and so the governor decided not to sign it, but rather to allow it to become law without his signature. Combs did not veto the bill because he felt that his veto would be overridden and he believed that getting something was better than getting nothing.

A bill to create the Industrial Development Financial Authority was passed in March. Both Combs and Lt. Gov. Wilson Wyatt attached great significance to the establishment of this body. The General Assembly also passed the "Senator Ware Act," SB 253, which answered the governor's appeal for more effective education for exceptional children. The term "exceptional children" as used in the bill referred to children who were mentally retarded or suffered from other forms of abnormality.

HB 521 was passed and signed by the governor who considered the bill to be of major importance. The provisions of the bill made it possible for students enrolled in the practice schools of the institutions of higher learning to obtain free textbooks.

The Combs administration forces encountered formidable opposition to the passage of two labor bills. SB 118 became the "failing" wage bill. However, after quite a struggle, a substitute bill barely scraped by in the Senate by an 18 to 14 count. The House passed the substitute by 55 to 21. That was the narrowest margin of victory for any administration bill to that time.

The second labor bill was the controversial Workman's Compensation Bill, HB 457. A companion bill was filed in the Senate. The showdown vote was due to take place on March 9, but administration leaders, fearing an adverse vote, asked for a postponement. In essence, as amended, the bill provided for an across the board increase of $4.00 per week for disabled workmen, raised allowances from $300 to $500, raised maximum benefits for total disability from $32 to $36 per week and raised the pool of employers from 200,000 to 300,000. These provisions were to be financed by employers and administered by the Department of Industrial Relations. When the battle was over and all the shouting had subsided, the House passed the bill 58 to 28 while it just barely cleared the Senate by a 19-15 count.

On February 29, Senator Ware introduced a pair of bills designed to supplement existing laws relating to turnpike construction and to provide alternative methods for financing turnpikes. The first of these measures was SB 223, which contained the following provision: "The Governor and Lieutenant Governor, Commissioner of Highways and the State Highway Engineer, the Attorney General and their representatives and successors in office, shall form a body corporate, a political constituency, constituting a public corporation, which will be a government instrument of the Commonwealth named the Turnpike Authority of Kentucky. The bill easily passed both houses of the General Assembly and was signed by the governor.

Closely related to the Turnpike Authority Bill was SB 251 which provided that unsold bonds amounting to $30 million remaining of the issue that was authorized in 1956, be sold for not less than par value and not for more than 3% interest if the bonds remained unsold by August 31, 1960. The bill also provided for submitting to Kentucky voters at the regular session in 1968, a proposal to authorize another bond issue in the amount of $100 million. It was stipulated that $10 million should be applied to the improvement and expansion of state parks with the remainder to be invested in turnpike construction.

The portion of the bonds allocated to parks was to be financed by taxing real, tangible and intangible personal property at not less than the rate existing in March 1960. The portion of the proceeds allotted to highway construction was to be supplemented by excise taxes, licenses and fees revenue from the Road Fund. The bill easily passed both houses of the legislature.

The Junk Yard Bill, as it was known, basically requiring fencing around the many junk yard eyesores around the state, got no further in the Senate than a second reading and placement on the Orders of the Day. The Junk Yard Bill was one of the few failures experienced by the Combs administration in the 1960 regular session.

During the 1960 Regular Session, Governor Combs vetoed five Senate bills, thirteen House bills and one House Resolution. Only once was his veto overridden. The one overridden veto came on HB 122 which had sixty-seven sponsors. The bill provided for a gradual increase in the per diem allowances of the members of the General Assembly. The increase was from $10 to $25 per day for regular and special sessions retroactive to the 1960 regular session (the current session). The governor's reason for vetoing HB 122 was that he was opposed in principle to public officials increasing their own compensation. The House overrode the veto 68-10 and the Senate overrode it by a margin of 28-7. Combs believed that the per diem increase should apply only to subsequent sessions. The governor handled this disagreement with the General Assembly very well. He handled the veto so well that no riff occurred between him and the legislators.

The regular session ended with the still new governor and members of the General Assembly having accomplished much for Kentucky. The new Sales Tax would become a tremendously important portion of state government funding for both the Combs administration and future administrations The Merit System greatly improved morale among state workers and attracted many able newcomers to state government. Combs had proven to be an able, efficient, thoughtful and trustworthy leader for the commonwealth. The members of the Combs' team and the public looked eagerly forward to more progress for Kentucky in the remaining almost full term of Gov. Bert T. Combs.

Governor Combs was progressive about a lot of things that surprised even his top people. At the cabinet meeting before Christmas, in 1960, the governor told his cabinet that they could not accept a Christmas gift worth more than five dollars. Well, Don Beecham and Wendell Butler proceeded to debate each other about the value of a country ham. They proved to the cabinet's satisfaction that a country ham wasn't worth five dollars. That was a major discussion at that cabinet meeting! I don't know how many of them got country hams, but it was pretty obvious that a good country ham was very important thing in those days.

17 The Birth of the Bluegrass Parkway & A Few Other Matters

I ALWAYS KEPT A briefcase on my credenza and I would put material in it that I wanted Governor Combs to see that day. Usually, when we drove or flew someplace, I would open the briefcase, dig through it, and brief the governor on everything that was in it.

On this particular day, we were flying to Bardstown for a luncheon meeting. When we finished reviewing the materials in my briefcase, the Governor stared out the window for a few minutes. I could tell that he had something on his mind. Finally, he turned to me and said, "Banksie, what we need is a toll road from E-town, by way of Bardstown, to Lexington."

Alarm bells immediately sounded in my mind. The problem I foresaw was that Happy Chandler would make a big issue of it in the 1963 campaign for governor. So, for the rest of the trip, I attempted to talk the governor out of building the road. He didn't say a word; he just sat there and politely listened to me.

The luncheon in Bardstown drew a big crowd of about 500 citizens. Governor Combs knew that when he began to speak I always left the room to make telephone calls back to the office in Frankfort. As he reached the podium to begin his speech, he said, "Banksie, don't leave."

Of course, that remark drew everyone's close attention. Then the governor went on to say, "I want to build a toll road from E-town, by way of Bardstown, to Lexington. But Banksie is against it."

Everyone stood up and shouted and booed and shook their fists at me! I can hear Governor Combs laughing to this day. He really enjoyed his joke at my expense. When the crowd quieted down, I went on out of the room and made my phone calls, but I kept my eyes open to make sure some well meaning local didn't come out and clobber me. And that's the way the Bluegrass Parkway was born—by poking fun at "Banksie."

When I became senior aide (chief of staff) to Governor Combs, my daily routine usually consisted of arriving at my office at 7:00 a.m. I would then telephone Henry Ward, the commissioner of Highways, and we would discuss all the problems that needed the governor's attention that day. In our conversations, Henry and I would fuss at each other a little and crack a joke or two before getting down to business.

Then, at 7:30 a.m., I would walk over to the Governor's Mansion to brief the governor on the coming day's activities. Mrs. Combs was always there waiting for me. We both had connections in Prestonsburg and she always wanted to know what was going on back there. After a few minutes, she would leave and the governor and I, now alone, would discuss the agenda for the day. I would brief him on anything he needed to know about, show him any letters he needed to read, and have him make any necessary telephone calls. Then, when we finished with these activities, we would walk over to the governor's office or leave in the car to go some place depending on what was on the day's schedule.

On a normal day, when the governor was in his office, I would be in and out of there many times to confer with him. When Governor Combs would have meetings that did not require my presence, I would deal with the various commissioners, sometimes by phone, but often by visiting them in their offices. While the governor had an open door policy, most of the commissioners preferred that I present their problems to him, which I was glad to do.

We had difficulties with a few of the commissioners. One had a very serious drinking problem. He was a brilliant tax attorney and commissioner of a critically important agency. The drinking continued until it became a real problem for the governor. One Saturday morning as I entered the Governor's Mansion, I found Governor Combs troubled and deep in thought. I said, "Your commissioner has you up a tree, doesn't he?"

"Yes, he does, Banksie, and I don't know how to get down," said the Governor.

I asked, "You want his resignation, don't you?"

Governor Combs replied, "Yes, I've got to have it."

At about that point in our conversation, a member of the governor's staff came in. I sat him down at a typewriter and dictated a letter of resignation and, when I was finished dictating it, I telephoned the commissioner and said, "I'm coming to see you."

A few minutes later when I knocked on his door, the first thing he said was, "Well, do you have it with you?"

I said, "Yes, here it is."

He walked over to a table, sat down in a chair, and signed the letter of resignation. We had become good friends during his tenure in office so I felt I could talk to him about his problem. I said, "If you don't watch out, you're going to lose your family."

He replied sadly, " Fontaine, I already have, they left me this week."

Realizing the situation was even worse than I had thought, I said, "You've got to stop your drinking or it's going to ruin your career too."

We continued to talk for about twenty minutes and then I left, leaving a nearly broken man behind the door. I did not hear from my friend for six months. Then one day, completely unexpectedly, he walked into my office and said, "Fontaine, I just wanted you to know that I haven't had a drink since that day. I've got a job, my family is back, and I just want to thank you for what you told me that day."

That man went on to a very successful career with a major Kentucky corporation and then, after he retired from that company, he had a very successful law practice. This man turned his life around completely. He took it back and I am grateful for the opportunity I had to play a small role in his success.

Another commissioner who found himself in trouble was the commissioner of Insurance who was ordered by Governor Combs to rescind an order, but refused. Quite naturally, he was fired.

Unfortunately, there is still another example. A lady from Floyd County had an important and high ranking position in the Revenue Department. One morning I received word that she was going to attend a luncheon in Louisville with Happy Chandler and was going to publicly endorse him for governor at the luncheon. I reported this to Governor Combs and he said, "Call her and see what she says."

So, as directed, I called her and said, "I understand you are going to make a speech at noon in Louisville today."

She answered, "Yes, I am."

I said, "Well, you'll have to do it as a private citizen because as of this minute, you're fired."

She replied, "What does that mean?"

I said, "That means that you no longer have a job."

I returned to the office and told the governor what I had done. After all, he hadn't told me to fire her, just to find out what she had to say about it. Governor Combs looked at me with a grim frown on his face. Then, after a few long seconds, his faced relaxed and he said, "Well, Banksie, you did right."

Surprisingly, the now ex-Revenue Department official didn't get angry with me, rather, he got mad at the governor. Strangely, she and I remained friends for many years after I fired her.

Overall, the Combs administration was served by an outstanding group of commissioners and other high-ranking officials. We had trouble with only a few. The administration's reputation for honesty and integrity ranks among the best in the history of the commonwealth.

18 Taking State Government to the People

AT THE TIME I began my career in state government in the first months of the Combs administration, the governor's staff members were attempting to figure out some way to get Governor Combs out among the people of Kentucky. Well, I came up with the idea of taking state government to the people. Kentucky is a relatively large state and it's a long way to Frankfort from far Western Kentucky or from the mountain counties of Eastern Kentucky. I proposed to take the governor's staff and other members of the Cabinet to the different areas of the state.

Temporary offices would be set up and citizens could come and meet with us and tell us about their needs. This would give the people access to the governor and officials of the various departments without having to bear the expense of driving to Frankfort. This would not only give our citizens access to the governor, but it would also accomplish the staff's goal of getting him out of the office and into the real world in which his constituents lived and worked everyday. We spent a great deal of time studying and planning the "State Government to the People" program.

Actually, we staff members called the program, "Portable State Government." No appointments were to be made. Visiting with the governor and other officials would be on a first come, first served basis.

The planning for these "Portable State Government" trips was my responsibility, but I was ably assisted by Ed Easterly, the Combs administration's press secretary and his assistant, Krista Finley.

In all, we made thirty-three trips, and "State Government to the People" turned out to be a big success.

On August 22 and 23, 1960, we made our first trip. It was a two-day session in the Western Kentucky town of Mayfield, the county seat of Graves County. Mayfield was a small industrial city about 175 miles southwest of Louisville. It was reported in the local press that ". . . scores patiently waited their turns to talk with Governor Combs."

The governor told the reporter, ". . . that his principal discovery on the first day was that people with problems are more tolerant if you let them know that you are interested in helping them and give them a chance to be heard."

Toward the end of the first day at Mayfield, the governor took time out to hold a press conference. When it was time for the press conference to end, a reporter asked Combs whether the governor thought that State Treasurer Thelma Stovall was justified in holding up the payment of entertainment promoters in New York City, something that had been in the news and was very controversial. The governor ducked the question by answering that he "... had come to Mayfield to get away from politics." Then he adjourned the press conference.

On the second day, the governor paid a visit to the State Penitentiary at Eddyville. He had said previously that he intended to drop in on state institutions unannounced. Penitentiary officials, however, got wind of his coming and, when he arrived, the penitentiary appeared to have been cleaned and dressed up for the governor's visit. So much for unannounced visits! It's very difficult to keep anything a secret in state government.

The governor inspected the interior and even visited the inmates on Death Row, including a brief talk with Kelly Moss, a notorious murderer. After his visit to the penitentiary, the governor stated that he had heard no complaints from prisoners about the quality of the food or about living conditions. The only complaint of any kind that he received was a rather dubious one from the death row inmate, Kelly Moss, who complained about body sores that he said had been inflicted by the prison warden.

At the end of the second day, Combs estimated that he had talked with more than 500 people including groups from all over western Kentucky. The governor was pleased with how the citizens had received the program. He believed that "Portable State Government" was going to prove to be a popular and successful way to allow all citizens an opportunity to talk to state government officials about their problems.

The second trip was to the Ohio River town of Maysville, the county seat of Mason County. Maysville lies about one hundred miles east/northeast of Louisville. Maysville is one of Kentucky's oldest and quaintest towns. Thus, on August 24 and 25, Maysville became the temporary capital of Kentucky. On the first day, Combs met with more than one hundred residents of the area. Taking government to the people seemed to be working quite well. Leaving by plane that evening to attend the Oldham County Fair that night, Governor Combs commented that the people who had visited with him that day seemed to be satisfied with what their state government was doing. Combs said that several visitors had offered to help with the selling of the proposed $100 million bond issue and that he felt encouraged about the bond issue.

Under the caption, "Governor Combs Confides in the People," the *Lexington Herald* of August 29, 1960, carried an editorial from which the following excerpt is quoted:

> Last week Bert Combs tried an experiment in mobile state government and it turned out to be a good democratic demonstration of taking government to the people. The governor was pleased by the experiment and expects to repeat it in the months ahead. Taking the state government to the people as the Governor has done is a novel and excellent idea. It serves the good purpose of giving the people a better understanding of the purpose and the problems of state government and gives the Governor a better opportunity to establish a person to person relationship with the people. On his visits out in the state, the Governor explains his programs to the people. He explained to them that economic, social and political progress cannot be achieved without cost and sacrifice by the people, notably by the payment of taxes and, in return, the people of Kentucky can advise state government of the people's needs as they see it and this is perhaps the principal advantage of Governor Combs' experiment of taking government to the people.

On October 26, 1960, Governor Combs opened his temporary governor's office in Manchester, the county seat of Clay County—the county in which the governor had been born. Clay County is in eastern Kentucky and was established in 1806 from parts of Madison, Floyd and Knox counties. It was named for Gen. Green Clay (1757-1826), a prominent pioneer surveyor and military leader in the War of 1812. He was a cousin of Henry Clay. Manchester lies at the junction of US 421 and KY 11. We traveled there by plane from Frankfort to London Airport and then by automobile to Manchester. We were an hour late in arriving and several members of the governor's staff had come ahead and set up the temporary offices, including big preparations for some of the activities that were planned for this trip.

One of the big events was to be a grand homecoming dinner put on by the citizens of Clay County honoring the governor who was born in their county. For this very special occasion, Governor Combs took along Rural Highway Commissioner Ted Marcum as a member of the official party. Marcum had stated earlier in the press that he had the distinction of having been the only Democrat ever elected to office in Republican Clay County. Marcum was along not only because he was from Clay County, but also because of his familiarity with the economic problems of Clay County.

About 400 citizens visited Governor Combs' temporary office in the two-day period of the visit. As usual, the visitors included representatives of several groups. For example, there was a sizeable delegation from Clay County High School from which the governor had graduated as valedictorian. There was a delegation of about one hundred people from nearby Leslie County led by County Judge Elmer Begley. Combs promised this delegation that the eleven-mile road from Hyden, the county seat of Leslie County, to Confluence, a small hamlet north of Hyden, would be paved.

At noon on the second day, Governor Combs made a five-minute speech on radio station WWXL. This speech was then relayed by radio station WKIC to Hazard where it was piped to a large crowd gathered there in support of the Constitutional Revision concerning the road bond issue.

On January 10, 1961, *The Louisville Times* made the following announcement regarding the Governor's setting up a temporary office in Louisville.

> Governor Combs . . . moves to Louisville for a two day stand starting at 8:00 tomorrow. The Governor and several representatives of state departments will set up shop in the state office building at Sixth and Cedar. Their mission is to hear gripes from taxpayers and to explain what the state is doing with their tax funds. Combs said he'd listen tomorrow and Thursday as long as anyone wanted to talk. With him will be representatives of four departments, Highways, Economic Security, Economic Development and Public Relations.

During the visit to Louisville, Governor Combs visited Kosair Crippled Children's Hospital, Waverly Hills Tuberculosis Sanitarium and the Kentucky Children's Hospital. At the Kentucky Children's Hospital, he was thanked for an emergency allotment of $40,000 that put the hospital over the hump until the end of the fiscal year. Joined by Highway Commissioner Henry Ward and Lt. Gov. Wilson Wyatt on Thursday, Combs commuted to Shively to announce plans for the early four laneing of US 31 between Shively and Louisville proper. The announcement was made near the spot where Combs and Wyatt had made a campaign pledge to four-lane the intersection.

Next, in late March, was the Lebanon project. Lebanon, the county seat of Marion County, is located at the junction of highways US 68 and KY 55 about fifty miles southeast of Louisville in the southern most part of the Bluegrass Region. Combs and his office staff set up in Lebanon at the Marion County Courthouse on March 30. The Lebanon trip chalked up another success for the "Taking Government to the People" program with most of the concerns being, as usual, about improving certain roads and highways.

The next trip was to Danville on April 4, 1961. Danville, the county seat of Boyle County, is located in the southern part of the Bluegrass Region and is the geographic center of the state and is also the home of Centre College, one of the nation's finest small colleges. In Danville, as in the five preceding trips, the majority of the callers were concerned with road problems; however, nine-year-old, Susan Hill, a Danville resident, said she just wanted to see a real, live governor. The usual procedure was to refer a particular road problem to the representative of the Department of Highways, but Combs was so deeply impressed with the appeal of the Danville-Perryville delegation whose members appealed for the reconstruction of US 150 between the two towns, that he promised to impress on Commissioner Ward the urgency of the project. By 10:00 a.m., about one hundred visitors, including a delegation from Hustonville and Stanford and other individuals from neighboring counties, had called at the temporary office.

Then Governor Combs took time out to visit the Kentucky School for the Deaf (KSD). Established in Danville in 1823, KSD was the oldest state supported school of its kind in the nation. Students from almost every state had attended KSD. The governor was extremely pleased and gratified by his visit to this very important and honored institution.

The next visit was to Irvine on April 13. Irvine, the county seat of Estill County, is located on the Kentucky River on the border between the Bluegrass and Eastern Coal Field regions. While there, Governor Combs exited his temporary office for short visits and talks at four of the local schools where he took the opportunity to boost the sales tax.

He was honored with a luncheon at Ruby's Café, a very popular spot, which was sponsored by the local Chamber of Commerce, Kiwanis Club, Women's Club and Garden Club and which drew a capacity crowd. After lunch, Combs told an extremely pleased courthouse audience, estimated at about 700, that plans were underway for the reconstruction of the seventeen-mile stretch of road between Irvine and Richmond.

A week later, we were off for two days to Owensboro, Wendell Ford's home. Owensboro, the county seat of Daviess County, is a thriving small city on the Ohio River in the Western Coal Field area of the state. The self-proclaimed "Barbecue Capital of the World," Owensboro holds the International Barbecue Festival each year in May. Owensboro is a port city located in a rich agricultural region and is the home of Brescia and Kentucky Wesleyan Colleges.

On the first day there, Governor Combs announced that Indiana and Kentucky would share equally in the cost of construction of a bridge across the Ohio River paralleling the existing Henderson-Evansville Bridge. Construction was expected to begin in fiscal 1961-1962. Governor Combs also announced that US 41 between Henderson and the existing bridge would be improved rather than relocated.

On the second day, Governor Combs made talks to students at the Daviess County, Western and Catholic High Schools and Kentucky Wesleyan College. At each school he urged the retention of the sales tax without exemptions that were now being proposed.

In May, we traveled to far Eastern Kentucky for a trip to Pikeville, the county seat of Pike County, my home county. Speaking to the Pikeville Kiwanis Club on May 11, Governor Combs said that as the sales tax became more firmly established, he hoped to be able to make reductions in the tax and he repeated his conviction that the tax should be retained without exemptions. He also announced that Congress had approved funding for construction of the Fish Trap Reservoir and said that he also expected an approval of an appropriation of $43,800,000 for the Big Sandy Flood Control project in time for construction to start in the fall of 1961. The governor spoke to a large crowd gathered at the courthouse. The trip was another in the string of successes that "State Government to the People" was producing.

Just a week later, it was on to Morehead. Morehead, the county seat of Rowan County, is located between Lexington and Ashland just south of I-64. It is the home of Morehead State College (now Morehead University).

The highlight of the trip was the announcement by the governor that a state vocational school was to be located in Morehead.

The next project was at Madisonville on July 11, 1961. Madisonville, named for James Madison who was Secretary of State at the time of the naming and would later serve two terms as president. Madisonville is the county seat of Hopkins County and is located in the Western Coal Field region of the state. A beautiful small city, more than one hundred residents turned out to visit the governor's "State Government to the People office." While there, Governor Combs announced the approval of three projects of much local interest: the early construction of a $400,000 District Highway Office Building, the construction of a 900-acre lake at Dawson Springs, and the installation of a runway lighting system for the local airport.

The governor took a little time out from the local visits and then, in late June, we visited Bowling Green, the county seat of Warren County. Bowling Green, at the time, was a thriving small city located along the Barren River in the Pennyroyal Region and was the home of Western Kentucky State College (now Western Kentucky University). While in the city, Governor Combs addressed a standing-room-only crowd in the Meador Auditorium at Western.

Western President, Kelly Thompson, who introduced the governor declared, "Until Bert Combs came along, I had never known a governor who had gone all out for education."

The governor ended his day and a half sojourn with an address to approximately 125 Chamber of Commerce members and guests at a luncheon held in his honor. During his visit, more than 200 citizens contacted his temporary office.

On August 21, we left for Hazard on our thirteenth trip. Located on the North Fork of the Kentucky River, Hazard—named for Oliver Hazard Perry, the naval hero of the Battle of Lake Erie in the War of 1812—is the county seat of Perry County, also named for the naval hero. Speaking to members of the Lions Club, with an audience of about 200, he received a roaring ovation when he defended the state's decision to spend $27,000 on re-paving a Hazard street that ended at La Citadel, the new resort hotel. About 250 citizens of the area appeared at the temporary office in Hazard. Governor Combs promised the delegation from the Open Door Children's Home at Leatherwood that a one-mile road to the orphanage would be maintained by the state. A delegation in support of the establishment of a two-year community college at Hazard appealed to Governor Combs. He stated that he favored the idea, but he advised the delegation to seek another conference with the State Commission on Higher Education.

Next was Prestonsburg, the governor's home and where he practiced law before becoming a judge of the Court of Appeals. The trip was a rousing homecoming for the governor. His reception equaled that of his other homecoming visit to Manchester and Clay County.

On that trip to Prestonsburg, a good friend of the governor and mine asked us to come by her house after we finished our work. When we got there, she came out of the kitchen with a tray of green peppers. I watched Governor Combs put two in his mouth. And she gave one of them to me, and I thought, "If he can have two, surely I can have one." I tell you I thought I was going to die! Oh, boy, were those peppers hot! And they both just roared laughing—they had planted it on me. Yes, Governor Combs liked hot food like that, but they sure were hot peppers that I got.

Next was Middlesboro, which is located in Bell County in Southeastern Kentucky very near the famous Cumberland Gap. Next was Shively in Jefferson County, our sixteenth trip. Shively was followed by Ashland in Northeastern Kentucky; then came Murray located in far Western Kentucky. It was then on to West Liberty in Morgan County followed by Elizabethtown in Hardin County. The next visit was to New Castle on August 30, 1962. In September, Somerset became the 23rd temporary office.

One of the most interesting visits of the "State Government to the People" program was the Haven project in Letcher County. Haven, also known as Cromona, was a once prosperous community that thrived on the coal mining business. Haven was now a community ravaged by unemployment brought on by automation in the coal mining industry.

Haven, which now had only about 500 residents, was the smallest town to be visited during the "State Government to the People" project. Combs said the trip was designed to focus attention on a distressed area. Haven was a busy town of about 2,000 until the mid-1940s when coal operations in the area were drastically curtailed. County Judge, James Corris, informed us that 60 percent of the residents survived only through public assistance and surplus food stamps.

A crowd estimated at 1,500 awaited Combs' arrival in the distressed little community. The temporary office was located in an old boarding house, which a church mission occasionally occupied. There being no restaurant in

Haven, Governor Combs and his party lunched at the school cafeteria eating food from the surplus commodities with which the school employees fed the children every day. The school children paid twenty cents per day for the lunch. The meal included tossed salad, peas, mashed potatoes, meatloaf and gelatin and was actually very good and enjoyed by all.

The 27th office project was set up in Owingsville, the county seat of Bath County. The 28th temporary office was set up in Bardstown on March 14, 1963. The 29th trip was to Burlington with shop being set up at the Boone County Courthouse. The 30th and final visit in the program was to Calhoun located in McLean County. The final trip occurred on March 21, 1963.

The "State Government to the People" program was a tremendous success by any type of measurement. It was great for the citizens who were presented with a rare opportunity to discuss their problems and complaints about government with the Governor and his top department heads. As for Governor Combs, the program gave him an opportunity to get out of the office, to get out of Frankfort, and to meet the people face to face and obtain a real feel for what their problems were. Governor Combs valued the trips highly.

19 The 1960 Extraordinary Session of the General Assembly

THE ORIGINAL VETERANS' BONUS law, which was enacted in February of 1960, authorized bonus payments to those veterans who were residents of Kentucky on November 3, 1959, the date of the bonus referendum. On that date, more than 100,000 Kentucky veterans lived outside the state. Remember that, when the Lower House voted on the Veterans Bonus Bill, nine of the twenty Republicans had managed to be in caucus when the vote was taken. Combs and his partisans in the legislature opposed the payment of the bonus to out-of-state veterans at that time because he felt that payment would place too much of a strain on Kentucky's budget.

Instead of including the out-of-state vets in the payments to be made under the bill, the governor decided to call for increasing the bond issue by about $36 million in order to include the out-of-state veterans. On September 7, 1960, the call for a Special Session of the General Assembly was issued. Shortly after having issued the call, Governor Combs mentioned the possibility of amending it in order to enable Kentucky to participate in the federal government's new medical care program.

On September 19, pursuant to the governor's call, the General Assembly met in an Extraordinary Session. It was during his address to the members of the General Assembly sitting in Extraordinary Session, that he requested the Kentucky veterans living outside the state be included in the bonus. The legislature began promptly carrying out the governor's recommendations. On the first day of the Session, following a favorable committee report, the House gave a first reading to House Bill 1, amending the Governor's Bonus Bill and appropriating $630,000 to cover the added cost of administering the act. The Senate made similar progress towards the passage of Senate Bill 1, appropriating $825,000 for medical care benefits and the administration of the bonus measure.

On Wednesday, with the quickest possible dispatch, each House passed the bill that it had originated, and on Friday, both bills received final passage and were sent to the governor for his approval. The Session lasted only five days, the shortest possible period for the enactment of a law.

Before the end of April 1961, the first bonus checks were presented in an impressive ceremony in the House Chamber with the governor and State Treasurer Stovall and other dignitaries participating. Presentation ceremonies continued for more than a year. The bonus bill and its payments were very popular with Kentuckians.

20 The Infamous "Truck Deal"

One of the most interesting situations that developed in the Combs administration was the famous or infamous, depending on one's point of view, "truck deal." On April 13, 1960, the *Courier Journal,* in a story written by Kyle Vance, disclosed that the Department of Highways had made a rental/purchase deal with Thurston Cooke's Louisville Equipment Rental Company for thirty-four tandem trucks. The contract stipulated that the vehicles were to be 1958 Model T-800 Ford Trucks.

On March 15, 1960, the contract was awarded to the Louisville Equipment Rental Company, but public knowledge of it was lacking until Vance's story appeared on April 13. If the usual routine had been followed (as it should have been) at this point in the process, a copy of the official "Award of Contract" form would have been attached to the contract. However, the form was not attached. The missing form cautioned vendors as follows: "This contract or any monies due or to come due hereunder, shall not be assigned without previous written consent of the Commissioner of Finance." Failure to attach this form, whether intentional or not, opened the way for the vendor to pledge the leased rental contract with the state to the Louisville Trust Company as collateral for a loan for $346,800. That action was taken on March 16. Two days later the mortgage was filed with the clerk of the Jefferson County Court.

Five trucks were delivered to the Central Garage in Frankfort. All of them were in poor condition. Harry C. Klapheke, who had been employed by the Department of Highways on Thurston Cooke's recommendation, had been Highway Equipment director since January 18. He found that the five trucks did not meet contract specifications; however, instead of informing Clements, head of Highways and Martin, the commissioner of Finance, he went to Louisville to convey the information to Cooke.

Now Cooke appears to have set up the Louisville Equipment Rental Company primarily for the negotiation of the truck deal. When Klapheke told Cooke about the unsatisfactory condition of the trucks, Cooke sent him to a St. Matthews dealership where the service manager promised him that the repairs would be made at Cooke's company. The night before, five more trucks had arrived at the Central Garage. They, too, were in poor condition and similarly failed to meet specifications.

On April 12, Kyle Vance heard about the deal and launched an investigation of the purchase at the Division of Records. As stated above, on April 13th, his first story appeared in the *Courier Journal.* On April 12, several other reporters also learned that a truck deal had been made on a limited purchase basis to extend for a period of two years. But only Vance seemed to realize the sensational potential of the story. The story exploded like a bomb. Citing the high cumulative cost of the two-year-old dump trucks that were found to be in such poor condition, the story conveyed the implication that either fraud had been committed or some sort of political payoff had been made.

The story precipitated a number of high level conferences. At one time or another during the next few days, these conferences included Governor Combs, Commissioner Clements, Commissioner Martin, Thurston Cooke and his attorney, a Mr. Grubbs. In retrospect, it appears that Cooke was not the only willfully dishonest person who was involved in the deal. It was obvious that Klapheke had demonstrated that his primary concern was for Cooke's financial interests rather than for safeguarding the legitimate financial interests of the commonwealth. Had he been a duly conscientious servant of the state, he would have reported the deficiencies of the trucks directly to Commissioner Clements and thus would have eliminated embarrassment for both Governor Combs and Commissioner Clements.

Apparently, he did not even inform Clements that any trucks had been delivered prior to the appearance of Vance's story and did not report the condition of the trucks until the following day. Belatedly receiving Klapheke's report, Clements notified Cooke and Grubbs that their trucks would not be accepted. He suggested they withdraw their bid and stated that he would accept their withdrawal without any comment about bad faith on the part of Cooke. Cooke requested time to consider Clements' proposal and disclosed to Clements that the contract had been assigned to the Louisville Trust Company. Here was an additional ground for cancellation of the contract, but the assignment hindered solving the problem with the simple withdrawal of the bid as Clements had suggested.

Late in the evening of April 14, the governor called Finance Commissioner Martin to ascertain his reaction to the publicity that the truck deal was receiving. Martin expressed the opinion that the contract should be terminated either by the vendor's withdrawal or by direct cancellation by the governor. The next morning, April 15, the governor instructed Commissioner Martin to discuss the whole matter with Clements.

That afternoon Martin conferred with Highway Commissioner Clements and Clements described the condition of the trucks that had been delivered thus far and declared that they were not acceptable by his department. According to Clements, he and Martin agreed that the best way to end the problem would be for Grubbs to withdraw his client's bid.

On April 16, Clements, Martin and Combs conferred in the governor's office. In view of the fact that the company had not fulfilled contract stipulations and had delivered trucks that were entirely unacceptable, it was agreed that the governor should cancel the contract unless the company would withdraw its bid. Clements and Martin went from Combs' office to Martin's office where they were joined by Cooke and Grubbs. Cooke seemed to be under the impression that the root of the difficulty was his identification with the ownership of the trucks—that this implied a political payoff. He had brought along a third party identified as a very wealthy contractor from Indiana who lived much of the time at the Brown Hotel in Louisville and who was willing to accept ownership of the trucks. Informed of this suggestion, Combs promptly rejected it saying that under no circumstances would he be a party to such a subterfuge. Nor would Clements and Martin budge from their position that the trucks were unacceptable under any circumstances and that Cooke and Grubbs should withdraw from the contract.

After a brief consultation outside Martin's office, Cooke and Grubbs reported that they were willing to withdraw from the contract, but would need time to clear up the assignment with the Louisville Trust Company. Martin said later that this was his first knowledge of the assignment of the contract. He was under the impression that the Award of Contract form with its caution to vendors had been attached to the contract.

The governor agreed to postpone cancellation of the contract over the Easter weekend allowing Cooke and Grubbs a limited opportunity to arrange for withdrawal. On Monday, finding himself unable to complete the arrangements for the release of the $346,800 mortgage within that amount of time, Cooke telephoned to request a further extension of time. Combs' impatience was aggravated by Kalpheke's report of defects, missing parts, needed repairs and other deficiencies of the trucks that had been delivered. He was indignant, too, because the contract had been signed in secret and because the required form had not been attached to it. He told Cooke so and made no commitment for any further delay.

On Tuesday, April 19, Cooke and Grubbs came to Frankfort, bringing with them a letter of withdrawal. Clements was willing to accept it and preferred to close the deal that way; however, by this time, Governor Combs had decided to cancel the contract and he so informed Clements. Combs was at the point of signing the cancellation order when he was informed that Cooke and Grubbs had brought their letter of withdrawal to Martin's office. Combs declined to alter his course, however, and shortly afterward, he informed the media that he had directed cancellation of the contract. The contract was officially cancelled on May 22, 1960. Three days later, Cooke's automobile empire collapsed. Before the end of June, Cooke and some of his business associates were indicted for fraudulent transactions and, on October 6, they pled guilty in criminal court. In due time, Klapheke was fired. While he was not charged with violating of the law, it was clear that he had shown little regard for the interests of his employer, the Commonwealth of Kentucky.

A few months later, on August 18, 1960, Governor Combs announced that Clements had tendered his resignation effective September 1. No reason for the resignation was given, hence newspaper editors, reporters and columnists jumped to the conclusion that the resignation was the outgrowth of the truck deal. At one time or another the Louisville, Lexington and Frankfort dailies and several other newspapers across the state, made speculations to the effect that Combs had fired Clements or he had resigned under pressure. Sometime later, Earl Clements told me that he had not been asked to resign, that he offered his resignation in order to help his friend, Lyndon Johnson, become President of the United States.

In summary, the Combs administration had legislated the first billion-dollar budget in Kentucky history, and administered it with no corruption attached to it. But this one situation, the "Truck Deal" came close to becoming a scandal.

We had anticipated a stepped-up highway construction program because of the federal interstate highway system and because of campaign commitments.

Thus, the Highway Department began immediately to increase its capabilities through the acquisition of more equipment and manpower.

Thurston Cooke, in addition to being a Louisville automobile dealer, had been finance chairman of the Combs campaign. When he contracted with the state to deliver thirty-four used trucks, a legitimate need was there. However, the trucks, secured in Alabama, were in an unacceptable condition. The trucks were run-down and virtually worthless.

The contract was with the Louisville Equipment Rental Company, but no one seemed to know who owned the rental company. Cooke stated that he sold the trucks, but had no connection with the planned lease to the state. With the situation already somewhat confusing, suspicions persisted even when Governor Combs stepped in and cancelled the contract.

Thus, even though the commonwealth never lost a penny in the "Truck Deal," newspapers, particularly the *Courier Journal,* continued to act as if a cover-up had been made. The principal focus of the media attack was Earl Clements, whose appointment as Highway Commissioner the *Courier* had found "troubling" and symbolic of factional politics. "It raises the question of his role and influence in the administration outside of highway matters," the paper cautioned.

Convinced that Clements' political practices somehow tarnished the otherwise pure image presented by Combs and Wyatt, the *Courier* kept up its relentless pressure. When Clements resigned in August to assist Lyndon Johnson in his campaign for the Democratic nomination for the presidency, the paper said that his departure was a contribution to Kentucky because he had become "the governor's greatest handicap."

Out of all this turmoil that began with the "Truck Deal," revelations evolved to create a rift between Combs and Clements that caused Clements, a former U.S. Senator and Kentucky governor to oppose Wyatt's U.S. Senate hopes in 1962, embrace Chandler against Breathitt in 1963, and work against Combs when he ran a second time for governor in 1971.

To me, this was a very sad outcome. In my opinion, Earl Clements was a very able man and undeserving of the political attack he received principally from the *Courier Journal.* The rift between Combs and Clements, caused by neither man, was costly to both in the long run. And, in my opinion, costly to Kentucky. A Combs-Wyatt-Clements team was a strong, progressive one. A team that would have been able to accomplish even more for the Commonwealth had they been able to continue as the natural allies they were.

21 Carter County

THE LAST SUNDAY OF February 1960, Richard Cherry published in the *Courier Journal* some of his findings in a case study dealing with the Carter County schools. The article dealt mainly with complaints against Superintendent Heman McGuire and his wielding of political power; however, the story kindled suspicions of gross misuse of public education funds. The allegations came during the 1960 Regular Session of the General Assembly when a House committee headed by Representative Harry M. Caudill of Whitesburg was investigating various aspects of public education.

Now, Harry Caudill was an attorney from Whitesburg (Letcher County) in southeastern Kentucky. He had been wounded in action in World War II and was first elected to the House in 1954. He was serving in the last of his three terms as a legislator. He was a tough investigator and a good leader. After he left the legislature, Caudill became a famous writer, an Appalachian historian and social critic while, at the same time, practicing law in Whitesburg. His first book, *Night Comes to the Cumberlands* is the story of how much of the mineral rich and beautiful land of eastern Kentucky was changed into an ugly, desolated place. It was about powerful coal operators bullying the neglected people of the area through the use of the broad form deed. Caudill wrote many books and later was a history professor at the University of Kentucky. He was a sharp investigator and a man looking out for the people's interests.

Not surprisingly, Caudill's committee decided to have a close look at the situation in Carter County. On Wednesday, March 2, the House Investigating Committee on Education devoted several hours to a hearing on the complaints of Carter County citizens followed by Superintendent McGuire's denial of the allegations. Chairman Caudill, whose investigating proclivities were strongly backed by other members of the committee, particularly Republican Marlow Cook and Democrat Ralph Bates, stated that the committee's role was to ascertain whether state money had been wasted and, if so, to place the responsibility for such a misuse of funds. This was the opening scene of an episode that turned into a long, drawn out battle to oust Superintendent McGuire and to recover a large amount of public school funds allegedly appropriated by him and the Carter County Board of Education.

Since Heman McGuire was not an employee of the Combs administration and, in as much as Governor Combs did not have the authority to remove him from office or revoke his certificate or to order an any official to do that, the complaining citizens who appeared before the House Investigating Committee on March 2, became the nucleus of the "Carter County Citizens League for Good Government." This group led the effort to clean up the education system in Carter County. Without the existence and actions of this League, it is quite conceivable that the misappropriation of public school money and chiseling done at the expense of the taxpayers of Carter County and the whole of Kentucky would have continued for years. To this League goes the credit for requesting that the State Auditor of Public Accounts initiate a recovery suit and for bringing it a successful conclusion.

The group began by securing the cooperation of Attorney General John Breckinridge and Assistant Attorney General Ray Corns. State Auditor Joe Snyder and his able assistant, George Stewart, made a very efficient audit of the expenditures of the Carter County Board of Education. They also did some clever sleuthing along the way. The audit revealed numerous financial irregularities, the most glaring of which was McGuire's alleged embezzlement of thousands of dollars which had been appropriated for the purchase of school buses that were never bought.

When the Carter County Citizens League for Good Government brought suit for the recovery of the misappropriated public school funds, entry into the case by the Attorney General was warranted by the fact that funds of the Commonwealth of Kentucky were involved. Assistant Attorney General Ray Corns was assigned to the case. He was an able and valuable attorney. He was optimistic throughout the case never losing hope that the prosecution would terminate successfully. On July 5, embarrassed by the publicity given to the scandalous affair, impatient with the slow progress toward correcting the situation, and without authority to intervene directly, Governor Combs used the occasion of the Governor's Day Convocation at Eastern Kentucky State College to suggest that Superintendent McGuire resign.

Three members of the State Board of Education promptly concurred with Combs' opinion that Superintendent McGuire should resign. Superintendent of Public Instruction Wendell Butler observed that the question of McGuire's guilt or innocence had yet to be settled in court and that one is presumed innocent until proven guilty.

While Governor Combs' immediate desire was the ousting of McGuire, his major concern was that no more situations similar to that in Carter County be allowed to occur in Kentucky. He expressed strong faith in the honesty and moral integrity of the great majority of public school administrators and members of the local school boards throughout the state. He stated that he was proud of the greatly increased financial support of public education brought about by his administration and he keenly desired that the confidence of taxpayers in those who spent public funds should not be undermined because of the McGuire mess in Carter County.

Two highly regarded members of the local legal profession, Attorney James W. Sykes of Louisville and former Chief Justice of the Court of Appeals and Circuit Judge, R.S.H. Rice of Irvine, investigated the Carter County situation on behalf of the State Board of Education. They made the report on which the State Board based its removal of four members of the Carter County Board of Education thus setting the stage for McGuire's removal. Judge Rice presided efficiently and admirably in the case and the Carter County Citizens League for Good Government won a judgment for the recovery of $36,291.00 from McGuire and from the four members the Board of Education. As part of his ruling, the judge ruled that the statute of limitations had run and thus precluded recovery of money misappropriated prior to McGuire's last five years in office. With the help of Governor Combs, however, his most important goal in the Carter County Case had been achieved—the early retirement of Superintendent Heman McGuire.

22 The Mountain Parkway

IN MY OPINION, ONE of the most interesting projects of the Combs administration was the construction of the Mountain Parkway. The Mountain Parkway was a major and critically important highway improvement. It ran from Winchester in Central Kentucky to Salyersville in eastern Kentucky.

During 1959, Bill May of Brighton Engineering in Frankfort voluntarily used his staff to draw up plans for a super highway to open up the mountains. He was determined to have the plans ready for Governor Combs before he was elected governor. So, when it came time build the road, Governor Combs advertised for road plans for the building of a Mountain Parkway. Of course, Bill May had his set of plans ready and his firm was the only one that was ready. Because of May's foresight, the Combs administration was able to start earlier than it would have been able to do otherwise. Governor Combs told me, "Banksie, we're going to turn dirt before the snow flies."

When it came time for the ground breaking ceremony, we had lunch at a school gymnasium in Winchester after which we were all going out to the site of the earth turning for the parkway. Unfortunately, the spot of the ceremony was far out in the country. To make things worse, while we were having lunch, a blizzard began. By the time we arrived out in the country at the appointed place, a huge bulldozer had to be pulled up to create a windbreak for us. The conditions were absolutely terrible—it was freezing cold with snow blowing hard. The governor and others had to turn their spades of dirt for the Parkway in a snowstorm so strong that they could barely see each other.

Wendell Ford and I had driven up together with S.C. Van Curon, editor of the *Frankfort State Journal,* and Paul Jordan who was the head of the Associated Press bureau. From the time we left the site of the ground breaking near Winchester to the time we arrived in Lexington was six hours. Wendell was scheduled to make a speech to in Lexington and we just made it in time.

Mrs. Combs was traveling in the car in front of us and everybody along the way would say, "Ms. Mable Combs is ahead, Mable is ahead." Vehicles all along the highway had pulled off the road. It was almost impossible to see well enough to drive. We had to creep along; it was an awful mess.

After we let Wendell off, Paul Jordan called in his story to the Associated Press. Meanwhile, Van Curon was asleep in the car and continued to sleep all the way back to Frankfort. Finally, we stopped at the Midland Tavern about 11:00 p.m. to have a bite to eat. Suddenly it dawned on me that Van Curon had not written his story. So Paul Jordan dictated a story and I copied it down on a napkin and took it to the *State Journal.* Of course, the folks there wanted to know where Van Curon was and I said, "Home in bed, here's his story," and the next day it appeared in the *State Journal* verbatim as I had turned it in.

We mountaineers watched eagerly as the work progressed on the Mountain Parkway. Before the completion of the parkway, the time for the trip back home had always been at least six hours. The parkway cut that time in half. Still, to this day, every time I travel the Mountain Parkway, I thank Bert Combs for having the guts and the courage, despite opposition, to build it.

23 The Floral Clock

ANOTHER INTERESTING PROJECT UNDERTAKEN by the Combs administration was the building of the Floral Clock that stands behind the Capitol on the grounds of the Capitol Annex. Governor Combs loved the Capitol and always insisted that the grounds be kept looking beautiful. He would walk around the Capitol building every day to make sure there were no pigeon droppings on the building or trash on the grounds.

One time he found a spot where pigeons had roosted and deposited something to remember them by. Governor Combs was furious and ordered me to fire the man who was responsible for failing to clean up the mess. He looked sternly at me and said, "Banksie, if you don't fire him, I'll fire you."

I hurried to the man and said, "If you don't clean up the pigeon droppings every morning, the governor is going to have you fired."

From that moment on, the pigeon droppings were cleaned up by daylight and Governor Combs never had a another problem with either the pigeons or the employee whom he thought had been dismissed.

As part of the beautification of the Capitol grounds, Bert Combs wanted to build a floral clock. He got the idea for the floral clock at Niagara Falls, Canada. When he saw the one there at the Falls, he was impressed and began thinking about constructing a similar one on the Capitol grounds.

When he told me about his plan to build the clock, I was very much against it because I was certain that Happy Chandler would make an issue out of the money spent on the clock. Wendell Ford agreed with me and helped me formulate some arguments against the clock's construction. To me especially, it looked like political suicide. The debate went on for some time. Finally, one day Wendell and I were standing in front of the Governor's desk. He was staring out of the window and finally he turned and said, "I want to build my damned floral clock." That settled the question right then and there!

The governor sent an aide to Niagara Falls to inquire about the clock and he made a drawing of it. The governor, himself, called watch companies to find out about the mechanical parts. He wanted to use prison labor to reduce the cost, but the labor unions threatened to picket the Capitol.

The project was going badly when the governor made a key move—he got the Garden Club of Kentucky interested in the project. The Garden Club folks agreed to help dedicate the clock and to make its construction the Garden Club project for that year. That sort of took the project out of politics.

The governor then proceeded with the idea of putting gold fish, turtles, and similar creatures in the pool around the clock. We started calling it a wishing well and people started throwing coins in the pool and making wishes. We decided to donate the money from the pool to handicapped children. After that, Happy and most of our other critics began talking about other things.

The clock cost $50,000, but, supposedly, it would be a very big tourist attraction. On April 27, Combs received congratulations for the Floral Clock project from the president and executive director of the National Association of Travel Organizations headquartered in Washington. On April 29, Governor Combs, speaking on the occasion of the annual convention of the Kentucky Daughters of the American Revolution, said that, for the time being, the Floral Clock was requiring more of his attention than the state's $12 million state park expansion program.

Floral Clock on the Capitol grounds

According to schedule, the Floral Clock was dedicated on May 4, 1961. Mayor Paul Judd of Frankfort spoke briefly expressing the hope that the clock would become as famous as the one in Scotland. Reverend W.R. Clark, pastor of the Louisville Presbyterian Church, spoke in nostalgic terms of Scotland's floral clock and said it was a superior tourist attraction.

The minute hand is twenty and a half feet long and weighs 530 pounds. The hour hand is fifteen and a half feet long and weighs 420 pounds. The entire structure, including the pool, is contained within a circular concrete wall. The pool is fifty-four feet in diameter. The coins tossed into the pool in the first two weeks amounted to more than $100. Combs announced that the first $100 was going to the Kentucky Training Home for the purchase of athletic equipment.

A few weeks after the dedication of the clock, Governor Combs and I were working in his office. We were both standing at the window and he was looking out and just kept looking at the east wing of the Capitol Annex building. All of sudden he turned toward me and said, "Banksie, we need something to balance off the clock."

I almost dropped in my tracks. *Oh, no, not another Floral Clock issue!* He looked at me and grinned and said, "How about a rose garden?"

I breathed a deep sigh of relief. And that's how the idea for the Rose Garden on the east side of the Annex originated.

There's another story about Governor Combs having to do with flowers, and I remember it very well. One morning I had been with Governor Combs, and he was in very good humor. A little later that morning, in came the groundskeeper for the Capitol grounds. And he told me, "Fontaine, the governor wants tulips to bloom on Derby Day, but they're going to bloom early. I said, "Let's tell him." So we walked in, the governor was looking down at his desk, and he didn't look up. I said, "Governor, the kid's got a problem." Governor Combs said, "What's your problem, kid?" He said, "Governor, the tulips are going to bloom early." Governor Combs looked up and said, "They better not." The kid said, "What do you want me to do?" The governor replied, as serious as he could be, "Pack them in ice." So we walked out, and the groundskeeper said, "Fontaine, what am I going to do?" I said, "Better call your ice man." It turned cold, like it can do on Derby Day in Kentucky, but the tulips bloomed early anyway. And the governor really didn't like it!

24 Northern Kentucky

In the 1920s, national prohibition gave birth to organized syndicate crime. Kentucky was not immune from this development. Syndicate crime became a dominant force in Newport and throughout Northern Kentucky. In the 1930s–1950s, Newport was a major headquarters for big-time gambling, especially lay-off betting in which one bookmaker, inundated with a large sum of money bet on a single horse, could move a portion of the bets to another bookmaker and if the horse won, the payoff was split. All through these decades, state government did not attempt to stamp out this illegal activity until the early 1960s when the citizens, themselves, began to attempt to do something about it.

On March 2, 1961, eight representatives of the Newport Protestant Ministerial Association delivered to Governor Combs' personal secretary, Mrs. Polly Gordon, a thirty-one page affidavit charging that eight law enforcement officers of Newport and Campbell County had permitted gambling, prostitution and illegal trafficking in liquor to flourish in the city and in the county. The names of the officers were Sheriff Norbert Rowe, County Judge A. J. Jolly, Circuit Judge R. L. Murphy, Newport Mayor Ralph Mussman, Newport Police of Chief George Gugel, Newport Detective Chief Leroy Fredricks, County Police Chief Harry Stewart and Detective Gardner Reed.

The delegation urged and requested that the governor remove these men from their respective offices. This action of the Ministerial Association came shortly after a Campbell County Grand Jury report found no widespread violations of law in the county and found that such violations as did exist had been greatly exaggerated by the ministers and the metropolitan newspapers.

At first Governor Combs moved cautiously. On March 4, he said that he had not had an opportunity to read the long affidavit. He also stated that he doubted he had the authority to oust Judge Murphy or Judge Jolly. He said that he would discuss the question with Attorney General John Breckinridge Governor Combs' first move was to request County Judge Jolly's attorney, Joseph Leary of Frankfort, a prominent attorney in the commonwealth, to state his reasons for claiming that his client was exempt from the proposed ouster proceedings. Leary's main point was that his client was a judicial officer rather than a peace officer and thus Jolly could be removed only by impeachment or by indictment and conviction.

On March 9, attorney Thomas Hurchfield asked Combs to drop any planned ouster proceedings against Mayor Mussman on the ground that the mayor was not a police officer. Attorney William J. Wyatt indicated he planned a similar defense for Gardner Reed.

On March 18, 1961, Clay Wade Bailey reported in the *Kentucky Post* and *Times Star* that Combs was proceeding with cautious restraint after a group of Campbell County businessmen appealed to him to go forward with an inquiry into charges of official laxity on the part of the Newport and Campbell County law enforcement officials. Bailey said that the petition they presented described the criminal conditions in Campbell County and alleged dereliction of duty in certain fields of law so severe that the situation had become tragically and urgently serious. The article stated that the group had been organized spontaneously by men whose intelligence was insulted by the report that had been issued by the Campbell County Grand Jury back in February.

Governor Combs was much encouraged by the action of this group of businessmen. He told them, however, that there was a strong possibility of his not having the authority to remove some of the officials who were named in their complaint. Challenging them to further action, the Governor said that he was quite willing to help with law enforcement, but would like to be certain that he would not be making a futile gesture for lack of authority to act.

On March 24, Governor Combs told press representatives that he had tentatively reached the conclusion that he lacked the authority to entertain ouster petitions against Judge Murphy, Judge Jolly and Mayor Mussman. He therefore rejected the initiation of the ouster proceedings requested by the Newport Ministerial Association against these three officials at least until there was a legal determination as to whether they were peace officers within the meaning of Section 227 of the Kentucky Constitution.

By the first week of April, a committee of about one hundred had been formed and had chosen a board of directors. The membership campaign was reported to have a goal of $5,000 to be raised for the Newport-Campbell

County clean-up effort. It was also reported that the committee would back an independent slate of candidates including a candidate for the office of Campbell County sheriff.

Next, the Newport Ministerial Association fired another blast at Circuit Judge Murphy in the form of a letter to the *Kentucky Post* and *Times Star* citing a half century old opinion of former Judge A. O. Stanley opining that a circuit judge is a peace officer and therefore subject to ouster proceedings.

On April 5, four leading members of the Committee of 500 (the Committee of one hundred was growing rapidly in numbers) including George Ratterman of Ft. Thomas, the committee's candidate for sheriff, presented a progress report to Governor Combs. Incidentally, they asked him to set up a temporary governor's office in the Newport area. They suggested that the best way for the state to combat vice in the Newport area would be through the enforcement powers of the Alcoholic Beverage Control Board (ABC). Governor Combs observed that this board could only cite illegal activities to the proper judicial authority.

Meanwhile, dissatisfaction with the slow and cautious moves of the governor was mounting. On April 6, the attorney for the Ministerial Association asked Franklin County Circuit Judge Henry Meigs for a ruling as to whether Governor Combs had the power and duty to hold ouster hearings for Judges Murphy and Jolly and Mayor Mussman. In addition, Combs' apparent reluctance to press ouster proceedings against Sheriff Rowe and the peace officers drew some very harsh editorial criticism.

On April 10, Governor Combs announced that he had ordered the ABC Board to the fight against gambling, prostitution and the violation of liquor laws in the Newport area. Commissioner Harold Moberly announced that eight to ten agents would be sent to Northern Kentucky within the week.

Governor Combs said that he would send State Police troopers to the area if the proper city or county official requested such action. He still did not believe that the situation warranted his declaring an emergency. He thought that taking such a step would bring more bad publicity and further damage to the reputation of the community and would be effective only for the duration of the emergency. At the same time, he announced the opening of ouster proceedings, making it clear that he would use the full power of his office if additional steps should be necessary.

On April 12, it was rumored that ABC Commissioner, Harry Moberly, was personally directing the drive to purge the illegal liquor business in Newport.

The report said this development had caused jittery nerves among some of the criminal element; it also made operators in the big casinos doubly worried as they were beginning to see that quite a few small places were refusing to pay off on pinball machines.

After about two weeks of stalking violators of the liquor laws, the ABC agents pressed charges against seven Newport taverns with hearings scheduled for sometime in May. Since both Combs and Moberly were not satisfied with what had been accomplished, Combs decided to seek the advice and assistance of Attorney General Breckinridge. Combs was convinced that additional measures were needed.

On April 24, Judge Meigs ruled that the Franklin Circuit Court had no jurisdiction in regard to the ouster of public officials. Governor Combs expressed disappointment saying that he had wanted the courts to decide the issue. The governor's calling on Attorney General Breckinridge to help in the clean up drive gave rise to speculation as to the next move that the Governor contemplated.

Meanwhile, in the second week in May, the hearings got underway for the owners of the nine establishments that had been cited by the ABC Board. On May 8, the liquor licenses of the Merchants Club and the Spotted Calf Bar were suspended for six months. Hearings for the seven others were set for later in May.

On May 29, Governor Combs received a big morale boost from a visit by a delegation of students from eight high schools in Northern Kentucky. They brought a petition signed by 1,300 students calling for better law enforcement and strong action against vice activities.

The petition declared, "We, the youth of Northern Kentucky, are disturbed at the vice and corruption around us. We want better law enforcement and more honest officials." Governor Combs' high regard for this group of young people of high school age gave him the morale boost he needed to initiate the ouster proceedings.

On June 7, Governor Combs issued four Executive Orders directing the Secretary of State to file for public review the affidavit charging Sheriff Norbert Rowe of Campbell County, Chief of Police Harry Stewart of Campbell County, Chief of Detectives Leroy Fredericks of Newport, and Chief of Police George Gugel of Newport with willful neglect their official duties.

In the middle of July, the hearings began in the conference room of the State Senate. Attorneys representing the Newport Ministerial Association assisted

Attorney General Breckinridge. He was also assisted by two members of his staff, Attorneys Roy Savage and William Watson. At one end of the long table sat Commissioner Jarnell Davis together with his stenographer and a chair for a witness. Attorney J.D. Buchman and his three clients, Sheriff Norbert Rowe, Police Chief Gugel and Detective Chief Roy Fredricks, sat at the opposite end of the table. Attorney Joseph Leary and his client, County Police Chief Harry Stewart sat on the south side of the table by Commissioner Davis. All five of the prosecuting attorneys sat on the north side of the table.

Generally, there were surprisingly few visitors and an atmosphere of decorum prevailed. However, several witnesses gave damaging testimony. At the end of the day, it was evident that the prosecution was scoring heavily. On July 19, Governor Combs was a surprise visitor. He came to officially file two documents whose purpose was to meet the defense attorneys' objection that the affidavits had not been filed according to law. The governor provided some brief testimony.

Probably the most damaging testimony was that of Mrs. Hattie Jackson. This woman had been sentenced to five years in prison for the operation of a house of prostitution in Newport. She named several of the accused officials as having received payoffs from the earnings of the prostitutes. She named George Gugel, Leroy Fredericks and former Mayor Robert Sennel, Circuit Judge Murphy and Commonwealth's Attorney William Wise. She said that the payoffs equaled half of the earnings of the girls. Her testimony was described in the media as "electrifying."

The Internal Revenue Service was interested in possible violations of federal income tax laws. Quite a few of those under investigation were caught in the federal net. Before the ouster hearings were resumed in September, there were many subpoenas to be served. They were connected with the 215 indictments that were returned in August by a Special Campbell County Grand Jury. The Special Grand Jury session was called by Circuit Judge Murphy who had been named by Mrs. Jackson as a party to the payoffs. During the Grand Jury Session, however, Murphy vacated the bench and was replaced by Judge Edward G. Hill of Harlan.

In order to guarantee and facilitate the serving of these subpoenas, Governor Combs sent State Police troopers into the Newport area on a limited emergency basis. The net was closing in on northern Kentucky vice.

Leroy Fredericks, as well as George Gugel, sought to escape penalties by resigning before the hearings began, but it was to no avail. The investigation convinced Combs that they were guilty as charged. Accordingly, on October 10, he issued an Executive Order reading as follows: "I hereby direct that all provisions and penalties of the statutes involved shall be applied to the said George Gugel the same as though he had been removed from office." A similarly worded Executive Order evoked penalties against Mr. Fredericks. The chief penalty was disqualification to hold public office. Attorney Buckman announced he would take the case to the Court of Appeals. The proceedings against Rowe and Stewart continued with the November election just ahead.

There was considerable speculation as to the ultimate effect on the clean-up drive if George Ratterman, the independent candidate of the reform forces, should be defeated in the election for Campbell County sheriff. Combs, in a televised interview in Cincinnati on October 3, said very emphatically that the fight would be continued without a let up. He conceded that the defeat of Ratterman would be a sharp setback for the reform movement, but would not end the investigation.

On October 27, the federal Grand Jury in Lexington indicted Newport Police Chief George Gugel and five accomplices and charged them with conspiracy to violate the civil rights of George Ratterman. Though the case was tried during the following summer of 1962, the indictments came at an opportune time to aid George Ratterman in his campaign for sheriff.

The voters of Campbell County rose to the occasion. Ratterman was elected by a substantial majority. On December 7, 1961, Governor Combs issued an Executive Order ousting Sheriff Rowe prior to the expiration of his term. In taking the case to the Court of Appeals, Rowe was able to remain in office until his term ended, but the Combs forces that had sought his removal at least had a noteworthy moral victory.

In another Executive Order, issued on January 20, 1962, Governor Combs ordered the ousting of Campbell County Police Chief Stewart. Campbell County Judge Jolly vigorously condemned the governor's order saying that Chief Stewart had conscientiously carried out his assigned duties. He challenged the governor's right to judge the validity of an order of the county court. Governor Combs stood his ground so Stewart took his case directly to the Court of Appeals.

Although most of Newport's gamblers and dispensers of prostitution had closed shop before the end of 1961, there was still a great deal of unfinished business for the clean up forces to accomplish. Gugeland Fredericks lost their appeals of the governor's ouster proceedings and their penalties were held to be applicable even though they had resigned. The Court of Appeals also upheld the governor's order ousting Stewart. The same thing befell Rowe somewhat later. Meanwhile, a federal Grand Jury had found Rowe guilty of four counts of having failed to file income tax returns.

Many of the eighty-seven people indicted by the Campbell County Special Grand Jury pled guilty and were fined while several others were tried and convicted. Most observers credited Governor Combs with having provided the necessary assistance that the Newport Ministerial Association and the Committee of 500 had requested. The attack on commercialized vice in Sin City, as Newport was known, and its environs achieved a great deal of success. The battle had been won and the good citizens of Newport and Campbell County enjoyed the victory that banished the organized crime syndicate element to other points outside the Commonwealth of Kentucky.

Before concluding the Northern Kentucky story, the George Ratterman story must be mentioned. George W. Ratterman was a former football player who played quarterback at Notre Dame and then played professional football for ten years, first with the Buffalo Bills and later with the Cleveland Browns. He was a well-rounded person who performed a piano solo with the Buffalo Symphony and he later wrote the book, *Confessions of a Gypsy Quarterback* (1962). After injuries ended his football career, he became an attorney and did sports commentary for network television broadcasts. While studying for his law degree, he worked as an investment counselor in Cincinnati. He helped form the National Football League Players' Association and was legal counsel for the American Football League. Ratterman was no lightweight—He was a very accomplished individual.

As we have previously discussed, in 1961, the alliance of ministers joined the Campbell County Citizens group known as the Committee of 500, in attempting to rid the county of organized crime which featured prostitution, bookmaking, other forms of gambling and illegal liquor activities. When the group decided to run its own slate of candidates in 1961, Ratterman, a Campbell County resident, agreed to run for sheriff as a high-profile candidate. He would be the main man; he would be the face of the reform forces.

On the night of May 9, Ratterman met with a syndicate member at a meeting set up by a business associate for the purpose of talking about the removal of casino operations from Campbell County. At the meeting Ratterman lost consciousness after he was served a drink that contained "knockout drops." He regained consciousness in the company of a nightclub dancer in a hotel bedroom, where the local police arrested him for prostitution and disturbing the peace.

In a sensational police court trial in Newport, it became obvious that the gambling interests were working with law enforcement officials to discredit Ratterman and the whole reform movement. A photographer testified that he had been contacted weeks earlier and asked to photograph such a scene. Charges against Ratterman were dropped and the reform movement, which had stood behind Ratterman throughout the long ordeal, gained momentum and became stronger.

In November, 1961, Ratterman and the other reform ticket candidates were swept into office by a landslide. Seeing the handwriting on the wall, the operators of the casinos and nightclubs cleared out of town. Four years later, Ratterman lost the election for county judge. Then, in 1966, he was again defeated, this time by Gene Snyder in a bid for election to Congress. By then Ratterman had had enough of Kentucky politics and, in 1967, he left the state and moved to Denver, Colorado.

The Ratterman star was a shooting star. It burned brightly, but quickly faded away. But Ratterman deserves much credit for agreeing to drop his many other profitable activities to aid the reform forces. The effort almost cost him his reputation, but he emerged from the set-up unscathed and went on to a much deserved victory in the sheriff's race.

During the whole period of the Northern Kentucky affair, I was deeply involved with Governor Combs as he carefully planned his actions. There were many times during the handling of this problem that members of the governor's staff felt uneasy. We had to be careful not to make any mistakes and hurt the efforts of the reform forces.

The governor acted cautiously throughout the entire affair. He never made a misstep. I was extremely proud of the manner in which the governor conducted himself. While members of the media and others were demanding quick action, Governor Combs took his time and with deliberate speed made all the right moves. All of the governor's staff members were extremely proud of the manner in which he handled the situation. The old saying goes, "the proof is in the pudding." Well, this pudding was cooked perfectly with the result that the citizens of Campbell County and the surrounding area were freed from the bad influences of organized crime.

25 The 1962 Regular Session of the General Assembly

Governor Combs worked diligently to convince the people of Kentucky that the state's first billion dollar budget was yielding satisfactory dividends in the form of expanded and improved services with major advances in education, health and welfare services, highway construction, conservation of resources, state parks and the rapidly growing tourism business.

Prior to the 1962 session, Combs' main effort had been directed toward showing that the sales tax was a splendid investment. The electorate had been bombarded with a considerable amount of demagoguery about the tax. Combs had read and heard allegations that the tax was "picking the pocket of the poor" and "taking food out of the mouths of the hungry."

In the May primary of 1961, leaders of the critics of the sales tax called out Governor Combs for a test of the voting sentiment for the tax. Had the voters been more impressed by the straight talk of Governor Combs and his warriors or by the smoke and camouflage of Happy Chandler and his followers? Chandler loudly predicted a vote against the sales tax. Chandler's relentless attacks on the tax created anxiety in the Combs camp; in other words, the candidates who had voted for the tax were running scared. So were several new candidates running for places in the General Assembly and who supported the tax.

The primary election was held on Tuesday, May 23, 1961. Newspapers on Wednesday began to tell the story; victory for the Combs administration and the proponents of the sales tax. By Wednesday, May 24, Combs was expecting a net gain of at least four seats in the Senate and at least ten seats in the House. The governor said that the results of the primary election were an endorsement of the progressive programs enacted by the previous General Assembly. Chandler commented that it was too early to tell and said that he would be nervous at this stage of the game if he were in Combs' position.

The official returns confirmed Combs' estimate of gains, with one exception. The General Assembly leaders who had supported the governor's legislative program in 1960 retained their seats and would be back. Representative Thomas L. Ray, the Majority Floor Leader in the House in 1960, however, had accepted the Democratic nomination for Sheriff in Jefferson County, but R.P. Maloney of Lexington, a brilliant attorney, would be back to ably replace Ray as the Floor Leader. Key Combs' supporters James Ware of South Fort Mitchell defeated Joseph Sumi of Covington, Alvin Kidwell of Sparta defeated Raymond Raffett, and Harry King Lowman of Ashland won handily.

In the Senate, Combs-backed victors over Chandler's partisans were Wilson Palmer of Cynthiana, Spencer Cobb of Nicholasville, J.D. Buckman of Shepherdsville, Cabbrell Francis of Stanford, Herbert Dickerson of Stanton, and John Turner of Jackson.

These six new senators represented added Combs' strength in the Senate. Two Chandler backed candidates, Marvin Edwards of Lawrenceburg and Casper Gardner of Owensboro, won nominations for the Senate.

Early one Sunday morning, Governor Combs called me and said he was going to go to the hospital to swear in Spencer Cobb as Senator and that he wanted me to go with him. We rushed over to Lexington's Central Baptist Hospital where Governor Combs administered the oath of office to Senator Cobb. When Combs arrived, Cobb greeted him with, "Thank God, you've come in time." After taking the constitutional oath, Senator Spencer Cobb's face glowed with satisfaction and he said, "Now I am a senator." He was expecting that his proxy would be used that evening at the Democratic caucus, but, just three hours later, Senator Cobb was dead.

Contrary to Chandler's prediction, shortly after the key primary victories by the Combs administration candidates, the governor's supporters easily controlled both houses of the General Assembly. In the Senate Democratic caucus, the pro-Chandler faction could not muster more than eight votes. Senator Kidwell was nominated for President Pro-Tem by a margin of twenty to seven. Senator James C. Ware was elected Majority Floor Leader by a vote of nineteen to five. Senator J.D. Buckman of Salt River was elected Caucus Chairman by acclamation, after Chandler partisans lost a motion for a secret ballot.

In the caucus of the House Democrats, Harry King Lowman was quickly nominated for a second term as Speaker of the House. R.P. Maloney was elected Majority Floor Leader and Thomas Fitzpatrick of Covington was elected Caucus Chairman. Lowman's nomination was equivalent to election since all Democrats were bound by party rules to vote for the caucus nominee. Governor Combs requested that I act as administrative assistant to R.P. Maloney, Majority Floor Leader in the House, which I did throughout the entire session.

On Tuesday, January 2, 1962, Governor Combs delivered his "State of the Commonwealth" address to a Joint Session of the General Assembly. As long as the Commonwealth of Kentucky endures, the speech Governor Combs gave that night will have an important place in the history of the state. Here quoted are some passages from that address:

> Since I spoke to you in 1960, the face of Kentucky and the mood of Kentuckians, the spirit of the people, all have been deeply and significantly effected. Your lieutenant governor and I were elected on a platform which had been submitted to and approved by the people. We have undertaken to carry out the programs pledged in that platform. What is needed is time to complete some of the measures and test others.
>
> It is traditional that the Kentucky governor approaches the second legislative session with some concern and perhaps apprehension. I come with confidence to report on the State of the Commonwealth and to join with you in officially opening what I believe will be a productive and hopefully historically significant session of the Kentucky General Assembly.
>
> I am confident that when the present session ends, our people will have cause to be grateful to you, the members of the 1962 General Assembly. I am convinced you will keep Kentucky on the progressive course charted two years ago. When I appeared before you two years ago, the problems we faced were the heavy accumulation of lingering needs, old wants and long neglect. We'd been accustomed to looking backward because the way ahead seemed too fraught with difficulties. We'd become accustomed to hearing Kentucky spoken of as a "problem state."

Governor Combs went on to enumerate some of the reasons for Kentucky's poor rating in the socioeconomic scale in comparison with other states. Then he observed,

> Today there is a new spirit in Kentucky. For the first time in this century, Kentucky has received more national publicity for our progress than for our problems. Neighboring states are beginning to regard us with respect. We no longer live in the past and, if we do what we can and should do here now, Kentucky need never again be classified as a problem state.
>
> We have taken the offensive and we can keep it by advertising Kentucky's business and tourist attractions to the world. Our annual growth in personal income has doubled the national average. In highway building, school construction and support, rate of salary increases to teachers and in health and welfare programs, we are among the leading states in the nation. Kentucky is the first state to qualify for regulation of atomic materials for peaceful use in private industry. A new industrial research center in Lexington is attracting national interest. Young Cultural Research Center is taking shape at the University of Kentucky and is one of the best in the nation.
>
> We are accelerating our geographic mapping program and expanding our vocational training. Through laws passed in 1960, we have controlled strip mining without crippling this industry or destroying the jobs it provides. This past year we opened seventy-five miles of interstate highway. Construction contracts for $123 million were let in the year 1961. While achieving this record on major highways, we have not neglected rural roads. In the past two years, the Rural Highway Division has spent roughly $34 million in constructing, repairing and maintaining approximately 17,000 miles of rural highways, bridges and culverts.

At this point in his address, Governor Combs credited the statutory merit system with having raised the morale of state employees to the highest level in history. Governor Combs continued by saying,

> That progress in social services has kept pace with that in education. Kentucky was the first state in the nation to

establish a Department for Child Welfare. We have begun a program for the care and training of our mentally retarded children; one more problem that desperately needs your attention. The Kentucky Training Home is completely obsolete and inadequate to the needs of these unfortunate children. We also started our program of medical assistance to the aged. We will increase assistance to the blind, the aged, dependent children and the permanently and totally disabled. We will use state funds so as to obtain maximum use of federal money.

The new Human Rights Commission has helped to maintain Kentucky's excellent reputation for progressive racial relations. In mental health, Kentucky has continued to make progress. We have one of the finest mental health departments in the nation. In the field of public health, six new community hospitals were completed in 1961 at a cost of almost $8 million. One nursing home and nine health care centers were dedicated. Ten hospitals, ten health care centers and two nursing homes are now under construction.

All of these projects have utilized federal funds. $12 million has been committed to expansion of the state parks system. Eight parks have been completely made over, three new parks have been added. Negotiations are in progress for the addition of three more. This program will give Kentucky the finest parks system in the world. It not only will be of tremendous value in building our tourism industry, but place the high quality, moderately priced vacation and recreation facilities within easy driving distance of Kentucky.

At this point in his speech, Governor Combs presented the proposals which he would ask that the General Assembly consider at this session. In substance they were as follows: The reorganization of certain departments of state government in order to improve the quality of services by grouping kindred activities; legislation in the field of education including the creation of two-year community colleges together with the implementation of some of the recommendations of the Education Commission. Other topics were confirmation of the Strip Mine Control Law and legislation authorizing the sale of bonds to finance additional vocational school construction.

Other subjects to be addressed included attending to the problem of automobile graveyards, the revision of absentee voting laws, regulation of industrial loan firms, expansion of the KRASS Program, better facilities for the Speaker of the House of Representatives including a year-round office and compensation on a per diem basis and reapportionment of the state into new congressional districts.

In order to demonstrate to the legislators that he had no further political aspirations, the governor promised that he would not allow politics to influence his conduct during the session. The governor urged that all members of the General Assembly join him in declaring a moratorium on politics for the duration of the session. He made it clear, however, that his commitment to "no politics" during the session would be binding only if all members of the General Assembly joined him in that pledge.

26 Senior Aide

When Governor Combs designated me as his senior aide, at my request, we did not make a public announcement of my appointment. The employees of the governor's staff were working well together and I feared that an announcement of my becoming senior aide might cause some jealousy and disturb the workings of our well-oiled machine of a staff.

Many key duties were assigned to me. For example, I was totally responsible for all legislative initiatives and efforts, a huge responsibility for just one person. I was in charge of contacts with all the governor's political friends and elected officials from all over the state. When a citizen had a problem with state government and desired to see the governor about it, I was the person who met with the citizen and attempted to resolve the problem or, at least, send the person to the proper official who could help him.

When I came to the governor's office, I brought Sarah Gordon with me from the Department for Personnel. I later added Tyree Gaines from Lawrenceburg and Pippen Carter from Woodford County. Those three ran my office; they knew what to do and didn't have to ask me. They were very able and efficient. I couldn't have handled all of my duties without their always competent assistance. They kept me informed; for example, when calls came through that they could handle, but were important in their opinions, they would inform me about them and how each was handled. They were truly outstanding employees and I will always be in their debt.

When a legislator or a citizen with a major problem with state government came to Frankfort demanding to see somebody, they usually ended up in my office. I would give them a cup of coffee, let them hang up their hat and coat, chat with them a little, get them relaxed and settled down and then I would take care of their problem myself or, if unable to do so, I would schedule an appointment for them with the department head who could help them. These folks, many of whom came to Frankfort fighting mad, usually left my office in a good mood.

Of course, my most important duty was to advise Governor Combs. He liked discussing problems, projects and issues with me because he knew that I would always give him my honest opinion with nothing held back. The last thing a governor needs on his staff or as an advisor is a "yes" man. Sometimes Governor Combs wasn't looking for advice from me; he just wanted someone to listen to him as he puzzled out a problem that he had been thinking about. I had to know the difference between those occasions when he wanted my opinion and the occasions when he wanted me to just be a good listener. Governor Combs valued my views on political issues and state government problems and often took my advice. When he didn't like my advice, he simply told me so. I always knew where I stood with him.

It was a great pleasure working so closely with Governor Combs even though the hours were long and the weekends sometimes nonexistent. We had a bond between us—a bond based on trust and the knowledge that each of us was totally loyal to the other. We seemed to almost automatically know what the other was thinking even when those thoughts were the opposite of what one of us hoped. I have always thought that our mutual Eastern Kentucky background and heritage was a contributing factor to our close relationship. We were more than governor and staff member, we were friends. Friends who knew they could rely on each other no matter the situation.

The manner in which we approached problems and issues was different. The governor was more intellectual in his thinking than I was. He was more concerned with the method of achieving a goal and with results while I was concerned with the political reaction to his efforts. He wanted to achieve while I wanted to protect—he was idealistic while I was practical. This made for a good combination. The ideal and the practical—each was a brake on the other.

We had a confidence in each other that was unique in my experience. We felt as if we were kindred spirits. We were comfortable with each other, and we could sit together in a couple of easy chairs and just talk. A governor needs to have someone to whom he can express his frustrations, someone with whom he can "let down his hair," someone with whom he can just be himself. For Bert Combs, I was that man. How blessed I was for Bert Combs was an uncommon man, an uncommon Governor, an uncommon statesman—he was a great Kentuckian and a great man.

Governor Combs laughingly told people that he could tell when I was angry with him by the way I slammed the door when I left his office. He said that the louder I slammed the door, the madder I was. One Friday afternoon, he and I were alone working in his office and were discussing some problems we had faced during the week. The week had been a rough one and, when I left the governor's office, I guess I slammed the door a little too hard. As I left the governor's office by the back door, somebody came in through the front door. In a few minutes Bill Leonard came by the office and said, "Banksie, I'll have you a new car Monday morning."

I said, "I don't need a new car."

Bill Leonard replied, "I don't care what you need; the governor said you'd had a rough week and he wanted you to have a new car." Sure enough, on Monday morning a brand new car was parked in my stall and I got in and drove it to Elizabethtown for a meeting.

The governor preferred that I relay information to the commissioners instead of having to talk to them himself. This saved the always busy governor a lot of time. But, for me, the result was that I was constantly on the phone with some commissioner about some problem in his department.

The governor's executive appointments came through my office and I had to process those and work them up and that was another time consuming job, but one that, I must admit, was very much needed.

The Minority Leader of the House had made speeches all summer that he was going to introduce a bill to change elections in Kentucky. On the first day of the session, he dropped his bill in the hopper. I had made Lawrence Langford, of Harlan, chairman of the Election Commission. Unfortunately, he had suffered a stroke and as a result was badly crippled. I sent for Lawrence and told him that, when he came to meet with me, to bring a copy of the bill and an analysis of its contents with him. It was a time consuming process for Langford, but he came to my office one day and said, "Fontaine, here's the bill, what do you want me to do with it?"

I took the bill from his hand, opened his coat and carefully placed it in his pocket and said, "Lawrence, leave the bill there until I need it."

Several times during the session he'd open his coat and say, "Fontaine, I've still got it." One day, I heard the gentleman from Lincoln County say he needed to see me. Of course, I knew he wanted to see me about his bill.

Well, he came into my office and said, "What did you do with my bill?"

I replied, "What are you talking about?"

He said, "You know, the bill I introduced on changing the election." Then he couldn't help but start laughing.

He said, "Fontaine, you're the only SOB I know that has the guts to take a bill and hide it. When are you going to give it back to me?"

I said, "Oh, it'll show up."

He said, "Yeah, I know, on the last day of the session."

On the last day of the session, my man, Lawrence, put the bill on the clerk's desk and it was, at last, in the process although it was going nowhere.

As the decades have passed by, I have had the opportunity to really think about the glory days, and they were glory days, of the Combs administration. I have come to the conclusion that Bert Combs and his administration deserve credit for bringing Kentucky, then in so many ways a backward state, into the twentieth century and, in many ways, also into the twenty-first century. I believe he had such an impact on state government and on almost all aspects of Kentucky life that we are still feeling and measuring his influence here in the first decade of the twenty-first century. He gave the state an impetus that is still going.

I think that, for the first time, he really made our people proud to be Kentuckians. Proud because of what he was doing and what he accomplished. I know that this feeling of pride was felt particularly deeply by the people of the hills and mountains of Eastern Kentucky. I know because I am one of them as was Bert Combs, himself. He brought the mountain people into the fold. Prior to Bert Combs, the folks of the hills and "hollers" were a forgotten people. Forgotten by all but the big-time coal companies that systematically, both literally and figuratively, stripped them of their heritage. With the building of the Mountain Parkway, Governor Combs began to open up this sadly neglected area whose people had so much to offer, but so little opportunity to give. His greatly improved funding for education, while benefiting the entire state, was especially important to the school systems and colleges of Eastern Kentucky.

In the final analysis, Bert Combs, himself, was a boon to the people of the Eastern Coal Field. There he stood, the perfect role model for the young people of the area. A man who had proven that it was entirely possible for a young person from Eastern Kentucky to overcome all obstacles and become a very successful and accomplished person.

As for the man himself, the "Little Judge" (as he was often called) was, in my opinion, a giant in the history of Kentucky. He was an outstanding governor and a great person. To me, he was the model governor—everything a governor should be. He was a man of integrity and good judgment. He had a brilliant mind filled with innovative ideas and yet he never got carried away with himself. He proceeded with caution and deliberation. He had a sense of humor and, unlike many politicians, he could laugh at himself. He was always in control; a man of great self control. I never saw him angry at anyone. He had the courage of his convictions, and he was always a gentleman and was courteous to everyone regardless of their station in life.

Bert Combs was a strong leader who tried to do the right thing even if public sentiment was against him. Rather than take a poll to decide which side of the fence to be on, he would attempt to lead the public to his view through logic and good old-fashioned reasoning. As a speaker, he wasn't gifted with a good speaking voice, but he spoke in well thought-out, understandable terms. He wasn't a great speaker, but he was an effective one.

The characteristic of Bert Combs that stands out the most in my mind was something that he didn't have—he was never concerned for himself. He was the least self-centered person I have known in my life. Oh sure, he wanted to leave a legacy, but not for himself, personally, so much, but rather for the people of this state that he loved so dearly. And what a marvelous legacy he left us—major improvements in virtually every area of government—roads, education, parks, human resources, human rights, and social services. His was one of the most progressive administrations in the state's history.

Often forgotten is the role he played in civil rights. He appointed the state's first human rights commission and, in 1963, issued an Executive Order that desegregated all public accommodations in the state. Bert Combs just wanted to do the right thing. He was never greatly ambitious for himself, but tremendously ambitious for Kentucky. The Kennedy Administration in Washington, serving during the same years as Combs, was called "Camelot." Well, it may have been so, but, here in the Commonwealth of Kentucky, we had our own "Camelot." I miss Bert Combs. I was privileged to play a role in his administration, and to count him a friend.

27 Breathitt's 1963 Campaign for Governor

Edward T. (Ned) Breathitt, Jr., was Kentucky's governor during 1963-1967, succeeding Bert Combs. And I do mean "succeeding." Breathitt was hand-picked, endorsed and backed by Bert Combs. Combs was so well-liked that, as a result of his popularity, he was able to name his own successor; something many other Kentucky governors have attempted to do without success. Breathitt had been Commissioner of Personnel in the Combs administration for awhile and played an important role in developing and implementing the new merit system for state employees. Later in the Combs administration, he moved to the Public Service Commission.

Ned Breathitt was born in Hopkinsville in 1924. After completing high school, he served in the air force during 1942-1945 in World War II. After the war, he enrolled at the University of Kentucky where he received a law degree in 1950. He opened a law practice in his hometown of Hopkinsville and proceeded to win three consecutive terms in the Kentucky House of Representatives. He gained political experience working in Adlai Stevenson's unsuccessful 1952 presidential campaign and in Alben Barkley's successful 1954 campaign for the U.S. Senate.

Thus, after a successful tenure as a member of the Combs administration and with the blessing of Governor Combs, in 1962, Breathitt announced that he would enter the 1963 Democratic gubernatorial primary. Breathitt made his announcement prior to the conclusion of the U.S. Senate race between Lt. Gov. Wilson Wyatt and the incumbent, Sen. Thruston B. Morton. Combs and Wyatt had an understanding that Combs would support Wyatt as his successor in the governor's chair. But after John F. Kennedy was elected president, Wyatt had second thoughts about succeeding Combs and decided to run for the Senate. The Senate seat had become much more attractive now that a Democratic president was in the White House and Congress was also in the hands of the Democrats. The glitz and glamour of the Kennedy

Camelot appealed to Wyatt.

Combs had no difficulty with Wyatt's decision not to run for governor, but he had to choose a successor candidate and then make an all-out effort to elect his choice. If Combs didn't do this, it appeared that Happy Chandler would be almost a shoo-in to be the next governor. This would mean defeat for Combs and the almost certain dismantling of his programs.

Fontaine Banks (far right) and James Wine, a Pikeville attorney and former ambassador to Guinea with John F. Kennedy supporters from Pike County

Chandler was already running. In fact, he had been running ever since Combs was elected. Well, there's an old rule in politics that says a party should run only one race at a time. Now Combs believed that, ordinarily, this was a sound rule. But Combs felt it was so important to elect his successor that an exception to the rule had to be made in this situation.

Wyatt lost to Morton and then blamed his defeat on Combs' decision to allow Breathitt to announce his intention to run for governor prior to the conclusion of the Senate race. Wyatt believed Breathitt's early entry into the governor's race cost him 50,000 votes because it caused Happy Chandler to oppose him and it split the focus and resources of the Democratic Party. He lost by more than 45,000 votes.

My personal view is that Breathitt's early announcement did not cause Wyatt's loss to Morton. The Chandler forces had already decided to back Morton. It was public knowledge that Happy was against any Combs-Wyatt candidate, especially when either one of those two was the candidate. Also, Wyatt, a capable and good man, just did not have the personality to connect with the average Kentuckian. No. Wilson Wyatt lost the race against Morton on his own.

Thus, the stage was set for a gubernatorial primary featuring the old war horse, Happy Chandler, against the almost unknown, Ned Breathitt.

Combs had agonized over the choice for some time. He carefully considered Congressmen Bill Natcher and John Watts, but they weren't interested, both enjoying safe Congressional seats. Combs considered Henry Ward, who he thought would be a fine governor, but he also thought Ward couldn't win. He strongly considered Court of Appeals Judge John Palmore and federal judge, Jim Gordon.

Combs finally settled on Ned Breathitt. He liked Breathitt because he was young, different and able. He would run an energetic, innovative campaign thought Combs. Even though he was not well known, he had a good ol' Kentucky name—"Breathitt." Combs also thought the element of surprise in his choice would prove psychologically important in an advantageous way. And lastly, Breathitt was an energetic, tireless campaigner who was a good speaker, backslapper, hand-shaker and joke-teller.

The Democratic primary turned out to be, as expected, a bitterly fought battle. The campaign focused on the three percent sales tax enacted during the Combs administration. When the dust finally cleared, Breathitt had won in a landslide.

The fall race was an entirely different matter. Breathitt's opponent in the general election was Louie B. Nunn, a Republican from Glasgow. Nunn was a more formidable opponent than the Democratic candidate for governor had had to face in past years. He was a World War II veteran and a successful attorney. He had served as Barren County Judge in a largely Democratic county. An able political organizer, he had run campaigns within the state for Senators John Sherman Cooper and Thruston Morton, and presidential candidates Dwight D. Eisenhower and Richard M. Nixon. His race for governor in 1963 was his first attempt at statewide office.

Combs played an active role in the 1962 fall campaign of Wilson Wyatt for Senator. He made speeches for Wyatt and did what he could to help with organization and strategy. Indeed, he did more than some of Wyatt's friends thought he should have.

In the 1963 race for governor, Combs did quite a lot of campaigning for Breathitt in the primary in which he defeated Chandler. In most of his campaign speeches, in addition to urging support for Breathitt, the governor asked voters to stand behind the sales tax and the expanded road program. He cut many ribbons opening new roads and parts of Interstate highways. Combs was not about to allow the voters to forget from whence came their blessings. It was not that he was seeking credit for himself, but rather that he wanted the people to realize the importance of the things state government, working with federal authorities in this case, could accomplish in the public interest.

Combs was ahead of his time in the extensive use of public relations to educate the public and gain its support for projects. He was concerned that future politicians would return to the old ways of doing things so it was important to him to ingrain in the minds of citizens the importance to them of his various initiatives, especially the sales tax. He dedicated projects at Eastern Kentucky State College, Oakwood Hospital, and at the Frankfort Training Home. These projects cost $6,750,000, a lot of money in the 1960s, but they were much needed projects. The governor took advantage of school meetings to ask teachers, school administrators and parent/teacher groups to support his program of increased aid to schools. He was pushing all the right buttons.

Meanwhile, Chandler was attempting to ignore Breathitt and attack Combs, but Breathitt was constantly reminding his opponent that he was a formidable adversary, himself. Breathitt began to ridicule Happy and even began imitating him to the delight of his partisans. For awhile, it seemed as if Breathitt was adopting Chandler's standard tactics of dirty tricks and outright falsehoods. He gave Happy every bit as good as he got. He began to give Chandler some real "hell" on the stump.

At many of Breathitt's rallies, there would be Ed Prichard in the crowd yelling at the top of his lungs, "Pour it on him, tell 'em the real truth about Happy, vote for Breathitt, he's clean, he's clean!"

A fresh, energetic group of campaign workers formed around Breathitt. A group whose members were dedicated, hard-working and full of new ideas. They worked day and night and on weekends. They made a real difference in the race.

Since Governor Combs controlled the money, he had a hand in the major decisions concerning campaign strategy. He wanted that role, but, at the same time, he didn't want to project himself too far out front. This was Breathitt's race, not his own.

Combs saw the governor's race in 1963 as a referendum on his administration. After all, Breathitt had pledged to continue the programs of the Combs administration. A Breathitt victory would mean approval of his administration and its initiatives.

The governor's race turned out to be closer than maybe it should have been. In addition to promising to continue the Combs' programs in education, highway development, state parks, agriculture and health and welfare, Breathitt promised a sustained economic development campaign to attract industry and create new jobs for Kentuckians.

A complicating factor for the Breathitt campaign was an executive order issued by Governor Combs in the summer of 1963 prohibiting racial discrimination in businesses licensed by the state. Among other things, the order desegregated public accommodations in Kentucky. Governor Combs, of course, realized that his executive order on civil rights would cost Breathitt some support and hurt him in the general election. Even so, Combs did what he always did—he did what he believed was right.

Remember, this is 1963, less than a decade since the U.S. Supreme Court's ruling in Brown vs. Board of Education, in which the court threw out the old "separate but equal" rule and desegregated public schools in America. Much resistance to the Brown decision still existed in our country and here in the commonwealth. The Nunn campaign immediately attacked the Combs order calling it "rule by executive decree." Nunn attacked both state and national commitments in the field of civil rights.

The introduction of race into the campaign and Happy Chandler's last-minute endorsement of Nunn clearly hurt Breathitt. Many Chandler supporters in the Bluegrass Region voted Republican while segregationists in western Kentucky stayed home and didn't vote. Breathitt's margin of victory, 449,551 to 436,496, was slim, at best.

Even after Nunn injected civil rights into the campaign, I was still very confident of a Breathitt victory. On election night, I had taken some friends to dinner downstairs at campaign headquarters at the Seelbach Hotel in downtown Louisville. About halfway through dinner, a man rushed in searching frantically for me. Finding me seated at the table with my unsuspecting friends, he rushed over looking very worried and said, "Fontaine, Breathitt wants you upstairs right now!" I said, "Hold it, I'm having dinner." Looking desperate now, he reached for my arm and said, "No you aren't, you have to come now."

Suddenly, I realized something was wrong. Had my confidence in victory for Ned Breathitt been misplaced? I hurriedly excused myself and raced upstairs. When I arrived in our candidate's room, Breathitt had a somber expression on his face. I glanced around the room. It was doom and gloom on the face of each individual. Breathitt's early, big lead had been cut tremendously. It was down to 13,000 and still falling.

I talked to Ned Breathitt trying to reassure him and then I called Governor Combs, who was at the Governor's Mansion. The governor told me in no uncertain terms to bring three or four people he named with me and get to the Governor's Mansion as fast as humanly possible. We were a very worried group as we sped toward Frankfort. We got there about 11:00 p.m.

We discussed what to do, if there was anything we could do, about our candidate's ever shrinking lead which, at least for the moment, appeared to be holding at about 13,000. After considerable discussion, we decided that the only possibly significant action we could take at this time on election night was to make telephone calls to our people in key counties directing them to keep a close eye on the ballot boxes and voting machines in their counties to make certain that no illegal activity took place in an effort to change the outcome of this suddenly extremely close election.

One man I called went to the courthouse and stayed there watching and guarding the voting machines. Three days later his wife called me and asked, "Fontaine, can George come home now? He won't leave the machines unless you tell him it's okay."

I had completely forgotten about him and told his wife to tell him that everything was fine and he could go home now. That's dedication! That's loyalty! That's a not so trusting Democrat! Thank the Lord for folks like him on whom you can depend in a tight political race. There aren't so many of them. There are always the many who want to jump on the band wagon at the last moment when victory appears assured, but they come late to the party and are virtually useless; I have always worked at developing and cultivating a small group of loyalists on whom I can depend without the slightest reservation.

Breathitt's majority held at a little more than 13,000 votes and the commonwealth had a new governor. Breathitt's win in the governor's race, although narrow in margin, was a big one. Breathitt's election to the state's highest office put an end to colorful career of Albert Benjamin "Happy" Chandler. In the Democratic primary, Ned Breathitt, at age forty-three had defeated the sixty-four-year-old Chandler by a shockingly large margin of 60,000 votes. On election night, Chandler had prepared to drive to Louisville for a victory celebration. Instead, he simply went home to his family and a few friends who had gathered there to offer their congratulations to him on another big victory. He even refused to concede defeat in the primary until the next day.

Illustrating the devastating extent to which the election had been a personal rebuke, Chandler's running mate, Harry Lee Waterfield, easily won the nomination for lieutenant governor. The results of the 1963 gubernatorial election were extremely painful for Earl Clements, too. He had opposed Breathitt, but even Union County, his home county, went for Breathitt. Even his own home precinct went for Breathitt by a vote of 317 to 274.

It is likely that for no one, Breathitt included, were the primary and general elections sweeter than for Bert Combs. He felt vindicated. He felt that his programs had received the endorsement of the citizens of the commonwealth. On the night of Breathitt's critically important win in the general election, as I have previously stated, the governor spent the evening at the Governor's Mansion eagerly watching the returns on television. As he watched Breathitt's lead shrink, he gave no outward sign of the tremendous strain that he was under. When the outcome finally became clear, he was greatly relieved. The popularity of his many state improvement initiatives, together with the deep respect the people had for him, had enabled him to anoint his successor. And in so doing, Bert Combs received the validation from the electorate that he had been seeking. The citizens appreciated Combs and his accomplishments so much that they indicated through the election of Ned Breathitt that they were ready for and desirous of another four years of the same. At last, Bert Combs could relax. His great works would not be torn asunder and Combs had placed in the Governor's Mansion the right man to continue his work—a man named Breathitt.

As the outgoing governor relaxed in his easy chair watching the television news reporters wrap up their coverage of the closer-than-expected election, he probably thought back over the middle years of the twentieth century here in the Commonwealth. During these years, state politics had been dominated by the three "Cs"—Combs, Chandler and Clements. Each man had left his impression on the state. Each had tasted a bit of glory.

Combs had accomplished much of what he set out to do and was more than willing to let history judge his administration. He had taken advantage of the opportunity given to him to improve his state. While much remained to be done, he had charted the course for Breathitt and others to follow.

Chandler, on the other hand, thought Combs, while leaving his impression on the state, essentially missed his opportunities to move the Kentucky ahead. This was a shame, he thought, because, with Happy's enormous popularity and resulting power, he could have written some of the brightest pages in Kentucky history. Instead, he wasn't willing to take risks today for the benefit of tomorrow.

Of Clements, Combs thought he had the best political mind of his generation, maybe of the entire century, in Kentucky politics. He regretted the manner in which they had parted. He thought Clements was a strong, courageous and intelligent governor. In Combs mind, when it came to pure intellect, Ed Prichard and Earle Clements were just about equal. I must add here, that having known Prichard, Clements and Combs very well, it is my opinion, that in the quality of intelligence, Bert Combs was the equal of the other two.

But now the scene was changing and a new leader had emerged—Ned Breathitt. And while he had pledged to continue the Combs' agenda, he also had ideas of his own.

28 Ned Breathitt & Me

NED BREATHITT AND I had been acquainted since I first came to state government and we had worked together many times. He was a strong supporter of Governor Combs and that threw us together on many occasions. Ned was a good Christian and we both attended the First United Methodist Church in Frankfort. Having frequent contact both at work and at church and having the same goal in our careers at that time (the success of the Combs administration), we became friends.

After Wilson Wyatt decided to run for the Senate taking him out of the upcoming governor's race, I became a strong advocate with Governor Combs for Ned Breathitt. I was very vocal and aggressive in my private conversations with Bert Combs arguing Breathitt should be the Combs' candidate for governor. I was much more vocal on the subject than I usually was when giving my opinion to the governor.

Fontaine Banks (l) with Gov. Edward T. "Ned" Breathitt looking at the 50th Anniversary stamps honoring the U.S. Marine Corps

There were times when Combs was considering others that I thought Breathitt might not get the governor's nod. Especially when the governor seemed to be leaning toward another possible candidate, I would talk up Ned Breathitt. I had nothing against any of the others under consideration; it was just that I thought Breathitt had the best chance to win. I knew no other candidate could out work him. On the campaign trail, he was tireless or so it seemed. He was extremely likeable, energetic and enthusiastic and had nothing detrimental in his background. He had not been in state government and politics long enough to have done much that was controversial. And lastly, although not as well known as some of the others Combs was considering, he had a great name for a governor—"Breathitt." On this point, the governor and I were in complete agreement. We both thought Ned's surname was an advantage, we just weren't sure whether it was a "big" advantage.

When the decision was finally made, we decided it was necessary to begin campaigning right away. We had to make the name, "Ned Breathitt," a household word throughout the commonwealth. When Ned announced his candidacy for the Democratic nomination for Governor, we kept Governor Combs away from the media. We didn't want Breathitt to look like he was just the governor's pawn.

Of course, Ned knew he could depend on me to be in his corner. While I continued in my role of chief of staff to Governor Combs during the primary and general elections, Ned and I talked daily about campaign issues. We had complete trust in each other and we did not hesitate to state our true feelings to each other even when we knew what we were about to say wasn't what the other wanted to hear. In other words, we were brutally honest with each other. We had to be—the stakes were too high for anything but the absolute truth as each of us saw it.

During his campaign for governor, Breathitt asked me to stay on with him in the governor's office through his first legislative session. After the session concluded, he wanted me to become the commissioner of Public Safety. I had been considering what to do next in my career, whether to remain in state government or return to the private sector, when Breathitt made his request of me. I knew we would be able to work well together as we had in the Combs administration and in Ned's campaign for governor. So, after giving his proposal some thought, I agreed to stay on and work as the new governor's legislative assistant as I had done under Combs. This arrangement worked well and we had a very successful session, something many a new governor hasn't been able to accomplish.

When the session ended, the next morning Governor Breathitt called me and said, "Fontaine, have every employee in the governor's office in my office in ten minutes." Well, it was obvious that something was up. I rounded up all the employees and brought them to the governor's office. Nobody said a word.

You could hear a pin drop, as they say. None of us, including me, knew what was coming next. Governor Breathitt walked in without saying a word to anybody. He sat down in his chair, looked at me and said, "Fontaine, is everybody present?"

I said, "Yes, Governor, everybody is present."

The governor speaking very deliberately and firmly said, "I just want to say one thing. Fontaine is the only person who stayed with me on every issue during the legislative session, and, for that, I am eternally grateful. Thank you, Fontaine. That's all."

Well, complete silence flooded the office. Everybody stood up and filed out. The governor never said another word about this, but it was obvious that all of the staff members had gotten the point. About two weeks later, thinking the governor was out, I opened the back door to his office and was half way in before I realized he was there. He had been sitting in his chair staring out of the window. When he heard me, he very quickly swung around, jumped up out of his chair and with tears streaming down his cheeks, came straight across the room to me, took me by the hand and said, "Fontaine, don't leave me please, please don't leave me."

I was shocked but I recovered enough to lead the governor back to his chair. He sort of sunk down into it as I, still greatly surprised, leaned against his desk to catch my breath. The governor looked up at me and said, "Everyone has let me down except you, Fontaine, don't leave me, stay with me."

I answered, "Governor, as long as you want me to stay in state government with you, I'll do whatever you want me to do."

Governor Breathitt sighed and began to calm down. About that time, Marian Hubbard, walked into the office. Marian was the person I had picked to replace me on the governor's staff when I thought I was going to the Department of Public Safety. The governor looked at Hubbard and said, "Marian, you're going to the Revenue Cabinet; you're going to head up the Division of Enforcement."

Marian looked shocked and just stood there without saying anything. Finally, after what seemed like a long time, Marian turned and, without saying a word, walked out. The governor and I talked for a long time. Finally, to conclude our conversation, Governor Breathitt said, "Fontaine, if you're willing to stay with me, you'll be my chief of staff."

I agreed and said, "Okay, but let's not make an announcement about it, it's enough that you and I understand what's going on." This was the second time I had been designated as chief of staff by a governor and also the second time I had requested that no announcement of the appointment be made. No point in possibly stirring up some jealousy or disappointment among the staff members, I thought.

Between the election when Governor Breathitt was elected governor and his inauguration, he came to visit with me in my office in the Capitol building, and asked me what Barbara and I were going to do on Inauguration Day. I said, "Probably freeze ourselves to death hearing your speech." He laughed, and said, "How about doing something else?" I said, "Tell me what." He said, "Could you have some refreshments and beverages in your office? And I can send my friends from Hopkinsville if they want something to drink or something to eat." And I said, "You sure can. I'll be glad to do it." So Barb and I set up a small bar in my office that day – we had some sandwiches, and some other things to eat, and a few things to drink in our office. It was a very, very, cold day, and I was pretty darn glad to be inside on such a day. And I walked outside a couple of times during the day, but came back in real fast. But it turned out really nice, and we had quite a few visitors to welcome that day because of all the folks from Hopkinsville who were there for Governor Breathitt.

My routine with Governor Breathitt was different than the one with Governor Combs. With Combs, I went to the Governor's Mansion early every morning and briefed the governor on the day's activities and other matters. Ned Breathitt had four children. So he and the First Lady had their hands full early. Each day, I would brief Governor Breathitt in his office shortly after his arrival. When we discussed matters on the telephone our conversations were brief and to the point.

One exception sticks out in my memory; it was a Friday and when I called him, he seemed to want to keep talking much longer than usual. He wanted to know the details about everything. The next morning he became seriously ill. It seemed as if our lengthy telephone conversation the previous day was the result of a premonition of the governor's that he might be out of action for awhile. Ned Breathitt was a wonderful person to work for. In all of our years of close association, there was never an ill word spoken between us.

29 The Further Adventures of Ned & Me

GOVERNOR BREATHITT AND GOVERNOR COMBS had entirely different types of personalities. For example, when Governor Combs made a decision, he stuck to it, you didn't have to worry about any backsliding afterwards. When Governor Breathitt made a decision, however, I had to know who was the last person he talked to because he would change his mind and reverse his previous decision without telling anybody after just a casual conversation with someone with a different point of view than his, usually a lobbyist. I found it necessary to keep close tabs on Governor Breathitt. It wasn't that he was so easily persuadable; I think it was more about his lawyer's way of thinking, constantly exploring both sides of a question. He could make a case for either side of a close question. Sometimes he talked himself right out of his own decision. It could be frustrating attempting to keep him on track. I spent much of my time trying to keep him focused on a decision he had already made.

The State Auditor during the Breathitt Administration was Henry Carter. Henry had a habit of bringing out a pitcher of ice water and a fifth of bourbon about three o'clock every afternoon in his office in the Capitol in plain view of anybody that happened to walk by. One day, the governor came into my office and I looked up and saw that he looked very tired. He said, "Damn it, I'm going to go home and take a nap."

It was three o'clock in the afternoon when Governor Breathitt walked down the hallway. As he passed by the Auditor's office, there sat Henry Carter behind his desk with his bourbon and water sitting on his desk top. Well, Henry invited the governor in and offered him a drink. Naturally, the governor refused and Henry began berating him. Carter actually cursed the governor. Breathitt turned around and walked back down the hall to my office. He was white as a sheet and mad as hell! After he calmed down, he told me what happened.

I said, "Governor, he starts drinking in his office at three o'clock every day, I just forgot to tell you. I make it a point to never go by his office from 3:00 to 4:00 in the afternoon. There's no telling what he will say."

Breathitt thanked me, left my office, and walked in the opposite direction from Carter's office headed for the Governor's Mansion and that badly-needed nap.

One night, Governor Breathitt, the governor's press secretary, Foster Ockerman, Ed Pritchard and I were all at the Governor's Mansion discussing how to handle a major issue that had come up. About ten o'clock, we made a decision about how we were going to handle the problem and after that the press secretary left for a late date he had. The rest of us stayed around and, after about thirty minutes of further discussion, we changed our minds and reversed our decision. In the *Courier Journal* the next morning there appeared a front page story reporting our original decision. Since we had reversed ourselves after the press secretary left, it was obvious that only one person could have been the source for the story and that person was, of course, the press secretary. He had leaked our original decision to a *Courier* reporter.

That morning the governor and I were to fly somewhere in eastern Kentucky for a state government event. I was waiting at the airport when a state trooper telephoned me and said, "Mr. Banks, please come to the Governor's Mansion right away."

I said that I couldn't come because I was waiting for the governor. The Trooper said, "Mr. Banks, please come to the Governor's Mansion now, there's a big problem down here. You'll have to drive to eastern Kentucky."

When I arrived at the Mansion, there were Governor Breathitt and the press secretary sitting there in silence waiting for me. The governor looked at me sternly and said, "Fontaine, I want you to fire my press secretary and if you don't fire him, I'll fire you."

That's when it dawned on me what had happened. The governor's press secretary just sat there slumping down in his chair and looking as if he would rather be anywhere else in the whole world, but where he was. He hung his head and didn't say a word. After what seemed like an eternity, an obviously angry governor Breathitt stood up and walked out of the room.

I went over to where the press secretary was sitting and said, "Since you have to go with us today, don't ride in the governor's car, get in the other one and be sure to stay away from him all day." We drove to eastern Kentucky and celebrated State Government Day. He followed my orders and stayed away from the governor the whole day. I sent him home early and then I rode back to the capital with the governor. After some small talk about the activities of the day, I said, "Governor, we can't fire our press secretary, we need him and I assure you that you made your point with him this morning. Governor, you scared him to death! It will never happen again—of that I'm sure."

Governor Breathitt sat there silently for a minute or two as we rode along and then he finally said, "Okay, Fontaine, but it better not happen again." I breathed a sigh of relief and so did the press secretary when I told him he was still employed by the Breathitt administration. No further leaks occurred during the Breathitt years. But that big leak almost caused the press secretary to be fired by the governor. What a career setback that would have been for him.

This was one of several instances in my career when I disobeyed a governor's order to me to fire an employee. I don't regret my actions in a single one of these cases. A governor is a very powerful individual. He is accustomed to having his way. Sometimes, when an employee makes a mistake that angers the governor, he reacts in the heat of the moment and orders the offending employee to be fired. The dismissal would, of course, be a crushing blow to the employee who would no longer be receiving a paycheck with which to support his family, but also would always be followed in his career by the disgrace of having been dismissed by the governor of the state.

To me, in most of these incidences, firing was too drastic a punishment. So my strategy was to allow a little time to pass in which to let the governor calm down and become focused on other matters. My strategy always worked and I never had to fire anybody that I thought didn't deserve to be fired. These incidents included several employees in the lowest type of jobs, such as the groundskeeper Governor Combs wanted me the dismiss because he hadn't cleaned up the pigeon droppings fast enough, to employees holding high profile positions such as the one held by the press secretary. The results were gratifying. In every incidence, the offending employee never caused another problem. It turned out that all were worth saving. I never had second thoughts about my course of action in any of the cases, and no governor was ever upset with me because of my failure to carry out the dismissal order.

Shortly after Governor Breathitt was inaugurated, on several occasions he told me to save a certain date open because we were going back to his hometown of Hopkinsville. I could tell this was important to him and I carefully kept the date free of appointments. When the day came, we flew to Hopkinsville. When we arrived, a big crowd of at least a thousand people was waiting for us.

This was his first trip back since he'd been elected governor. During his address to the large crowd of supporters he said, "Whenever you have a problem with state government, the man you want to call is Fontaine Banks."

To this day, I can hear Governor Breathitt laughing because of the distraught expression on my face. I wasn't happy. Now, thanks to Ned Breathitt, everybody in Christian County was going to call me with every kind of problem imaginable. The governor had a big laugh out of my reaction. But I knew that he really meant what he said. He wanted the good people of his hometown taken care of when they had a problem with state government.

There's one more story I'll tell about Governor Breathitt's administration, and something that I did as he was leaving office. We had some funds left over from the Breathitt campaign, and when we went on political trips, the staff couldn't route their receipts to the state to get reimbursed, so we used the extra funds to pay those expenses. About a month before the Breathitt administration ended, I remembered that fund that we hadn't used in some time. We opened up the safe, and there was $700. I thought, "What am I going to do with it?" Then I thought of Mrs. Breathitt. I called her, and went over to the mansion. We sat down on the couch, and we talked. I finally said, "Francis, we had this special fund, and there's $700 left. I don't know what to do with it, but I'd like to give it to you." She took it and cried and said, "Fontaine, thank you, this is the only money we have," which proved to me that Breathitt was an honest man.

30 Accomplishments of the Breathitt Administration

THE CHIEF GOAL OF Governor Breathitt's administration was to complete the projects begun by Governor Combs. Breathitt's administration worked almost full-time on these projects and programs. His administration did a magnificent job of completing the Combs projects. One of the reasons for such success was that the 1964 and 1966 sessions of the General Assembly were composed of almost the same membership as in the 1960 and 1962 sessions in the Combs years. The great majority of the members of both houses of the legislature were anxious to see these projects, which they had passed, completed.

Another reason for our success in dealing with the membership of the General Assembly was that we virtually organized the legislature. We decided on who would hold the positions of leadership. We discussed these matters with certain key members of the legislature, but we made the final decisions on who would hold the leadership positions. We even made committee assignments.

In those days there was no such thing as "legislative independence." That didn't begin to come on the scene until John Y. Brown, Jr. was governor. I must say I was sorry to see the governor's power reduced by the coming of legislative independence, but now, as I think back about it, it has been a good thing overall. In the days of Governors Chandler, Combs and Breathitt, "Governor of the Commonwealth of Kentucky" was a title that might as well have been "King of the Commonwealth."

Early in the Breathitt administration, I placed my emphasis on the further development and improvement of the merit system for state employees. Beginning in 1961, the merit system had been closely followed by all—the Combs administration, the media, state employees and the public. As the Breathitt administration got rolling, I created a team of experts on the merit system and members of the team visited each department and trained each supervisor in the requirements of the merit law. As a result, during both the Combs' and Breathitt administrations, the merit system functioned almost perfectly. This was a pleasant surprise to us, but we came to realize that the time and effort put into educating all the department supervisors about the merit system had been a key to the system's outstanding performance. My decision to create the team of experts and send them into the field to train the supervisors was, in my opinion, one of my best ones.

Governor Breathitt continued the Combs' program of "State Government to the People." And, once again, the program was a big success. We had many nice trips to places where the people normally had little opportunity to sit down face to face with the governor or department head who could assist them with their problems.

Overall, I thought that Breathitt's first session of the legislature was successful although most others, including the media, thought his first session was a big disappointment. We did face some problems and had some disadvantages. Breathitt's youth and inexperience, the narrowness of his victory in 1963, the untimely death of Richard P. Maloney, Sr., a key legislative leader, and the still lingering civil rights controversy combined to undermine Breathitt's effectiveness with the 1964 General Assembly. Much of the session was spent arguing over an unsuccessful effort to adopt a public accommodations law. But we did secure a model purchasing law, improved teachers' benefits, and strengthened legislation regulating strip mining. But, most important, he won legislative approval for a referendum on a $176 million bond issue that was vital to his administration.

Ned had promised "no new taxes" during his administration, a pledge he was determined to honor. Yet, at the same time, he wanted to continue the road building, state park development, education improvements, and social service programs initiated under Combs. In education, the need for physical facilities was absolutely overwhelming. In addition, Breathitt took office at a time when unprecedented funding was available for the taking from the federal government in generous dollar-matching programs. The combination of funding requests and dollar-matching opportunities far exceeded current state revenues. The only answer to this dilemma was the $176 million bond issue that was structured to provide funds for capital improvements only.

Most of the issue was designated for highway construction; however, funds for education, state parks, and other public facilities were also included.

Breathitt very carefully designed a campaign to win approval of the critically important bond issue. The campaign was most effective and the bond issue won approval at the polls by three to one despite the opposition of Lt. Gov. Harry Lee Waterfield and Happy Chandler. This bond issue approval was key to a successful Breathitt administration. Now funding would be available to complete the Combs' agenda.

The 1964 General Assembly also adopted enabling legislation to draft a new state constitution. Thirty-eight distinguished Kentuckians worked for many months preparing the new constitution. As with the bond issue, Breathitt planned and mounted a very impressive statewide campaign to insure its adoption. But this time the Breathitt public relations campaign failed and failed miserably. The voters rejected the new constitution by an overwhelming margin.

Looking back on the outcome, there were many obstacles to passage of the new and badly needed charter. Changing the terms of the constitutional officers was not popular; voters thought that the new document threatened the independence of local governments; it appeared as if more power was being given to the governor and Frankfort; and also there was the ever-present aversion to constitutional change that was and still is a Kentucky tradition. All of these together were a rock-solid roadblock to adoption of the new constitution.

Fontaine Banks (standing on left) with John Y. Brown, Sr. (seated second from left) with members of the Kentucky General Assembly

I thought that the document's defeat was a missed opportunity for the state to move ahead a little farther into the twentieth century. It was a missed chance to modernize the machinery of state government and improve its effectiveness. The people had voted against their own best interests for, if the new constitution had been adopted, they would have received faster, more effective services from their government. All those scholars, all those constitutional experts, all their work for nothing. To me, the defeat of the document, while inevitable, was still a shame.

I had the opportunity to head the campaign for the adoption of the new constitution, but I turned it down in order to manage the campaign of my old friend, John Y. Brown, Sr., who was running for the U.S. Senate. I had been asked to do both and, on the very day I returned from summer camp with my Marine unit I found former Governor Wetherby waiting for me in my office. He said I had to make a choice as to which campaign I would manage and make the choice that day. Because I felt certain that both the new constitution and John Y. Brown, Sr. would be defeated at the polls, I decided that I should try to help my old friend. I told former Governor Wetherby and Governor Breathitt that I would take on the senate campaign.

When John Y. and I had our first meeting, I told him that he would lose by 200,000 votes no matter how well we ran the campaign. He laughed and said, "Yes, Fontaine, but we'll have a lot of fun." John Y's campaign had no money and he was running against the well-heeled and popular incumbent, John Sherman Cooper.

Well, John Y., Sr. was able to get his son, John Y. Brown, Jr., of Kentucky Fried Chicken fame, to fund our efforts. Among other things, he furnished 3,000 chicken boxes for a picnic for state employees. Johnny Jr. even paid for a train tour similar to Harry Truman's 1948 classic. John Y. lost the election by 220,000 votes, but he was right—we did have fun!

One of the reasons for the failed constitutional effort was the problem caused by the famous Russman vs. Luckett case in which the Court of Appeals, then the state's highest court, in 1965, rendered a stunning decision that ordered the enforcement of a previously unenforced constitutional provision that required property to be assessed at 100 percent of its fair cash value for property tax purposes.

This unexpected decision was a bombshell and the public, confused by all the legal wrangling, blamed Governor Breathitt. If nothing was done to alleviate the effect of the decision, property taxes would soar. Voters immediately poured the pressure on Governor Breathitt to do something about the decision. The governor's only two options were to call a special session of the General Assembly to deal with potentially skyrocketing property tax bills and also venture into the uncertain area of constitutional reform. Breathitt tried both.

During the special session, Breathitt proposed a reduction in property tax rates that would be in proportion to the increased assessment amounts. In the middle of this crisis, Governor Breathitt saw an opportunity to help the public schools. Thus, he included in the remedial legislation a provision for a small increase in property tax rates primarily for the schools. As usual, the governor's plan was opposed by Lieutenant Governor Waterfield who submitted an alternative plan. Breathitt beat back the Waterfield plan and secured passage of his plan. When the session was over and the property tax crisis averted, Breathitt found himself with greatly increased political prestige. He was learning how to govern. I could see him gaining in confidence and self-assurance every day. The Russman decision had presented Breathitt with a crisis and an opportunity. In the end, he averted the crisis by seizing the opportunity it offered him. From then on to the end of his term, Breathitt was a dominant governor.

The next year, 1966, the legislature met in its regular session. This time we were ready for them. Breathitt was now a much stronger leader. In addition, the administration's economic development program, spurred by an upturn in the national economy and the garnering of federal dollars for the state, had generated an additional $100 million in state revenue. Breathitt, negotiating from a position of strength, submitted a budget that was 27 percent higher than the one he presented in 1964, and it included generous appropriations for most political districts. The budget was approved by a wide margin in the now comfortably Democratic legislature.

In addition to the favorable budget, Breathitt was able to obtain passage of a civil rights bill that prohibited discrimination in employment and in public accommodations. I was especially pleased with passage of the civil rights bill. In 1964, the Reverend Martin Luther King, Jr. led a civil rights march on the Capitol in Frankfort. The many marchers gathered on one of the side streets off of Capitol Avenue. Amazingly, there were at least 10,000 people. They marched up Capitol Avenue to the Capitol building where the Reverend King addressed the crowd of marchers. Dr. King requested an audience with Governor Breathitt to which the governor agreed.

I met Dr. King as he entered the outer office of the governor's suite. He had a stern look on his face—there was no chit-chat. We shook hands and I led him into the governor's office where Governor Breathitt was waiting for him. Again there was no chit-chat. Dr. King got straight to the point. He wanted civil rights legislation passed now—in the 1964 session. We told Dr. King that, while we favored civil rights legislation, we would not be able to gain passage of it in the 1964 session. We told him that we thought we could obtain passage of a bill on civil rights in the 1966 session and that we would make every effort to do so. Dr. King looked disappointed at the news of a two-year delay in the passage of civil rights legislation in Kentucky. I do think, however, that we were able to convince him of the sincerity of our commitment to make every effort to acquire passage of the legislation in 1966.

Gov. Edward T "Ned" Breathitt greets civil rights leader Rev. Martin Luther King in the Governor's Office in 1964
Source: Kentucky Dept of Libraries & Archives

King knew of Breathitt's reputation as a member of the new breed of Southern Democrats who accepted the directions of the New Deal and Fair Deal. Democrats who viewed state government as a proper tool with which to tackle social, economic, political, and human problems and who rejected the traditional demagoguery of race and states' rights. Breathitt believed in states' rights, but he also believed in state responsibility.

Dr. King, while not getting what he wanted from his visit, went away, I think, believing he had found an ally in Kentucky and a powerful one—the governor of the state, Ned Breathitt. I noticed that during the meeting, Dr. King's stern look never changed. He was polite and cordial, but he maintained his stone-like expression the whole time. To me it seemed to be like a mask, but I was unable to tell what he was hiding behind that stony, stern expression. When the meeting ended, I escorted Dr. Martin Luther King, Jr. to the door. As he departed, he gazed at me with that severe expression still in place, and simply said, "Thanks."

When the civil rights legislation was enacted in 1966, I don't recall if we heard from Dr. King. There was no real need to. We had done only what we said we would do. We had done only what was right. You don't need or deserve congratulations for that.

The passage of the civil rights legislation in 1966 made Kentucky a national leader in implementing civil rights for all citizens. It also brought Ned Breathitt a great deal of political prestige and his name, so very recently almost unknown in Kentucky, was becoming known on the national stage.

Other 1966 legislative successes, in addition to the budget and the civil rights bill, included adoption of a strong strip-mining law, creation of an authority to regulate water, soil, and forest resources, enactment of an extremely controversial compulsory automobile inspection bill, enactment of tightened state regulations governing political contributions and expenditures by candidates, and adoption of a Breathitt-sponsored Congressional redistricting plan.

Unlike the 1964 session which had some successes, but was not considered to have lived up to its potential, everyone, including the media, agreed that the 1966 session was an unqualified success and most believed it to be the most productive session in memory. Governor Breathitt had exhibited outstanding leadership during the session. He was assisted during the session by a small group of advisors whose judgment he respected and on which he relied. The small team of advisors was composed of Foster Ockerman, Ed Prichard, Smith Broadbent, Jr., and me.

Kathryn "Katie" Peden was a very good friend to Governor Breathitt. The governor appointed Kathryn as the commissioner of Commerce, which was a very influential position in state government—it was the first time a woman had been appointed to that position. Of course, at that time, it was somewhat novel in Kentucky for a woman to be appointed to such a high position, but for Governor Breathitt it didn't make any difference. Katie Peden was an absolutely wonderful person. But, she was all business, there was no foolishness around her! She enjoyed a good evening with friends, and would get very involved in their activities. But she was sort of a star of the Breathitt administration, and I always valued her friendship. We never had an ill word between us, and she always welcomed any suggestion

Katie Peden shakes hands with Pres. Lyndon B. Johnson

I made. She took care of everybody. Governor Breathitt admired and trusted Katie Peden, and she proved that she could do a good job—better than any man. She was a very important person in the Breathitt administration, and I will say that she was instrumental in helping the governor accomplish his goals for economic development.

I will close the chapter on the accomplishments of the Breathitt administration by relating the one incident of which I am not proud. Before the 1966 session of the General Assembly convened, Governor Breathitt had promised the school teachers of the state that they would be given a much deserved salary increase with funding coming in the 1967-1968 budget that would be enacted by the legislature. Well, there just wasn't enough money available to make the appropriation. We needed an extra $18 million. When the governor was informed that there was just no way the salary increase could be funded, he thought about it for a minute and then ordered me to change the revenue estimate to add the needed $18 million. I said to him, "Governor, I can't do it, the money just isn't there."

Governor Breathitt very calmly replied, "I know, Fontaine, just go do it." So I obeyed orders like a good soldier does and $18 million was added to the revenue estimate and the teachers got their raise. But, as a result, when Governor Nunn took office succeeding Governor Breathitt, the first major problem confronting him was a budget shortfall. Nunn suspected what had happened, but I never admitted that it was done or that I was the one who did it.

Over the years, incoming governors have often charged their predecessors of shady dealings with the budget leaving the cupboard bare for the beginning of the new administration. I don't know how often budget estimates were improperly "adjusted," but I know it happened at least once. Now, some people I've worked with in state government over the years would say that, in the case of a much needed and deserved salary increase for teachers, the "adjustment" to the budget estimate was okay because the end justified the means. I can't buy that. If the philosophy of "the end justifies the means" prevailed in our society, we would be in bad shape because that approach to problems can be used to justify almost anything. In my situation during the Breathitt administration, I am happy that the teachers got their raise, but I regret that I took part in a subterfuge to accomplish that worthy goal.

31 Summary & Assessment of the Breathitt Administration

DURING HIS TERM AS governor, Edward T. Breathitt achieved almost all of the goals he had laid out in his 1963 campaign. The road building program of the Combs administration was continued and expanded. In 1967, Breathitt's last year in office, Kentucky had more miles of highway under construction than any other state. Education also benefited during the Breathitt years. Teachers received salary increases; four state colleges were elevated to university status; a statewide vocational education program was greatly expanded; much needed physical facilities including libraries, classroom buildings and dormitories were constructed in record numbers; and a statewide educational television system (KET) was established.

The state park system was expanded and Kentucky joined with the Tennessee Valley Authority in the development of the 170,000 acre Land Between the Lakes in Western Kentucky. Agriculture also benefited, particularly through Breathitt's conservation efforts and his campaign to increase farm income. The governor also created a new state agency to regulate the use of the state's natural resources.

The Breathitt years were a period of unprecedented prosperity in Kentucky, despite the continuing poverty in eastern Kentucky. This monumental problem of poverty in Appalachia bothered me especially. I was from there and so I lobbied Governor Breathitt for more resources to go to programs that benefited the area. It was easy to get the governor's ear on the issue of poverty in eastern Kentucky even though he was from currently prosperous western Kentucky. He wanted to help and he did much to assist the people of the mountain area. The governor was very aggressive in pursuing federally-funded projects and programs. He got good results from his efforts. There were many construction, conservation, health, education, and welfare projects that would have been otherwise impossible to bring to fruition had not Ned Breathitt gone the extra mile in pursuit of them.

Although expansion of the national economy contributed much to Kentucky's prosperity during Breathitt's term, so did the work of the Breathitt administration. A strong effort to increase tourism was successful and a substantial increase in tourism income won the administration several awards.

Breathitt's industrial development program produced 749 new industries or expansions of existing plants, 57,000 new jobs and more than $1 billion in new plant investment. By 1967, manufacturing jobs had increased by 23 percent and nonagricultural employment was up 20 percent. In 1964, the Breathitt administration received an award for the best state industrial development program in the nation.

Following his term as governor, Breathitt went on to a successful career in the private sector. He never again ran for public office. He became special counsel to the Southern Railroad. His work for the railroad led Breathitt to relocate to Washington, D.C. Later the railroad was consolidated with the Norfolk and Western Railway and was reorganized as the Norfolk Southern Corporation, which Breathitt served as vice president of public affairs and senior vice president until his retirement in 1992.

During his years with the railroad, Ned Breathitt also gave much of his time to public service. In 1968, the Ford Foundation named him director of the Institute for Rural America where he continued the work he had begun as Chairman of President Johnson's Commission on Rural Poverty. Later, he served as chairman of the Coalition for Rural America, an organization he helped found that was designed to implement the work of the Institute for Rural America.

In 1992, upon his retirement from the railroad, Breathitt returned to Kentucky, settling in Lexington and joining the law firm of Wyatt, Tarrant and Combs. After so many years, Breathitt's name was once again associated with that of Bert Combs.

Bob Bell, Betty Smither, Ruth Murphy, Linda Breathitt (daughter of Governor Breathitt), Wells Lovett, Fontaine Banks and Cattie Lou Miller at an event honoring the late Governor Breathitt

Unfortunately, however, Combs had died in December of 1991. In his last years, Ned Breathitt worked tirelessly in a series of volunteer and community service activities.

On October 10, 2003, while giving a speech at the University of Kentucky, Breathitt collapsed and never regained consciousness. He died on October 14 from heart problems. His body lay in state in the Capitol Rotunda.

I was so privileged to have known and worked for Edward T. (Ned) Breathitt. He was an outstanding governor of the Commonwealth of Kentucky. He ranks right along with Bert Combs as one of the twentieth century's greatest governors. Our state was so very fortunate to have had their services as our leaders for eight years back to back. These were the glory years—years of great accomplishment.

Ned Breathitt was a man of great integrity. He was a servant of his fellow man. He was brilliant, enthusiastic and, to the end, energetic. He was a good and decent Christian man. John Ed Pearce, the author and journalist, put it best when he said, "No finer monument could be raised to a man but that which reads he left the world better than he found it." I feel the same way about Ned Breathitt as I feel about Bert Combs—I miss him.

32 From Political Enemy to Personal Friend: Happy & Me

For many years, A. B. "Happy" Chandler and I had been political enemies. It wasn't a personal thing—we had never even met. It was more of an organizational enmity. For years the battle in Kentucky politics was not between the Democrats and the Republicans. It was between the two Democratic Party factions—the Combs organization versus the Chandler organization. Each side had tasted both victory and defeat. The members of each organization disliked the members of the other organization. Members of each organization could not understand how any citizen in his or her right mind could vote for the candidate of the rival faction.

These Democratic Party factional battles were every bit as fierce as any Democratic versus Republican battles in any state or on the national scene. Yes, while it wasn't so much a personal matter, Happy Chandler was by far my biggest political enemy. And what a tough, determined enemy he was.

"Happy" Chandler was born in the late nineteenth century (1898) and lived almost to the end of the twentieth century (1991).

He was born in Corydon, four miles southwest of Henderson in Western Kentucky. Rejected and abandoned by his mother at age four, he was raised by his father and relatives. He grew up in poverty and worked selling newspapers and doing chores for neighbors. By the time he was seven, he was virtually supporting himself.

The hardships of Chandler's childhood resulted in a character of unusual strength. He overcame his hardships and grew up cheerful and self-assured. He developed a very friendly, happy personality and was a very popular young man. Chandler never forgot his early experiences and these memories influenced his political views throughout his long career. He was always in favor of any program that gave poor children a better opportunity to have the necessities of life.

Chandler went to Transylvania College (now University) in Lexington. His list of possessions he brought with him is a part of Kentucky folklore. He said, "I had a red sweater, a five dollar bill, and a smile."

He was a star athlete while at college, but he had to work his way through doing odd jobs such as baby-sitting, washing windows and serving tables at a boardinghouse. Besides his degree, Chandler acquired something else at Transylvania that was of great value to him throughout his whole career in politics. He was given the nickname, "Happy," which fit his friendly personality perfectly.

Happy went on to Harvard and then on to the University of Kentucky Law School graduating in 1924. After his school days concluded, he settled in Versailles and married Mildred Watkins whom Happy referred to as the "Secretary of War," but who became known to Kentuckians as "Mama." A Virginia native, she had extraordinary insights into the nature of people and politics. She was always more than just a wife; she was Chandler's advisor and colleague.

In 1929, Happy won a state senate seat and his political career was off and running. In 1931 he won the lieutenant governor's race running on a ticket with Gov. Ruby Laffoon. In 1935, he was elected governor. In 1938, while still governor, he challenged incumbent Sen. Alben Barkley and suffered his first defeat after Pres. Franklin Roosevelt came to Kentucky in support of Barkley. But fate treated him generously and in 1939 he became a U.S. Senator after the death of Sen. M. M. Logan. Happy resigned the governorship to take the senate seat. He won a full term in 1942, defeating his old friend and ally, John Y. Brown, Sr.

In the fall of 1945, Happy resigned his senate seat to accept the prestigious position of National Commissioner of Baseball. He served in that capacity for six years and oversaw the admission of the first black players into major league baseball. The always aggressive Happy soon alienated the baseball owners and he was not reappointed in 1951. He returned to Versailles and soon was back in his old profession of Kentucky politics. In 1955, he again ran for governor and won a second term. The most important accomplishments of his second term were his enforcement of the U.S. Supreme Court's desegregation decision and the founding of the University of Kentucky Medical School and hospital now named after him.

Three more times Happy ran for governor (1963, 1967, and 1971), all unsuccessfully. After his defeat in 1971, Happy never ran for office again, but throughout the last decades of his life he remained active in politics, several times in opposition to his own Democratic Party. In his post political career, Happy engaged in many business and public activities, such as serving on the board of trustees of both of his alma maters, Transylvania and the University of Kentucky. In 1982, he was elected to baseball's Hall of Fame.

(l-r) Gov. Bert Combs and Gov. Happy Chandler

Happy died in June of 1991. When talking about his life, Happy always said, "I wear the world like a loose jacket. I live each day like it's gonna be my last, and sleep each night like I'm gonna live forever."

My first encounter with Happy was in the 1955 Democratic Party primary race for governor. Of course, as a young man, I supported and worked with all my might for Bert Combs, but in this, my first confrontation with the irrepressible Chandler, I found myself on the losing side. But in 1959, I found myself on the winning side as Bert Combs defeated Chandler's candidate, Harry Lee Waterfield. In 1963, in the Democratic primary, we defeated Happy, himself, when Ned Breathitt beat him in a landslide.

Through these three gubernatorial campaigns, I had never met Happy Chandler. Then, early in the Breathitt administration, I unexpectedly got the opportunity although I wasn't looking for it. Frankfort attorney, Clifford Smith, had decided he would try to arrange a reconciliation between Chandler and Breathitt, the man who crushed Happy in the primary. Well, Clifford Smith didn't like me and I didn't care for him. So his plan deliberately left me out of the picture. Smith's plan was to one morning bring Happy over to the Capitol Annex cafeteria where he would meet with Bill Bevins, a member of Governor Breathitt's staff, and Bevins would escort Smith and Chandler over to the governor's office to meet with Governor Breathitt and, if the plan worked out, Chandler and Breathitt would bury the hatchet—the same hatchet they had used to cut up each other in the gubernatorial primary.

When I arrived at the office that morning, I found one of the secretaries crying and asked her why she was upset. She said, "Fontaine, I'm not supposed to tell you."

I said, "You better tell me now or you can find another job."

She raised her eyes from the typewriter keys, looked at me and said, "Clifford Smith made this arrangement with Bill Bevins to come over here and patch things up between the governor and Happy Chandler."

I could feel my face getting red. Then the secretary said, "Fontaine, Bevins is nowhere to be found."

I grabbed a phone and called Sarah, the cashier at the cafeteria, and said, "Sarah, this is Fontaine, is Clifford Smith there?"

Sarah said, "Yes he is, Fontaine."

I said, "Sarah, get him right now and put him on the phone."

She brought Smith over to the phone and I said, "Clifford, this is Fontaine; it looks like your plan fell through, your man, Bevins, is nowhere to be found. He probably skipped town, will I do?"

A very surprised Smith said, "Yes, Fontaine, please come."

So I headed for the cafeteria and, when I got there, the place was packed. Nobody was leaving. Everybody knew something big was up. I spotted Smith and noticed there was an empty chair between Smith and Chandler. I went straight for it, pulled it back and sat down. Before we had time to be introduced, Happy grabbed my arm and held on tight. He never let me loose the whole time we sat there talking. After a preliminary chat, I said, "Let's go across the street to the governor's office."

I was anxious to leave the cafeteria because I could see members of the media gathering in the cafeteria. So we got up and then had to make our way through the crowd in the now completely jammed-packed cafeteria. Even the hallway outside the cafeteria was packed with onlookers. Everybody was excited, everybody was curious, everybody wanted to know what was going on. As we walked over to the Capitol, Happy still clung to me, hanging tightly to my now almost numb, right arm. Reporters were waiting for us and it was clear that Happy was going to be interviewed. I kept trying to get my arm loose from Happy's iron-like grip because I didn't want to be interviewed and I didn't want to be seen on TV standing arm in arm with Happy Chandler. But all my efforts were in vain. Happy held on to me the entire time he was in the Capitol—through the interviews, through the meeting with Governor Breathitt, through chit chat with folks in the halls of the Capitol—until he and Clifford Smith finally departed.

I think that Happy clung to me so closely during his visit because he was somewhat embarrassed being in the camp of the folks who he had opposed him and crushed him. I think he wanted to show the many onlookers that he knew a Breathitt confidant and was welcome. I think I saved him from some embarrassment. At any rate, this entirely unexpected meeting between me and the former governor, was the beginning of what turned out to be a wonderful friendship. He invited me to his birthday parties and I went. I began to realize the old warhorse, my political enemy of so many hard-fought campaigns, wasn't such a bad guy when you got to know him. We would never agree on many political issues and candidates, but, on a personal level, I, like so many others before me, found it impossible to resist the old-fashioned charm of his sparkling personality. As I think back now on my friendship with my old adversary, I remember it fondly and treasure my memories of this remarkable Kentuckian.

I have several memories of our meetings. For example, not long after my meeting with Happy and Clifford Smith, I began to hear persistent comments that Happy was telling everybody that he had "a man in Frankfort." Well, this worried me. I did not want it to appear as if Happy had some special friend in the Breathitt administration who was doing his bidding. That seemed to me to be the implication of his remark about "his man in Frankfort." Then one day I ran into Chandler's old friend and aide, Foxie DeMoisey.

I said, "Foxie, What's all this business about Happy having his man in Frankfort?"

Looking surprised, Foxie said, "Why, Fontaine, it's you; Happy's telling everybody you're his man in Frankfort." I was simply speechless.

One day, several years later, I walked into the lobby at the Campbell House in Lexington and there sat Governor Chandler, alone. As I approached his table, I could see that he was upset. I said hello and he jumped up and grabbed hold of my arm and sat me down. Just like in our first meeting years before, Happy wouldn't let go of my arm. He was so thrilled to see me that I realized he had been embarrassed to be sitting alone. He was still used to being the center of attention. He was used to being surrounded by admirers. I stayed with him until his friends arrived. They were apologetic about being late. They never knew what discomfort they had caused Happy.

33 Wendell Ford & the 1967 Campaign for Lieutenant Governor

EARLY IN 1960, I met Wendell Ford for the first time when Governor Combs asked me to come to Frankfort to discuss working for him in his new administration. Wendell was working on the governor's staff and, when Governor Combs finally persuaded me to leave my job at IBM and join his administration, I ended up working with Wendell much of the time. We got along well, enjoyed working with each other and became friends.

A few months later, Wendell left state government and it was, at this time, that Governor Combs designated me his chief of staff. Then one day about six months later, Wendell came to me and told me he was going to run for the state senate and asked that I help him. I promised him I would help in any way I could.

During the next several months, I found everyone working in state government who was either from Daviess County, Wendell's home county, or had a contact in the Owensboro area. I personally contacted each of them and asked them to go to Daviess County and help Wendell win his senate race. I was gratified by the fact that not a single person refused to help. I also sent extra gravel and blacktop to Wendell's senate district and made sure he received the credit for the additional paving that was done. I did everything I could possibly have done to elect Wendell Ford to the state senate. It was a close race and Wendell squeezed out a win by 280 votes.

By way of background, Wendell Hampton Ford was born in Daviess County in 1924. While attending the University of Kentucky, he left to enter the army during World War II. After his discharge in 1946, Ford graduated from the Maryland School of Insurance and entered the insurance business with his father. He joined the Combs administration and was the governor's chief administrative assistant until he left and I took over that position. Two years after winning the state senate race, Ford decided to run for lieutenant governor.

One day, just as he did when he decided to run for the state senate seat, Wendell came to my office unannounced and told me he was going to file to run for lieutenant governor. His most likely opposition would probably be Robert Matthews, the attorney from Shelbyville. Wendell once again wanted my help, but Governor Breathitt had asked me and others in his administration to stay neutral in the Democratic primary race for lieutenant governor. I and the others had promised the governor that we would do so.

The campaign proceeded and I watched its progress with interest. Then on a Thursday morning, two and a half weeks before the primary, I was given a copy of the opinion polls in the race. A member of Wendell's campaign staff had recently told me that he expected to lose the election. I spent several hours studying the polls. Wendell was right. He was headed for defeat at the hands of Bob Matthews.

That afternoon I sent for Bill Leonard of the Department of Highways to come to my office. I explained the situation to him and, after some lengthy discussion, we decided the best thing we could do for Wendell was to quickly raise some money over the weekend and then leave on Monday morning for Eastern Kentucky where Wendell was trailing and spend the next two weeks prior to election day working to pull out a win for Wendell. It was a formidable task and we knew it would take working day and night and on weekends over the next weeks if Wendell was to have any hope of winning. We kept our plans secret until Monday morning and then we took off for the mountains.

But before leaving Frankfort, I had one important matter to attend to. That Monday morning I went to Governor Breathitt's office and, fortunately, found him alone working at his desk. In my coat pocket was my letter of resignation. Before I pulled it out of my pocket and handed it to the governor, I said, "Governor, I can't stay neutral in the lieutenant governor's race any longer. I'm for Wendell and he's behind, and I've got to help him."

Governor Breathitt jumped up from his chair, clicked his heels together, saluted me and said, "Major (he always called me "Major," my Marine rank at the time), what can I do to help?"

I said, "Governor, you can organize Christian County for Wendell."

I then told him that I would be in eastern Kentucky for the next two weeks, but would call him every day. With that I turned, resignation still in my pocket, and left the governor's office headed for the hills of my old home in the east.

Over the next two weeks, Bill Leonard and I were all over eastern and southeastern Kentucky. We telephoned every county official and county campaign chairman and asked them to meet with us right away. No one refused our invitation. When we met with them, we explained that we wanted Wendell Ford to win the lieutenant governor's race. Several of the local officials had already organized their counties for Matthews. One county judge cried like a baby when we told him we were for Wendell, but he went home and, although reluctantly, changed his county organization from Matthews to Ford.

I have no idea how many politicians in eastern and southeastern Kentucky we talked with and convinced them to be for Wendell, but it was a big number. Whatever support they needed we offered, whatever they wanted in exchange for supporting Ford, we promised it. Whatever it took to get those committed to Matthews to switch to Ford, we provided or promised it. In reality, we didn't have much trouble getting most of those already organized for Matthews to switch. After we made our case for Wendell, a typical remark from them was, "Okay, I'll switch. Who the hell cares who the lieutenant governor is anyway?"

After two weeks of working night and day and all day long on the weekends, on election day we were exhausted. But our efforts were worth it. Our efforts proved decisive. Wendell Ford won the election by a razor thin margin of 650 votes. The only regret I had was that was that we should have begun our efforts two weeks earlier, but I didn't have the results of the polling then. At no time from election day to this day did Wendell Ford or J. R. Miller, his campaign manager, ever say a word of thanks to either Bill or me.

A few days after the election, one morning I looked up from my desk to find Bob Matthews leaning against the doorframe. After a few seemingly long seconds, Bob directed an insulting remark, not printable here, to me. His insult implied that my efforts on behalf of Ford had cost him the lieutenant governor's post. I replied to his rather degrading remark, "Bob, if you want to give this ol' country boy from the mountains credit for winning the race for lieutenant governor, I'll gladly accept."

Matthews just glared at me for another seemingly long, slow number of seconds, then he turned and left my office without another word. For a very long time, years actually, Bob Matthews would not speak to me.

The lieutenant governor's race of 1967 proved once again the best lesson I ever learned in politics—a well-organized effort for a candidate makes all the difference in the outcome of an election. Organization is everything! Many of the pundits and so-called experts say that in the world of the twenty-first century this is no longer true. That good TV and other media advertising is all that is needed. I couldn't disagree more. Yes, media is much more important today than fifty years ago, but, in order to win, the candidate must still have a good organization. The candidate needs a group to organize, among many things, house-to-house canvassing, a telephone calling effort, a mailing of campaign literature project, and to organize an effort to assist voters to the polls on election day.

In a statewide election, you need dedicated supporters in each county to help with these efforts. You need a few dependable supporters in each county that you can call and get a good assessment of how things are going in the county or area. No, TV and other advertising—although critically important to a candidate—are just part of the effort, maybe even the most important part, but, without an organization and I mean a good one, a candidate is doomed to defeat in a statewide Kentucky race.

I have never regretted my role in the 1967 race for lieutenant governor. Wendell made an excellent lieutenant governor and catapulted from that position into one of the greatest political careers of the twentieth century in Kentucky politics.

The 1967 race was a clear demonstration of the importance to a candidate of having a good organization. The hastily put together organization in the eastern part of the state, made the difference in the outcome of the race for lieutenant governor. Of course, Bill and I had the backing of Governor Breathitt and his administration and of the Combs' Democrats. When a campaign is supported by strong allies like the Breathitt-Combs faction of the Democratic Party, it is much easier to organize a victorious campaign. During the 1960s, it was easy to elect a candidate who had the support of the Combs-Breathitt faction. If Breathitt had not requested that the members of his administration remain neutral during most of the campaign, I believe Wendell would have been able to win by a comfortable margin instead of squeezing out such a narrow win.

34 Robert F. Kennedy & the Campaign that Never Was

On November 22, 1963, I had gone to lunch with some friends on that beautiful, sunny fall day and, after I had returned to my office and made a few telephone calls, just as I sat down in my chair, my assistant, Willard Gibson, came running into the office and shouted, "Fontaine, the president has been shot."

The press room in the Capitol was on the third floor at the time. Without saying a word, I quickly walked out of my office and up the steps to the already jammed-packed press room. The reporters and others of the Capitol work force were crammed in shoulder to shoulder around the teletype machine. Suddenly some of the crowd, all with expressions of shock on their worried faces, turned around and saw me and then quietly stepped aside making a path for me to the teletype machine. Just as I got to the machine, a bell rang signaling that a message was coming over the wire. I held my breath as the message came spilling out of the machine. Pres. John F. Kennedy was dead!

Pres. John F. Kennedy in the motorcade in Dallas on November 22, 1963
Source: Wikipedia, photo by Victor Hugo King

As the news spread like lightning around the crowded room, there was a great collective cry of anguish. A deep sigh was released from the depths of each soul in that small overflowing room. I was dazed. This horribly shocking news didn't seem real to me. This couldn't be! This was twentieth century America. We were more civilized now than in the long ago nineteenth century that saw the Great Emancipator, Kentuckian Abraham Lincoln, assassinated. But as I watched the reporters begin to run to their typewriters and the rest of the crowd stumble their way out of the room, I knew it had happened and the world had changed in an instant when gun shots rang out in Dallas, Texas, U.S.A.

I had admired President Kennedy, not so much for what he had actually accomplished as for the renewed spirit of enthusiasm and optimism and "can do" attitude he had brought to the White House and the country. A feeling of utter depression came over me as I told myself that I had work to do and I had better get to it. I did return to my duties that afternoon, but it was as if I were working on a different planet. My world was not the same. Our world was not the same. And the change was not for the better. I left the office a little earlier than usual. I wanted to get away from this devastating news, but, of course, there was no place to hide.

Even in such a dark moment of American history there was work for the Combs administration to do. Decisions had to be made. Governor Combs, whose term was almost over, did not want to attend the president's funeral. Governor Combs and I had visited with the Kennedy's on several occasions. Kennedy had campaigned in Kentucky while running for president and Governor Combs had introduced him when he spoke on a Saturday morning at the University of Kentucky. I told the governor that he should go and listed several reasons. I told him he must go. He relented and did attend the funeral. A friend of ours who owned an appliance business in Frankfort set up a TV in my office and we sat and watched the funeral that day and, of course, didn't get anything done. Somehow, even without the TV, I don't think much work would have been done on that sad day. Nobody felt like doing anything. It was as if those bullets had hit us and drained from us all of our energy. But they say time heals all wounds. Time passed and the governor's torch passed from Bert Combs to Ned Breathitt. The busy years passed quickly.

On the national scene, in 1968, President Johnson found himself mired in the quicksand of the Vietnam War and had announced to the nation that he was not going to be a candidate for re-election. This surprising announcement resulted in a Democratic field of Vice President Hubert Humphrey, Wisconsin Sen. Eugene McCarthy and New York Sen. Robert Kennedy, the assassinated president's brother. It was a highly interesting race with the last candidate to enter being Senator Kennedy.

Robert F. Kennedy was John F. Kennedy's younger brother and, when John became president, he appointed his brother U.S. attorney general. As attorney general he became one of the president's closest, if not the closest, advisers and supervised the enforcement of civil rights legislation in the South. After his brother's death, he inherited leadership of the liberal wing of the Democratic Party. After resigning from the office of attorney general in the Lyndon Johnson administration, he moved to New York and ran a winning campaign for a seat in the U.S. Senate.

One day in 1968, I was working at my desk when the telephone rang and, when I answered, the caller identified himself as a representative of Robert Kennedy and said he was calling from New York. He asked me to meet with him at Bluegrass Field (the Lexington airport) on a certain date, gave me his flight number, said he would have one hour to talk to me before his return flight, and hung up.

When the appointed day arrived, I drove over to Lexington to the airport and met the gentleman who had called me. He stated that Robert Kennedy wanted me to be his campaign chairman for Kentucky for the remainder of the presidential campaign. Before the hour was up and before Kennedy's man boarded his return flight to New York, I had accepted Robert Kennedy's offer.

During the next few days I considered the different options available to me as Bobby Kennedy's state chairman. My former political science professor at the University of Kentucky, Jack Reeves, was state chairman of the Eugene McCarthy Campaign; so I called him and we met. As a result of the meeting, we each agreed to join forces with the other if one of our candidates won and the other lost. We recognized, of course, that both could lose to Humphrey.

I proceeded to make my statewide contacts and quickly I developed a statewide organization for Kennedy. It was much easier than I had expected.

I decided to use the California Democratic Primary win, presuming a Kennedy victory, to begin our statewide run to capture Kentucky for Robert Kennedy. In other words, if Kennedy won the California Primary on June 5, I would immediately implement my campaign plan to win Kentucky for Kennedy.

I felt certain Kennedy would win California. On television it was obvious that the people loved him. He was generating excitement and enthusiasm not seen since the death of his brother, Jack. He was calling for a different direction for the Vietnam War. He was calling for a different direction for America, generally. He had not run just to oppose Lyndon Johnson or Hubert Humphrey. He ran to propose new policies for his country. He said he wanted to end the bloodshed in Vietnam and in our city streets. He wanted to close the gaps between black and white, between rich and poor, between young and old both in this country and around the world. I was very excited about participating in the campaign of such a dynamic leader. It was clear to me that if Kennedy won California, he would win the Democratic nomination.

Robert Kennedy, 1964
Source: Wikipedia, LBJ Library photo by Yoichi R. Okamoto

In the early morning hours of June 6, 1968, the morning after the California Primary, I turned on my radio to learn the stunning news that Robert Kennedy had been shot and was barely hanging onto life in a California hospital. He had won the California Primary and my plan of action on his behalf was only waiting for me to step on the starter. Of course, I did not begin the campaign. Robert Kennedy passed away and joined his brother and Dr. Martin Luther King who had been assassinated just a few months earlier in that terrible year of 1968.

I watched television ever so sadly the day they buried Robert Kennedy. I remember the slow train ride from New York to Washington, Kennedy's last ride. The thousands of people all along the railroad tracks waving goodbye to this great American. I remember night falling and seeing Kennedy's casket draped with the American flag in the lit-up railroad car. I remember turning off the television set and with it my hopes for a rejuvenated America. I didn't say a word. I just sat there in the dark and thought about what might have been. Indeed, what should have been.

Hubert Humphrey went on to capture the Democratic nomination at the Chicago National Democratic Convention amid students rioting and Chicago's police officers beating the protesters with clubs. The unruly Democratic Convention sealed Humphrey's fate and he narrowly lost the general election to the comeback kid, Richard M. Nixon.

About three months after Robert Kennedy's funeral and then burial in Arlington Cemetery alongside his brother, I was informed that Massachusetts Sen. Ted Kennedy, the only remaining Kennedy brother, wanted to come to Kentucky to thank those who had helped his brother.

My old friend, James Wine, came with Senator Kennedy. James Wine was from eastern Kentucky and had been my friend for twenty-five years. He was the person responsible for the famous and critically important meeting between Jack Kennedy and the Protestant Ministers group in Dallas during the 1960 presidential campaign.

When the day of the meeting arrived, we met at a hotel in Louisville. I immediately found my old friend, James Wine, and we proceeded to a corner table where we sat and talked for an hour. When Senator Kennedy entered the room, he walked over to our table and said, "This must be Fontaine Banks." James Wine nodded and introduced us. Senator Kennedy was very gracious in his comments to me. We talked for about an hour.

The death of Robert Kennedy was a tragedy for our country and a personal loss to me. I had such hopes for a Kennedy victory. I felt that my campaign strategy was good and would lead to victory for Kennedy in Kentucky. His senseless death sent me into the depths of depression. I shall always be proud of his selection of me as his state chairman and I shall never forget the kind comments made to me by Sen. Ted Kennedy concerning my efforts on his brother's behalf.

35 The 1971 Democratic Gubernatorial Primary Campaign: Combs vs. Ford, The Race That Should Not Have Been Run

At the close of the Breathitt administration, I took a position as special assistant to the president of the Appalachian Regional Hospitals, Inc. (ARH), a position I held from 1968 to 1975. Louie B. Nunn was governor succeeding Ned Breathitt. Nunn had been defeated in 1963 as the Republican candidate running against Breathitt who defeated him by a mere 13,000 votes. Encouraged by Nunn's strong showing in 1963, the Republican Party nominated him again in 1967, but only after a tough race in the primary against Jefferson County Judge, Marlow Cook. In the general election, Nunn defeated Democrat Henry Ward by 454,123 to 425,674.

Nunn's campaign had taken advantage of disarray in the Democratic Party. Nunn attacked the "Democratic machine" as inefficient and the party that increased taxes. He was one of the earliest of candidates to say that he would run government like a business. He attacked Henry Ward as a tax-and-spend Democrat. His upset victory made Nunn the first Republican governor of Kentucky in twenty-one years.

During Nunn's years as governor, 1967-1971, serving as lieutenant governor was, of course, Wendell Ford. While my position as special assistant to the president of ARH was challenging, I still had time to keep up with politics in the state. As possible candidates for governor on the Democratic side began jockeying for position, I got busy and talked to literally hundreds of supporters of Bert Combs from all over the state. Combs had served as a federal Court of Appeals judge from 1967 up until his resignation from the Court in 1970. While on the federal bench, much like me, former Governor Combs kept an active interest in state politics.

During this period, Combs had also divorced his first wife, Mabel Hall and married Helen Clark Rechtin. Another unfavorable factor in the possible candidacy of Combs was that many Democratic officials and voters felt that it was Wendell Ford's turn to be governor. He had earned it. Combs' divorce and his resignation from the Court of Appeals both being unpopular with a large number of voters, together with the general feeling that it was Wendell's time caused me to become convinced that Bert Combs couldn't win. I was certain of it, but many others disagreed with me. When I discussed my beliefs with the former governor, he told me that I was the only member of his inner circle who did not want him to run. I replied that I was sorry and wished that I felt differently, but the election returns would prove me right.

At this point in our conversation, Combs paused a few seconds as if he was formulating an idea in his mind and said, "Banksie, go see Wendell and try to find out if there is any way we can resolve this problem."

Combs' remark brightened my outlook. Maybe I was making some headway in convincing the former governor not to run. I said that I would go talk to Wendell. Optimistic that I could work things out so that Combs would not become a candidate and we could field a united Democratic Party behind Ford, I went to the lieutenant governor's office to see Wendell. I waited awhile, but didn't get in to see him. It was clear that he was there and that he wasn't busy with anybody in his office. Wendell just wouldn't talk to me.

I remain convinced to this day that had Wendell talked to me about the situation and allowed me to explain what I was attempting to do, Bert Combs would not have been a candidate for the Democratic nomination for governor. I feel certain that Wendell did not know of my opposition to Combs becoming a candidate and thought I was solidly in the Combs' camp. He must have thought I was there to try to convince him to drop out of the race in favor of Combs.

It was an extremely frustrating experience. I felt sure I could make a real difference if I only had the chance to talk to my old friend who I had helped elect to the very position he held at that moment. What a shame and what a waste for a great governor like Bert Combs to go down to defeat at the hands of one of his former assistants, a man he mentored.

I also have thought over the years that Bert Combs was too good a politician not to know that I was correct about his inability to win in 1971. I believe one of the chief reasons that he ran was because he received pressure from his second wife to do so.

My efforts at reconciliation between Combs and Ford led to another unfortunate consequence besides Combs' defeat. This development was personal. As soon as I left Wendell's office, a number of his staff and friends, not knowing of my opposition to Combs as a candidate, began a well-organized campaign to have me fired as special assistant to the president of ARH. The campaign against me became so heated and critical of me that the ARH Board of Directors felt it necessary to give me a vote of confidence. The members of the board all assured me of their support.

One of my most loyal supporters on the ARH Board was Garvice Kinkaid, the Lexington real estate developer, bank president, insurance executive and radio and television station owner. Kinkaid's unwavering support was very helpful to me in weathering the totally unjustified storm against me. Politics can be mean and small at times. I attempted throughout my political career to avoid using dirty tricks and to find out the facts of a situation before acting. I tried to assume as little as possible. Here my good intentions were completely misinterpreted due to the fact that I never got a chance to explain myself to Wendell Ford.

But, back to the campaign. When Bert Combs made the mistake of deciding to run for governor, he immediately made a second one. He appointed Bob Matthews as his campaign manager. Bob just wasn't willing to put out the maximum effort the Combs' campaign required to have a chance. During the primary campaign, Matthews spent most of his time at the Pendennis Club in Louisville rather than in the trenches at campaign headquarters. The situation had left me with virtually no choice but to support Combs in the primary. Unfortunately, I spent most of my time in the campaign visiting with Combs' supporters that Bob Matthews had angered. I had to be the peacemaker attempting to keep these important supporters on the Combs team. All of such activity should have been unnecessary. Instead of spending my time attempting to win, I had to stick my finger in the dike and try to keep it there.

J.R. Miller, Ford's campaign manager, wanted very badly to defeat Bert Combs and his running mate for lieutenant governor, Julian Carroll of McCracken County in far western Kentucky. Combs chose Carroll to be his unofficial running mate because he, being from eastern Kentucky, needed a western Kentucky native to provide the ticket with balance. Miller's animosity toward Combs and Carroll made it difficult for me to support Wendell Ford in the general election with any degree of enthusiasm, especially after the way I had been treated concerning my job at ARH. I began to consider supporting the Republican candidates, Tom Emberton and his running mate for lieutenant governor, Jim Host.

A few days after the primary in which Ford had defeated Combs, but in which Julian Carroll, combs' running mate, had won because of receiving mountain votes from Combs' supporters, Gov. Louie Nunn invited me to the Governor's Mansion for a friendly conversation. We met for one solid hour with no one else in the room and with no telephone calls. I found Governor Nunn very pleasant and easy to talk with. We were both surprised to discover how close we were in our political philosophies. Finally, toward the end of our conversation, Governor Nunn said, "I have several important appointments to make, would you accept one?"

I said, "Governor, it would depend on the position offered and, if I did accept, my appointment would be immediately interpreted as an endorsement for Tom Emberton for governor."

Nunn said, "Fontaine, would you accept an appointment to the Council on Higher Education?"

I said, "Yes, I will and I will begin my efforts on behalf of Tom Emberton and Jim Host right away."

I did not know either Emberton or Host, but, after meeting them, I quickly became friends with both. Both were intellectuals who wanted what was best for Kentucky. They were totally honest, shrewd, hard working and very good campaigners. Joining me in this effort were R.L. Combs, the brother of Bert Combs, and former state senator Everett White from western Kentucky. We were successful in recruiting many other Combs' supporters to join our effort on behalf of the Emberton-Host ticket. I worked harder for Emberton and Host than I had in any previous campaign. I knew from the beginning, however, that the odds were stacked against us.

During the general election campaign, I spoke with Bert Combs and told him that J. R. Miller was doing everything in his power to defeat Julian Carroll in the lieutenant governor's race. This was true even though Julian was the Democratic candidate. I told Governor Combs that, if he would not become involved in the fall campaign, I would obtain complete financing for Julian Carroll. Combs looked at me with a very serious expression on his face and said, "Banksie, I didn't realize until just now how deeply you are involved in supporting Emberton and Host. They must trust you and be relying heavily on your experience."

I was trying to keep Combs from supporting Ford. After much more discussion, Combs said that he would have to support Wendell Ford, the man who had defeated him in the primary. I had no further contact with former Governor Combs during the campaign. Happily, after the election was over, Bert Combs and I forgot the past and once again became the good friends that we had been previously. By the way, Combs did acknowledge to his inner circle that "Banksie" had been correct about the outcome of the primary and that I had given him good advice.

Election Day 1971 found me attending a Marine meeting in Philadelphia. I was having a drink in the hotel bar with some friends when I received word that my being out of the state on election night was going to cause some difficulty with the campaign's plans for the evening. So the Emberton-Host campaign arranged for a small jet to pick me up and fly me to Louisville for the hoped-for victory celebration. By the time I arrived the election had been decided and Wendell Ford and Julian Carroll had defeated my candidates, Tom Emberton and Jim Host. I must say that to me our defeat was no surprise. I expected it, but hoped for an upset. Since the election had already been decided, I flew back to Philadelphia and found my friends still sitting at the same table in the hotel bar. I rejoined them. It had been a long and sad day for me.

Emberton and Host ran an excellent campaign. They were honest about the issues and they worked as hard as any candidates I have ever been associated with. It was a losing effort, but I couldn't have been more proud of them. To this day, I still have great respect for each of them. Ford's majority over Emberton was a little more than 60,000 votes. But based on past history, Ford should have won by 125,000 to 175,000. His win was much narrower because of the great campaign of Emberton and Host.

Jim Host has told me on more than one occasion that, considering his post-campaign career success, he is happy that he didn't win. Of course, he didn't feel that way at the time of his loss to Carroll in the lieutenant governor's race. Jim has been one of Kentucky's most successful businessmen and a tried and true supporter of the Commonwealth.

Like Host, Tom Emberton went on to great success. He became a highly respected judge of the Court of Appeals and served as its chief judge. Ironically, when Tom retired from the bench, he was succeeded by Judge Sara Combs, the widow of Bert T. Combs.

After the 1971 gubernatorial election, my contacts with Wendell Ford were few and far between. Finally, in 2003, when Ben Chandler, grandson of Happy Chandler, ran for governor, Wendell and I both worked for his election. We did some work together and, after more than thirty years, finally "buried the hatchet." Our friendship will never be as close as it was prior to the 1971 race for governor, but we can now talk civilly to one another and work together in campaigns.

Of course, Wendell Ford went on to have one of the most successful careers of any Kentucky politician in the entire history of the state. He was a good governor who streamlined state government, emphasized higher education, removed the sales tax from food and had the courage to raise motor fuel taxes, in spite of his campaign pledge not to raise taxes. He served four terms in the United States Senate where he achieved respect and status. And I must say that Wendell, while serving in the Senate, always looked out for the best interests of Kentucky. He took national leadership roles as chairman of the Senate Rules Committee, as Democratic Whip and, in 1996, as Presidential Inaugural Chairman when Bill Clinton was elected to his second term.

Wendell contributed a remarkable thirty-four years of elected service to the commonwealth, in the State Senate, as lieutenant governor and governor, and in the U.S. Senate. I am very happy that I am now, after three decades, back on speaking terms with my old friend that I worked for so hard in eastern Kentucky in 1967 in order to give him a chance to win the lieutenant governor's race—the victory that sent him on his way to such outstanding success in his political career.

I have no regrets about my efforts in 1967 to elect Wendell lieutenant governor. My regret is over Wendell's unfounded assumption that I was supporting Combs instead of him in the 1971 governor's race. My experience of being attacked personally and having my job placed in jeopardy was a difficult way to learn the lesson of "never assume anything." If only Wendell had granted me the common courtesy of a visit with him that day so long ago, I could have explained my position on Combs' running and avoided this long unwarranted period of coldness between us.

They say politics makes strange bedfellows—how true that is. In 1971 I found myself receiving an appointment from a Republican governor and working to elect a second Republican governor whose opponent had been one of my closest friends in the Combs administration. Sometimes life is difficult. Sometimes it's strange. Sometimes it's just plain confusing.

As for Governor Nunn, I was pleased with his interest in me. He opened some doors for me that could never have been opened by anyone else. Even though we often found ourselves on opposite sides in political campaigns, we remained close friends until his untimely death on January 29, 2004.

Although never elected to office again, Nunn remained active in Republican politics. In 1972, a year after his term as governor ended, he ran for the U.S. Senate against Walter "Dee" Huddleston and was defeated by about 34,000 votes. In 1979, he again ran for governor falling at the hands of John Y. Brown, Jr. by over 75,000 votes. Louie Nunn continued to practice law in Lexington until his death. He had been the strongest Republican governor in Kentucky history.

36 Kentucky's First Woman Governor: Martha Layne Collins (1983-1987)

IN 1974, GOVERNOR FORD resigned the governorship after winning a seat in the U.S. Senate. He was succeeded by Lt. Gov. Julian Carroll who in 1975 won a full term as governor. Carroll was followed by Gov. John Y. Brown, Jr. who served from 1979 to 1983. Brown, in turn, was followed by Martha Layne Collins, Kentucky's first and, so far, only woman governor.

Martha Layne Collins was born Martha Layne Hall in Bagdad—no, not that Bagdad—a small community located in Shelby County. As a youngster, she was encouraged to participate in extra-curricular activities in addition to working hard at her studies. Collins was selected the Shelby County Tobacco Festival Queen and in 1959 became Queen of the Kentucky Derby Festival. She graduated from the University of Kentucky that same year with a degree in home economics. Two years later she met Billy Louis Collins of Hazard, a student at Georgetown College. Martha Layne and Bill married on July 3, 1959, and then Martha Layne taught in Louisville at Fairdale and Seneca high schools while Bill obtained his degree in dentistry from the University of Louisville Dental School.

Fontaine Banks and Gov. Martha Layne Collins

In the mid-1960s the couple, now with two children, moved to Woodford County where Bill started his dentistry practice and Martha Layne taught at Woodford County Junior High School. In Woodford County, Martha

Layne became interested in politics. She worked her way up by working in campaigns. After Wendell Ford was elected governor, Collins was chosen to be Kentucky's Democratic national committeewoman. It was then that she quit teaching and became a full-time worker at the state Democratic Party headquarters under J. R. Miller, who had been Ford's campaign chairman. In 1975, after having helped many candidates win elections and at the urging of her husband to work on her own campaign, Collins decided to run for the state office of Clerk of the Court of Appeals. Collins won the general election over Joseph E. Lambert of Mt. Vernon who later served as Chief Justice of the Kentucky Supreme Court.

In 1979, she ran for lieutenant governor and squeezed out a razor-thin victory of about 4,000 votes in the crowded primary field of five candidates. In the general election she defeated Republican and later to be Congressman Hal Rogers of Somerset by more than 200,000 votes. As lieutenant governor, Collins was not assigned a significant role in Governor Brown's administration. Free to do as she pleased, she traveled the state making speeches, cutting ribbons and doing things the governor didn't like to do. She visited all 120 counties, some of them many times. She was building an organization.

Collins' campaign for governor began officially a full year and a half before the primary election in May, 1983. She was a well-funded candidate with an effective fund-raising team headed by her husband. The Collins' campaign raised about $2.8 million for the primary and nearly $5 million for the primary and general elections combined. She ran an excellent campaign and won a close race over Louisville Mayor Harvey Slone and former Human Resources Secretary Grady Stumbo, both of whom were physicians. She received 33.97 percent of the vote while Slone received 33.28 percent and Stumbo got 30.34 percent.

The Democratic Party patched-up its three-way split in the general election and the state elected its first woman governor and only the third woman governor in the history of our nation. She also made history by receiving more votes than any previous candidate for governor (561,674). She won by more than 100,000 votes over Republican State Senator Jim Bunning of Fort Thomas, a former major league baseball pitcher who is now enshrined in the Baseball Hall of Fame and is currently serving his third term as a U.S. Senator.

As the primary race was getting under way, a group of former supporters of Bert Combs and Ned Breathitt met and discussed who we should support. We debated back and forth with some for supporting Martha Layne and some for supporting Mayor Harvey Slone. Finally we decided to take a vote. It was close, but Slone won. I did not know either Martha Layne or Bill Collins. I had never met either and no one from her campaign approached me on her behalf. So, based on the vote of the group, I decided to go with them and support Harvey Slone.

As the primary campaign progressed, it became obvious to me that Collins was well organized and out-campaigning Slone. If there are two things I am especially good at in politics, they are my ability to recognize a good organization and a good, hard-working campaigner. Martha Layne had spent her years as lieutenant governor building an excellent organization and she was a tireless campaigner. To say the least, I was not surprised when she won the primary over my candidate, Dr. Slone.

Following the primary election, for the next few weeks I did absolutely nothing politically. Then one day I received a phone call from Eddy Coleman, Collins' campaign manager for Franklin County. He asked me to come to Collins' headquarters and meet with him. I agreed and, when I arrived, I found that several people were awaiting my arrival.

We all sat down and Eddy told me that the Collins' campaign was having a difficult time obtaining the help of the Slone forces. He asked me if I would be willing to help get the Slone supporters on board the Collins' bandwagon. When I said I would be willing to help, everyone looked relieved.

They set up a desk for me at Collins' headquarters. My desk was next to the desk of my ol' friend and Marine buddy, Al Austin. For the remainder of the campaign, I spent most of my days at my desk at headquarters assisting the full-time staff and organizing the Slone troops for Collins. For that entire summer and fall, Al Austin and I worked very closely together. We worked day and night, even spending some nights at headquarters. We sent out mailings, we made phone calls, we did everything we possibly could in the time we had. We felt good about the reception we were receiving from folks. It was gratifying to see that we were making progress.

When I started we had a split Democratic Party, but by about midway in the general election campaign, I could say with confidence that we had a party united behind Martha Layne Collins. By election day, I thought Collins would defeat Jim Bunning by around 100,000 votes. She won by 107,000. She received the largest margin of victory in the history of Franklin County.

On several occasions during the campaign, Al Austin asked me which position he should take in the Collins administration. If she won, Al would have a choice between working on her staff in the governor's office or becoming secretary of the Human Resources Cabinet. I was very clear in my advice to him. I told Al that he should take the position of secretary of Human Resources because that is where he had spent his working years and he had gained the knowledge and experience to do this very important job very well. I also told Al that, with his type of personality and way of doing things, he would not do well working in the governor's office. I told him that he had the choice of being an excellent head of Human Resources or a disaster as an assistant to the governor. Since I had so many years of experience working in the governor's office, Al felt that he was getting good advice from an old hand. A few days after our last discussion on the subject of his future employment, he came into the office and said, "Fontaine, we are going to Human Resources."

I said, "What do you mean by 'we'? I was for Slone, remember."

Al said, "Dr. Collins and I convinced Martha Layne that you should come with me."

Needless to say, I was surprised, but pleased. I was happy about the confidence both Dr. Collins and the governor-elect had shown in me especially since I had opposed Martha Layne in the primary. I also looked forward to working in a responsible position with my friend, Al Austin. After the election, Al and I maintained the transition office until Inauguration Day.

One day just prior to our taking over at the Cabinet for Human Resources, we were over there and asked a question of the chief counsel of the outgoing crew. He didn't know the answer so he made a telephone call to someone in the Cabinet. In a few minutes, a young man bounded into the room and introduced himself as John Cubine. When we asked our question, Cubine had an immediate and full answer. So we asked him another question. He answered that one with knowledge and enthusiasm. We kept on asking questions for more than an hour. He answered every one without the slightest hesitation. When we finally ran out of questions to ask and Mr. Cubine had left the office, I told Al that, while I didn't know anything about John Cubine, we were damn sure going to keep him on and keep him close to us. Al just laughed, but he agreed.

When we finally took over operation of this giant cabinet, the first item of business was to put our management team in place. We chose Sue Sykes as our secretary. The rest of our excellent team was composed of John Cubine,

Ben Lawson, Mike Robinson, James Thompson, Bill Gardner, Brad Hughes, Dr. Teague, Anna Grace Day and Matt Amato.

I had only a few meetings with Governor Collins, but one thing was clear to me—of all the governors I have known, she was by far the hardest worker. When she had to leave on a trip, she would fill a legal size sheet of paper with assignments for secretaries of cabinets to complete before she returned to Frankfort. In meetings with members of the General Assembly, she was always in complete control.

Meanwhile, back at Human Resources, Al was beginning to be away from the office too much of the time. Many times Governor Collins called Al on his private line which, when he was away, I had to answer. The governor would always say, "Fontaine, where is Al?" I usually told her that he was just out of the building for awhile. She would always reply, "Fontaine, you know he's not. You find him and tell him to call me right away."

During the term of Governor Collins, my relationship with her husband, Dr. Bill Collins, was wonderful. He would call me whenever he had a problem that involved the Human Resources Cabinet. Fortunately, I was always able to solve his problems. Dr. Collins was always extremely supportive of his wife. For that matter, he was also very supportive of Al Austin.

Martha Layne Collins had a very successful administration. Through a combination of determination, grueling hard work, long hours, a willingness to transform herself from the tough taskmaster to the team player, the courage to make necessary personnel changes, and the intelligence to change course on issues when necessary, made her an outstanding leader. As Kentucky's first woman governor, she had different aspirations and approaches to problems than her male predecessors. In a state where politics is often simply low-down mean, she withstood the attacks against her husband and herself and remained focused on her goals.

As she began her term as governor, she was startled to discover that the state cupboard was bare. The state treasury was short of funds for budgeted programs by more than $300 million. She had realized during her campaign that a revenue shortfall existed, but she didn't realize how large the shortage was. She had emphasized in her campaign that she did not intend to raise taxes despite the revenue shortage that lingered longer in Kentucky than in most states, which were recovering from the 1982-1983 national recession. But as the call for improvements in education became more insistent and revenue forecasts continued to be discouraging, she changed course and asked the General Assembly for tax increases amounting to $324 million. She was unable to get the votes necessary for passage of the tax bill and so conceded defeat before the end of the session. She had to settle for a continuation budget. Her first session left many disappointed because of the bare-bones budget, but some successes were achieved. Mandatory kindergarten was enacted, testing and internship for teachers, remedial programs for early grades, and academic receivership for schools failing to perform.

Governor Collins signs a bill into law

Governor Collins attracted national attention during the summer of 1984 when she chaired the Democratic National Convention in San Francisco and was one of the potential running mates interviewed by presidential nominee Walter Mondale. Mondale ended up choosing a woman, but not Collins. He decided upon Geraldine Ferraro of New York.

Collins received a setback near the end of 1984 when, during a trip to Europe to investigate acid rain, she swallowed a shard of glass. Emergency intestinal surgery kept her in a London hospital for more than two weeks and, when she was released, she was given strict orders to take it easy for the next several months. But by January she was back in stride.

Speaking of stride, in my opinion, Martha Layne Collins hit hers beginning with the special session she called in the summer of 1985. Gone were Finance Secretary Mac Thompson and Transportation Secretary Floyd Poore, both closely associated with her husband and fund-raisers in her gubernatorial campaign, and both major contributors to quarrels within her administration. The other factor in her emergence as an effective leader was a much more focused message on the dual benefits of economic development and education reform. Her message was simply "better jobs require better schools."

Her program called for increased salaries and longevity bonuses for teachers, reduction in class sizes in the lower grades, and a career ladder program for teachers tied to performance. The business community supported these education reforms and thus also supported a large increase in the corporation license tax to fund most of the reforms. The legislature enacted the reforms in the special session.

Next, Governor Collins turned to economic development. Collins and her economic development team headed by Commerce Secretary Carroll Knicely put together trips to Japan, Europe, Korea and Taiwan. The biggest victory by far was convincing Toyota Motor Manufacturing to build its $800 million assembly plant in Georgetown, bringing thousands of jobs and dozens of satellite industries to the state.

A bidding war between several states had broken out and Collins was determined to win. She brought Toyota officials to Kentucky and treated them to the best Kentucky had to offer. She wined and dined them and charmed them right into choosing Kentucky as the home of the new plant. More than 3,000 workers were initially hired. Later Toyota added a $300 million engine plant to their Scott County facility. With this tremendous success, Governor Collins made Kentucky a player in the global economy.

I was there when Governor Collins played hostess to the Japanese, and I was there for the fireworks that the Japanese loved so much! Some of her advisors thought she was going too far, but she didn't care. She knew what she was doing and was successful with it. We looked all over Louisville trying to find sushi for that dinner, and I'm glad to say everything worked out fine that night. The Japanese were very happy. They had Maker's Mark bourbon there . . . they were very happy. They must have carried a ton of that stuff to Japan. It worked out fine, especially for Kentucky.

Negotiations for the purchase of the land, the need for water and sewage lines and the use of union employees raised some opposition to the project, but the vast majority of Kentuckians welcomed the new plant with its many jobs. Collins developed a $125 million incentive package, which included training and deferred taxes. The incentive package was immediately attacked as corporate welfare and challenged in court. In a landmark precedent, the Kentucky Supreme Court ruled that the state's incentives and other efforts for Toyota were constitutional and justified in order to attain the public goal of reducing unemployment. And that goal of reducing unemployment was achieved far beyond the initial projections. Unemployment dropped from almost 10 percent in October 1983 to just a little over 7 percent four years later. During her administration, almost 85,000 new jobs were created.

The major environmental issue during the Collins administration was water management. The Collins Cabinet for Natural Resources and Environmental Protection developed and implemented the state's first comprehensive water management plan. The cabinet also successfully negotiated the state's continued primacy over surface mining enforcement.

Another major accomplishment occurred in the state's Workers' Compensation program which faced an almost $2 billion deficit. After a legislative task force recommended changes, Governor Collins called a special session of the General Assembly that enacted a package that placed the program, once again, on a sound financial footing.

While there were no scandals among employees of the Collins administration, the legacy of the state's first and to date only female governor was damaged to some degree by the business affairs of her husband.

In 1986, the *Courier Journal* revealed in a major article that almost half of the investors in the real estate and thoroughbred horse partnerships of Bill Collins also held contracts with or appointments with the Collins administration. Collins responded to the article by denying any *quid pro quo* between those who invested in her husband's company and those who did business or received appointments with the state. Even though Dr. Collins never held a position in the Collins administration, allegations that investors had been forced to invest in his company or make contributions to the campaign in order to win contracts with the state or appointments to positions in the Collins administration became the subject of seemingly endless federal grand jury investigations.

In the end, Bill Collins was indicted in 1992 on charges of extortion, conspiracy, and tax fraud. Martha Layne was called to testify, but no charges were ever filed against her or any member of her administration. Bill Collins was convicted and served the majority of his five-year sentence in federal prison in Alabama.

The Dr. Bill Collins' affair was in many ways a tragedy for the governor. She not only had to see her husband go to federal prison, she also suffered greatly in her future political career. Just think about it—she had been a rarity, a female governor and a very successful one. The Toyota plant acquisition for Kentucky put her on the national political map. Her political future appeared extremely bright. But the fallout from her husband's activities probably cost her an appointment in the Clinton administration and discouraged her from running for a seat in the U.S. Senate.

Ruling out running for office, Collins, still energetic and hard-working, found other ways to serve the Commonwealth. She concentrated on the field of higher education. She lectured in international business and public policy at Harvard, the University of Louisville and the University of Kentucky. She served as president of St. Catherine College from 1990 to 1996, she directed UK's International Business and Management Center for two years, and then became executive scholar in residence at Georgetown College. Today she still continues to encourage economic development within the state.

I was extremely disappointed about the Bill Collins' mess. While Governor Collins had a very successful administration, it could have been even more successful had it not been for the nearly constant distraction during the final two years caused by the Bill Collins' affair. For me personally, I was always treated well by both the governor and her husband. I appreciated the faith she placed in me by giving me a responsible position in the Cabinet for Human Resources when I had been a Slone supporter during the primary campaign. I admired her work ethic, her courage and determination and her "team player" attitude that enabled her to bring rival groups together. I also marveled at her knowledge of and abilities in international businesses affairs. She could go anywhere in the world and be comfortable in representing the economic interests of her beloved Kentucky. In my opinion, she was one of the best Kentucky governors of the twentieth century.

37 A Non-Native Becomes Governor: Brereton Jones (1991-1995)

BRERETON C. JONES WAS governor of Kentucky from 1991 through 1995, succeeding Wallace Wilkinson. He was born in 1939 and grew up on a prosperous dairy farm in the small West Virginia town of Point Pleasant. In his childhood, Jones learned the rural values of community and family and developed strong Christian beliefs, which he later demonstrated in his public life.

A football star in high school, he went on to play college football at the University of Virginia. He graduated from Virginia with a degree in commerce and public finance. Upon graduation he returned home to West Virginia and developed a successful real estate and home construction business.

In 1964, Jones was elected as a Republican to the West Virginia legislature, becoming the youngest person ever elected to that legislative body. He was reelected in 1966 and became minority leader of the House Republicans. Jones, however, grew disenchanted with Republican politics after he perceived corruption in West Virginia state government, which was led by a Republican adversary of Jones.

Jones quit politics in 1968 and concentrated on his Huntington real estate development business. His long-time interest in horses brought Jones on numerous trips to Central Kentucky where he met Elizabeth "Libby" Lloyd—they were married in 1970. In 1972, the couple moved to Libby's childhood home, historic Airdrie Farm in Woodford County between Versailles and Frankfort. Jones then leased a portion of the farm from his father-in-law, former Adjutant General A. Y. Lloyd, and began to work with horses. Airdrie Stud, now a large and successful thoroughbred operation, has grown to 2,700 acres and almost 300 horses, including winners of classic races in both Europe and America.

In 1975, Brereton Jones changed his party registration from Republican to Democrat, but remained out of politics (at least out of elective politics).

Gov. John Y. Brown, Jr. appointed him to the University of Kentucky Board of Trustees and the University of Kentucky Chandler Medical Center Board. He also became involved in fund raising for a cancer center at UK. In the mid-1980s, he founded the Kentucky Health Care Access Foundation to provide free health care to thousands of Kentuckians who fell below the poverty level, but were not poor enough to qualify for Medicaid.

But Brereton had not yet moved to Kentucky when one day in 1972, I received a telephone call from Libby's father, the former Adjutant General, A. Y. Lloyd, whom I had known since the years of the Combs administration. He didn't say why he called; he just invited me out to Airdrie for a talk. I accepted the invitation and when I arrived on the appointed day, General Lloyd showed me all around the farm and we talked about our relationship during the good old days of the Combs' and Breathitt administrations.

After walking and chatting for almost an hour, General Lloyd said, "Fontaine, I have a huge personal favor to ask of you."

He went on to say that his daughter and her husband had decided to move to Kentucky and to develop the farm into a successful horse operation.

He said, "Fontaine, Brereton has been in West Virginia politics and I expect him to do the same when he arrives in Kentucky. Would you watch out for him, help him, and support him if he becomes a candidate for office?"

I answered, "General, I will do anything and everything I can to be of help to his candidacy for any office."

The general smiled and looked relieved. We shook hands and I departed the beautiful rolling pastures of Airdrie. I thought to myself that this land was perfect for a really major horse farm. I could see in my mind's eye, mares and their foals romping in those lovely fields. I hoped that the general's son-in-law would be a frisky young colt of a politician. One who would go romping through the campaigns of the future without breaking his stride.

It turned out in the end that Brereton Jones was that frisky young colt I had hoped he would be. He did romp through the Kentucky politics without a hitch. But it would be a few years before this colt entered the starting gate ready to race. Like in the case of the thoroughbreds he raised, there would have to be a period of preparation; a period before Brereton Jones would have a real chance to make a successful entry into the stormy world of Kentucky politics.

As related previously, during the Collins administration I served as deputy secretary of the Cabinet for Human Resources. During my tenure there, a time came when the administration needed to form a Medicaid Advisory Committee. I saw this as an opportunity for Brereton. Fortunately, my efforts turned out well, even better than I expected. I was able, not only to have him appointed to the statewide committee, but to have him chosen as its chairman. As chairman, Jones did an outstanding job of protecting the state's interests and, at the same time, protecting the people who needed Medicaid.

I considered his appointment as sort of a coming out party. I felt that now was the time to get Brereton introduced to the citizens of our commonwealth. I made it my business to make certain that Jones was introduced to all the Democratic and Republican political leaders throughout the entire state. I took him around the state, county by county, until I felt we had been successful in bringing the name "Brereton Jones" to the attention of all of our state's leaders.

This critically important task proved much easier to accomplish than I expected. Brereton always had a smile on his face and was friendly and sincerely interested in whoever he was talking with. He was tireless; always ready to move on to meet some other officials. It was obvious that Brereton Jones was going to be a formidable candidate no matter which office he might decide to seek.

(l - r) Fontaine Banks, Gov. Brereton Jones and Barbara Banks

I had worked extremely hard to get Brereton known in Kentucky political circles. I felt good about my efforts. It appeared to me that I had accomplished my goal. It was all up to Brereton now. If he wanted to run for office, the preliminary work had been successfully completed. He was no longer the "out-of-state, rich, conservative Republican, blue-blooded horse farm operator." He was "Brereton Jones, the friendly, charming, moderate Democrat farmer from the little village of Midway, Kentucky."

As my efforts to make Brereton well-known to the movers and shakers of Kentucky politics met with more and more success, most political leaders began to feel that soon Brereton Jones would announce that he was a candidate for public office. The questions were when and for which office?

I had been on the Brereton Jones bandwagon for a long, long time when in 1987, he took the plunge and announced his candidacy for lieutenant governor. His candidacy ensured that I would not be able to support my fellow Pike countian, Paul Patton, the three-time Pike County judge executive who would later serve as both lieutenant governor and governor.

Campaigning for Brereton Jones in the lieutenant governor's race was both difficult and easy. This was his first run for public office in more than twenty years and he was a bit rusty. Also, in both the primary and general elections, he was accused of being a carpet-bagging Republican from West Virginia. Brereton responded well to this type of attack. He would say, "I was and am very fond of my mama, and I wanted to be close to her when I was born. She just happened to be in West Virginia, but I got here as quickly as I could."

The other difficulty I faced in the campaign was working with Brereton's campaign staff. They were all well-meaning, but they were young and almost totally inexperienced. I had to spend much of my time teaching, advising, and answering questions posed by these youngsters.

The easy part was that the candidate was so appealing. And when you combined him with his beautiful wife Libby, he was an even more appealing candidate. He always had a smile on his face and he was always friendly and patient with the public and the media. He was a very open and honest candidate. He answered questions; he didn't dodge them. He used TV advertising extensively, emphasizing in the ads his business and health care experience and leadership. Brereton spent more than $2 million on television advertising. He was a different kind of candidate than I had worked with in the past, but he was a good one.

We were all exhausted each night trying to keep up with him. He was a great campaigner, but I still say that his biggest campaign asset was his wife, Libby. She was not only a beautiful lady, but also most gracious, courteous and patient all the time. Brereton and Libby together made this old campaigner grin from ear to ear. They were magnificent. Brereton was a winner and I knew it. He defeated Attorney General David Armstrong, Paul Patton and two others by a 7 percent margin in the Democratic primary election. In the general election, he won easily against Republican Larry Webster. Brereton won by an almost three to one count.

After Brereton won the primary, he looked like an almost certain winner in the general election. It was then that I began to consider whether I wanted a position on the lieutenant governor's staff. So it was early in the general election campaign that I decided not to seek a position on Brereton's staff. I decided that I could do far more good for him if I immediately began campaigning for him for the office of governor. When Brereton announced his candidacy for governor, I had already invested three years of campaigning for him. During those three years, I spent most of my campaigning time contacting old friends from the Combs' and Breathitt administrations and asking them to join me in helping Brereton become governor. I generally received warm responses and pledges of help and support for Brereton. All this work was a bit tiring on an old campaigner, but well worth all the effort. When Brereton Jones announced his candidacy for governor, I had participated in ten gubernatorial campaigns (counting his in which I had already been working) and had been active in Kentucky politics for forty-five years. I never would have dreamed then that I would play an active role in several more campaigns for governor.

But I'm getting ahead of my story. Brereton's term as lieutenant governor was disappointing to him in several ways. In the first place, his relationship with Gov. Wallace Wilkinson, like that of so many others, was in Brereton's own words, "terrible." Secondly, Wilkinson gave him almost no opportunity to play any kind of significant role in his administration. These were disappointments.

On the other hand, Brereton came up with his own initiatives and, under difficult circumstances, accomplished quite a lot. For example, he received praise for his efforts to attain a "Made in Kentucky" label for homegrown produce. He was also a very strong advocate for the preservation of family farms and for education reform. His friendly, cooperative, courteous manner enabled him, as president of the Kentucky Senate, to develop a good working relationship with most members of the general assembly.

While the bitter relationship with Governor Wilkinson left Brereton with little power, the office of lieutenant governor made him the front runner for the Democratic nomination for governor in 1991. The lack of any real power or any duties worthy of mention was helpful in that it left him with plenty of time to concentrate on winning the race for governor.

During the primary and the general election campaigns for governor, I found myself involved in many different activities. From time to time, I worked with Jack Hall arranging fund raisers. I even had a big one at my home in Frankfort. I was very pleased at the number who attended and the amount of funds raised. Many who attended either currently held or, in the past, had held positions of leadership in the Kentucky Democratic Party.

Much of my time was spent assisting and teaching younger staff members who were new to politics. I met with Brereton on several occasions to brief him on certain campaign issues. Overall, Brereton's gubernatorial campaign was one of the most exciting and interesting ones in which I have participated.

In the Democratic primary, Jones faced some formidable opposition. As the frontrunner, he was the chief target of the other candidates who were Martha Wilkinson, the incumbent governor's wife, Scotty Baesler, former mayor of Lexington and Congressman Dr. Floyd Poore, and Gatewood Galbraith. Brereton had to contend with a lot of negative campaigning from Martha Wilkinson running to succeed her husband, but she dropped out of the race about three weeks before primary election day. With Martha Wilkinson's withdrawal, Brereton defeated one of his major rivals before the voters had had a chance to go to the polls.

Brereton's campaign consisted chiefly of his call for campaign finance reform and his emphasis on ethics in government. He contrasted himself with Wallace Wilkinson's image of dishonesty and business improprieties. With the strong support of labor, teachers, and many other groups, he took his campaign to every county in the state. His campaign was well organized and thus he was able to contest every county. On the stump he exhibited personal charm and charisma.

On primary election day, I felt very confident although I did not expect a landslide. When the votes were counted that evening, Brereton had won by a margin of about 35,000 votes over second place finisher, Scotty Baesler. He defeated Dr. Poore by more than 50,000 votes and Galbraith by more than 150,000 votes.

But the days of tough Democratic Party primaries and easy general election victories were over. The Republicans were now fielding formidable candidates for governor and the 1991 general election was expected to be a dogfight between Jones and the Republican candidate, seven-term Sixth District Congressman Larry Hopkins of Lexington. Hopkins had narrowly won the Republican Party primary over Lexington attorney, Larry Forgy. To my surprise, what was expected to be a hotly-contested close race turned out much differently. No big issues emerged and Hopkins ran an unexpectedly lackluster campaign in which he was outspent by Jones by more than two to one. By election day, I was totally confidant of a big victory. Some of our campaign staff members were worried and it usually pays to be worried because worry keeps you on your toes and looking over your shoulder to see if your opponent is gaining any ground on you. But here, a very cautious old campaigner like me, just couldn't worry. Jones had run brilliantly and I just couldn't see the plodding Hopkins campaign gaining any ground. In fact, the Hopkins' campaign just kept slipping further behind. I had been prepared for a down-to-the-wire, knock-down-drag-out battle in the general election. Thankfully, it didn't happen.

Brereton felt comfortable throughout the race and crushed Hopkins by a count of 540,458 to 294,452. Winning by the largest margin in the history of Kentucky governor's races, Brereton won by a startling margin of almost a quarter of a million votes.

Between the election and the inauguration day, I telephoned Brereton and let him know that I wanted to be a part of his administration. We discussed several possible positions, but did not come to any decision. Then, about two weeks before inauguration day, Jack Hall called and asked me to come to see him. When Jack and I met, he said that the governor-elect would be pleased if I would accept the position of deputy secretary of the Cabinet for Human Resources. This was the exact same position I had held during the Collins administration. When I agreed to accept the offer, Jack immediately introduced me to Len Heller who was to be the cabinet secretary. Over the next few days, Len and I had several discussions in which we became acquainted and discussed my role as deputy secretary.

Finally, Len and I began to discuss who we wanted on our cabinet staff. I suggested we keep Kay Hill, who had served as secretary to Dr. Harry Cowherd when he was secretary of Human Resources, as our joint secretary. Kay had an outstanding reputation and possessed tremendous talent and experience. She was loyal, intelligent, friendly and extremely helpful to members of the cabinet. She had excellent computer skills and knew everyone in the cabinet.

I asked the director of Personnel to approach Kay to see if she was interested. She was, she accepted the position, and the rest is history.

Others who joined us included Ron Keal, Sharon Stumbo, Dr. Rice Leach, Bill Hampton, Bill Gardner, Paul Mauer, Kevin Peyton and Matt Amato. Since I had served previously as deputy secretary for four years, it was not difficult to get Human Resources moving early in the Jones' administration. For the first few months, I was very busy managing the cabinet and was completely unaware of the difficulties Len Heller was having with personnel in the governor's office. To my great surprise, one day I was called and asked to meet with Governor Jones who, when we met, told me that Len was being transferred to the governor's office and that I was to be named secretary. Later I learned that Len had experienced problems in dealing with the governor's cabinet secretary.

When I became secretary of the Cabinet for Human Resources, the secretary of the Governor's Cabinet told me, in no uncertain terms, that I was not to do anything that might negatively influence the governor's plans for health care reform. I said that I would cooperate in any way I could and would make every effort to help with health care reform. I had my "marching orders."

The problem with an order not to do anything that would hurt the chances for the success of some program is that it is often very difficult to tell what might become a negative influence on a proposed program. The only way to make certain that you and your cabinet exert no negative influence is to do nothing. And if you do nothing, you are robbing the taxpayers who pay your salary and the salaries of all of your employees. Well, I never was a "do-nothing-guy." Prior to receiving the appointment as secretary of the Cabinet for Human Resources, I had developed a reorganization plan for the cabinet that would have saved millions of dollars and greatly improved efficiency and the delivery of services throughout the cabinet, especially in the critically important Medicaid program. Time and time again, I requested permission to implement my reorganization plan. Each time I was given a very definite "no" by the secretary of the Governor's Cabinet. I kept trying, but to no avail. Each time my request was turned down without explanation. I can only assume that the cabinet secretary must have thought that my reorganization plan would impact negatively on the governor's plans for health care reform. But I couldn't see it that way. It appeared to me that my plan would have no impact, either negatively or positively, on plans for health care reform.

At this time, Sen. Mike Maloney, a Lexington attorney, was chairman of the Senate Appropriations and Revenue (A&R) Committee of the General Assembly. Members of the governor's staff accused me of divulging information to Senator Maloney. Mike's father and I had worked together several years before the Jones' term and Mike had affection and respect for me as a result of his father's friendship and working relationship with me. Mike's friendship with me was considered by some on the governor's staff as protection of me. This was a complete misinterpretation. Mike was a tough, straight-shooter. He and I were friends, but he wasn't about to protect me if I made a major misstep.

The problem was that someone in the Jones' administration was providing Mike Maloney with delicate information. Some members of the governor's staff thought that, because of my friendship with the senator, that I was the one divulging information to him. It turned out that the person providing the unauthorized information to the senator was the Director of a very important state agency. Mike told me that they met every morning at Mike's health club.

I took this information to the secretary of the Governor's Cabinet and told him of the disloyal acts of the director of the state agency. The cabinet secretary became very upset and asked me, if he decided to inform the governor of this disloyalty, to go with him. I replied that I would go, but nothing ever happened.

After having had the implementation of my reorganization plan for the cabinet turned down over and over again and being falsely accused of divulging information improperly, I began to analyze my position as head of human resources. I came to realize that my reorganization plan was not going to be approved and that, with my orders not to do anything that could possibly injure the chances of health care reform, I was not going to be allowed the freedom to accomplish much of anything. With these thoughts in mind, I felt that my only honorable choice was to resign, which I did.

Today, more than a dozen years have passed since the Jones' administration ended in 1995. I feel that it is important that I treat the years of the Jones' administration with absolute fairness. Many have not. In my opinion, Brereton Jones is a greatly underrated governor.

In December, 1991, the Commonwealth of Kentucky faced a $400 million revenue shortfall. The state had been forced to make budget cuts in twelve of the fourteen years just prior to the Jones term. Governor Jones cut waste, reduced the state's payroll by attrition and stimulated private sector growth. Jones reorganized the Cabinet for Economic Development and established the Economic Development Partnership Board. As a result of these actions, Jones raised the budget revenue trust fund balance to $200 million.

At the end of his term, there were 200,000 more Kentuckians working than there were in December, 1991. The unemployment rate had dropped to the lowest level in twenty years. Standard & Poor's upgraded the state's credit rating to A+, which was the best rating in the Commonwealth's history.

During the 1992 session of the general assembly, Governor Jones pushed for campaign finance reform. The general assembly obliged and passed a good bill. In 1993, Governor Jones called a special session of the legislature in order to pass an ethics code for legislators which turned out to be the best ethics code in the nation. Although falling short of his goal of health insurance coverage for all Kentuckians, Governor Jones did win passage of a comprehensive health care bill which put Kentucky at the forefront of reform efforts in America. After the conclusion of a three-year process, Governor Jones announced that the federal government had approved an amendment that allowed Kentucky to implement managed care. This action alone saved Kentucky $170 million in Medicaid expenses. Jones also called a special session of the legislature to authorize a bond issue for renovation work at Kentucky's state parks.

In January 1995, Governor Jones called yet another special session to consider three construction projects:

1. The Kentucky History Center;
2. A convention center in northern Kentucky; and
3. Expansion of the Commonwealth Convention Center in Louisville

All three projects were approved.

Governor Jones also instituted a unique program called "Open Door after 4:00" which provided citizens with an opportunity to meet with the governor to discuss problems and seek assistance from state government.

During the special session in 1995, Governor Jones recommended reducing taxes by more than $120 million. This was achieved by cutting the income tax on private pensions and reducing the state inheritance tax. Jones also pursued a bold new economic development recruiting program that allowed Kentucky to better compete for jobs throughout the nation. The Kentucky Technology Service was established while he was governor.

For the first time since the program began in 1990, Governor Jones was able to authorize full funding for local school building programs. In 1994, nearly $75 million was transferred to support local schools.

During the first three years of the Jones' administration, the Transportation Cabinet built more roads and spread more blacktop than at any other time in history. In 1995, Governor Jones won legislative approval to designate $50 million in road fund surplus for rural and secondary road improvements.

In his budget address in 1994, Governor Jones stated, "I strongly believe that it is government's responsibility to help those citizens who are unable to help themselves. However, it is not government's responsibility to help those who are unwilling to help themselves."

During the Jones' administration, a project called "Kentucky Outlook 2000—a Strategy for Kentucky's Third Century," involved Kentuckians from all walks of life in planning in order to address the future needs of the commonwealth.

When the Jones' administration began, the Commonwealth of Kentucky did not have a "rainy day fund," at least not one with any funds in it for use when that rainy day came. In 1994, Governor Jones built the fund to $100 million.

When the Jones' term began, Kentucky had a budget imbalance of nearly $400 million and when his term ended, the state had a surplus of $300 million—a turn around of $700 million. In 1995, *Financial World Magazine* ranked Kentucky seventh among the fifty states in financial responsibility, up from a ranking of twenty-sixth in 1994.

The Department of Personnel implemented Governor Jones' direction to downsize state government through attrition. By the end of the Jones term, 2,000 full-time positions had been eliminated. At the same time, Governor Jones implemented salary increases of 5 percent annually for state employees.

I believe historians will be extremely kind to the Brereton Jones' administration because Jones was successful in every area in which he attempted to make improvements. Brereton Jones came to Frankfort promising renewed cooperation in state government and determined to achieve enactment of an ambitious legislative program. At the end of his term, a budget surplus existed of more than $300 million, improvements in relations with the general assembly had been achieved, an array of ethics and government reform legislation had been enacted, welfare rolls were declining, lower unemployment rates existed, and the administration had been scandal-free. Governor Jones failed to achieve his most ambitious goal of health care insurance for all Kentuckians, but he left office with a record 61 percent approval rating. Overall, a very fine record.

When Brereton ended his term, he returned to Airdrie tending to the breeding of thoroughbreds. He also founded Commonwealth Broadcasting, through which he and his partners purchased numerous radio stations in Kentucky and Tennessee. He has continued to be involved with the important issues of today, such as promoting campaign finance laws, health care reform, and dealing with casino gambling proposals. He has said that the duty of a former governor is to continue to lead by example and to voice concerns.

Brereton Jones has not sought further public office, although he has considered it, but Kentuckians can be sure that he will continue to be heard from in the political debate on the issues important to his adopted state.

38 It's in the Genes: Ben Chandler & the 2003 Gubernatorial Campaign

I HAVE TOLD THE story of how Governor Chandler and I became close friends. This friendship continued from March 1964 until Governor Chandler's death on June 15, 1991.

The last time I was with Governor Chandler was at his last birthday party. As I walked into the building, Mrs. Chandler was standing behind her husband. She saw me enter the room and came to meet me. She took me by the arm and said, "His man in Frankfort." I asked about her husband's health and Mrs. Chandler said, "Fontaine, he isn't doing very well."

When I reached the spot where the governor was sitting, I leaned down and he placed his arm around my neck and pulled me to my knees. In that position, down on my knees, I remained for my entire visit with him. Governor Chandler said, "Fontaine, I have a personal favor to ask of you. Will you do it?"

I told him I would do whatever he asked me to do. He repeated himself, saying, "Will you do it?"

I again said, "Governor, if it's within my power, I will do whatever you want me to do."

He paused and stared at me for a few moments and then said, "Will you watch out for my grandson and help him be elected governor?"

I told Governor Chandler, "Yes, I will. I will do exactly what you have asked me to do."

Governor Chandler said, "Thank you, Fontaine. I knew I could count on you."

We talked for a few more minutes and then I departed, Foxy DeMoisey walking me to the door.

When I got to my car, I realized I had seen Governor Chandler for the last time. I found myself crying like a baby.

Ben Chandler is the grandson of Governor A.B. "Happy" Chandler and was destined to be a political figure to be reckoned with here in Kentucky.

Ben entered state politics by running for Auditor of Public Accounts. Aided by name recognition, he won his first race and became Kentucky's State Auditor. With about one year remaining in his term, Ben and I had lunch during which he asked me what I thought about him becoming a candidate for governor. I very quickly told him it was not yet the time for that. I told him that he was too young and needed more experience. I recommended that he run for attorney general and serve two terms in that important post. I told him he would gain great experience as attorney general and that the office would provide numerous opportunities to be in the public eye and to be seen as an experienced, competent leader. Ben took my advice, ran for attorney general, won, and did serve two successful terms in that post, just as I had advised.

After serving eight years as attorney general, it was time to make a run for the office of governor. Ben filed and became a candidate, in fact, he became the front runner for the Democratic Party nomination. Unfortunately, Kentucky was in the midst of one of the worse political scandals in the history of the state.

The scandal involved two-term Democratic governor, Paul Patton, and a woman named Tina Connors. The scandal involved an affair occurring on state time and then, when the story broke, the governor lied claiming that the affair never happened. After the media exposed him as having lied about the affair, Patton apologized, but refused to resign from office. Patton hung on and finished his second term, but irreparable injury had been done to the Democratic Party. The bad publicity had been relentless and prolonged. The public was in a "throw the rascals out mentality!" Nothing could have been worse for the Democratic Party nominee for governor. It was against this background that the 2003 race for governor began. But, once again, I'm getting ahead of my story.

During March and the first part of April 2003, on numerous occasions former Gov. Ned Breathitt and I discussed Ben's race. Each time he asked me if I had heard from Ben or from someone at his headquarters. Each time I had to answer, "No."

Finally, my old boss, Governor Breathitt, ordered me to meet with him at Ben's headquarters. When I arrived at the appointed time, Ben made me feel welcome and Governor Breathitt really went overboard in telling Ben's campaign manager all about my background and experience. Evidently, this did me no good with the campaign manager.

I was asked to come to headquarters and help, but I was given only the smallest possible nook in which to try to work. The first thing I did when I settled into my nook was to ask for a copy of the campaign organization. I was stunned to learn that no such document existed. Why not? Because there was no political organization for Ben's campaign. I quickly realized that many horrible mistakes had already been made by Ben's inexperienced staff. For the next two days, I talked to everyone at campaign headquarters in an effort to determine where the campaign needed the most help. While there were many needs, the most desperate need was for the creation of an organization. I decided this was where I had to start. A campaign for governor underway with no organization throughout the counties! It was hard to believe, but it was true.

I quickly listed forty, strongly Democratic counties and began a fast check with people I knew in order to determine who were the Chandler leaders in each county. This was only five weeks before the primary election. Only five weeks to build an organization. I wasn't sure it could be done, but I was going to do everything I possibly could to do the nearly impossible.

In the meantime, I quickly realized that Ben's campaign manager was uninformed about Kentucky politics and didn't have a clue about what to do. I tried to advise him with no success. I tried to help him with no success. He didn't want any advice. He didn't want any help. I also quickly determined that he didn't want to work either. He spent much of his time batting a ball around the headquarters and refusing to take his phone calls. He was a loser. My hope was that he hadn't already made Ben a loser in the primary. I got to work. By primary election day, I had organized fifty-one counties.

Meanwhile, the primary campaign had started to heat up. The candidates started spending tons and tons of money for television advertising. Ben faced two major challengers although he was the favorite. One was businessman Bruce Lunsford who spent a record $8 million of his own money on the race. The other was House Speaker Jody Richards who had little money to fund his campaign. Candidate Lunsford was extremely anti-Chandler and sponsored some rather vicious television ads against Ben. Finally, seeing he couldn't win, but still wanting to defeat Ben Chandler at any cost, Lunsford dropped out of the race with just four days to go and endorsed Jody Richards. This was a shocking move by Lunsford and it damaged Ben. Even so, on election day, I felt certain that Ben would win in a close race.

During our last bus trip before the primary, Ben and I sat in the back of the bus and discussed several important topics. I had just asked Ben what role he wanted me to play after the primary election when Charles Owen, his running mate for lieutenant governor, joined us. Ben said that he wanted me to work on the organization. Owen made the statement that he lost a Senate race and $8 million dollars because he didn't have a statewide organization. I assured them that within one month after the primary election I would have a Chandler-Owen statewide organization in place. I now knew the challenge that lay ahead of me. I liked that—I always want to know what is expected of me.

As I had thought, the primary election proved to be very close. It was late in the evening before House Speaker Richards conceded. Ben, who had been heavily favored, won by only 3.7 percent of the vote. I had been correct that Ben would win, but that the race would be close. It was clear that Lunsford's departure from the race and endorsement of Richards had hurt Ben. The returns also proved that my organization of fifty-one counties during the five weeks prior to the election made the primary victory possible for Ben Chandler. It was the difference. I breathed a long sigh of relief when Richards appeared on the TV screen to concede. But, in my heart, I knew the close race, with its small margin of victory for the big favorite, was going to appear to many voters like a defeat.

For the next month, Ben, having taken my advice about his campaign manager and other matters, reorganized his campaign. Meanwhile, during that same month after the primary and while Ben was reorganizing the campaign, I spent my time organizing more counties, analyzing the entire primary vote county by county, and reviewing the Republican effort. Sadly, I came to the conclusion that, because of Patton's problems, the Chandler-Owen ticket would lose the November election. It wasn't that Kentuckians didn't like Ben and wanted to vote against him; they simply wanted a change. It didn't really matter who either party put up for governor; the Republican candidate represented the change that the people wanted so badly. Ben could argue for months that he represented change as much or more than his Republican opponent did, but, in the minds of the voters, a change of party in the Governor's Mansion had to occur to have meaningful change. Yes, it was a "throw the rascals out" year and Paul Patton was the rascal who would defeat Ben Chandler, not the Republican candidate. Patton had made the long Democratic hold on the governor's office untenable.

This did not stop our efforts, however. All summer, I put on my smiley face and was very positive. Those who helped me build the organization during the campaign were Eric Evans, Josh Zik, Slick Melvin, Susan Turner, Frank Fitzpatrick, John Black, Mae Girkey, Jim Gray, and Bob McWilliams.

Ben replaced his primary campaign manager with Mark Nickolas, a more experienced campaign manager and the man who had managed the campaign of Jody Richards so well. This change was a decided improvement. Along with my assigned duties, I also began to spend more time advising and helping Charlie Owen, the lieutenant governor half of the Democratic ticket. Charlie is a multi-millionaire attorney and businessman who had planned on running for governor, but instead joined with Ben to form what appeared to be at the time a strong Democratic team.

As I look back on the entire general election campaign, unlike the primary, I can find no fault in the management of the campaign. Ben's primary campaign manager had been weak and ineffective, but Mark Nickolas did a fine job with the fall campaign. The Patton scandal was simply too much to overcome.

Two people who contributed immensely to the general election campaign were State Senator Bob Jackson and former State Senator Joe Prather. Those two always came in when we needed them and were of tremendous help. Joe Prather's wife also gave many weeks of her time to the campaign. Two other ladies who contributed a lot of quality time to the campaign were the Chandler ladies—Jennifer, Ben's wife, and Toss, Ben's mother. They were on the go all the time.

In my opinion, headquarters did not support Charlie Owen in the way I thought it should have. He should have been assisted on a daily basis. Part of the responsibility of headquarters was to Charlie Owen. I will admit, however, that at times he seemed to want to do his own thing.

Ernie Fletcher, a congressman from Lexington, was Ben's Republican opponent. Fletcher had won the lightly voted Republican primary with only about 91,000 votes. This, however, was 57 percent of the vote. The defeated adversaries were Jefferson County Judge Executive Rebecca Jackson, State Rep. Steve Nunn of Glasgow (the son of former governor Louie Nunn), and State Senator Virgil Moore of Leitchfield.

Fletcher, born in Mount Sterling, besides being a medical doctor and politician, had been an Air Force fighter pilot and had moonlighted as an ordained lay minister of his church. He was a three-term congressman and emerged from the primary as the clear favorite to win in the fall. As the polls showed Fletcher running comfortably ahead, he began to draw heavy support and contributions from contractors and other state government vendors who had favored Democrats in past races for governor. Republicans had an overall financial advantage of nearly two to one because the Republican Governors' Association ran ads for Fletcher and state senate Republicans won de-funding of the eleven-year-old system that subsidized the campaigns of gubernatorial candidates who limited their spending, which Chandler preferred.

The candidates campaigned against two main backdrops: the sex-for-favors allegations and related scandals involving Democratic Governor Patton and a revenue shortfall that had forced Patton to reduce appropriations and warn that the next budget would be $710 million short of meeting the state's obligations.

Fletcher promised to "clean up the mess in Frankfort." Both candidates said they could balance the budget without raising overall tax revenue. Both favored revenue neutral tax reform that would not raise additional revenue initially, but would make the state's tax collections keep pace with economic growth.

Fletcher had the high ground. Ben and Charlie faced an impossible task. The Patton scandal had permeated our whole society and it was just impossible for voters to ignore it. Fletcher won by the greatest margin ever for a Kentucky Republican in an election for governor. The final tally was Fletcher 596,284 to Chandler's 487,159.

After the election, polls showed that voters did not cast their votes to defeat Ben Chandler. They just voted for change. In fact, after the election, polls showed that Ben Chandler had a high favorability rating. The voters liked Ben; they just wanted to make a change. And while a vote for Ben Chandler was, in reality, a vote for positive change, most voters just didn't seem to understand that. Looking back with hindsight, it is absolutely clear that Ben Chandler was the real candidate for change in the 2003 gubernatorial race.

The Chandler-Owen team had some great people working for their election. Mae Girkey did an outstanding job of keeping all financial aspects of the campaign under complete and legal control. Mae had been involved in Kentucky politics for many years. She had started out working with Thelma Stovall. Between Mae and me, we were acquainted with almost all of Kentucky's political leaders.

Another person who performed in an outstanding manner was Veronica Judy, who coordinated Ben's office (he was still serving as Kentucky's attorney general) and the headquarters agenda without a mishap.

Two young men who performed very well were Eric Evans and Josh Zik. Eric had managed campaigns in western Kentucky and thus he understood the daily routine and realities of campaign staffers. He was a whiz on the computer and always gave me excellent results very quickly. He was always on schedule and worked late hours almost daily. When the campaign was over, he went to work at State Democratic Headquarters and later was recruited for employment by the Kentucky Trial Attorneys Association.

Josh Zik was an intense, intelligent, loyal, hard charging young man who assisted former University of Kentucky head basketball coach, Joe Hall, in all of his travels on Ben's behalf. Whenever I needed assistance, Josh and Eric were always ready and willing to help.

One of Kentucky's most famous Republican politicians, Slick Melvin, came to see me and offered his help in Ben's campaign. He and I knew all the political leaders in Kentucky on both sides of the aisle. From the first day, he made a tremendous contribution to Ben's campaign. Slick was a very close friend of Gov. Louie B. Nunn. About three times each week, Governor Nunn called me to give me his opinion on moves to make to assist Ben's campaign. We were indeed very fortunate to have former Governor Nunn and Slick Melvin assisting in the Chandler-Owen campaign.

Another person who performed brilliantly in her position was Barbara Hadley Smith, who was our communications director. She was always correct in her timing of press releases and in their content. In my opinion, she did not make a mistake in the whole campaign. She was very kind and helpful to everyone. She always had time to assist me no matter how difficult and time-consuming were my needs.

After the primary, Tony Miller, Jody Richard's running mate for lieutenant governor, came to our headquarters and volunteered to campaign for Ben and Charlie. I had known Tony for many years. Tony was extremely helpful in all sections of Kentucky. He never declined a campaign request and he was also very helpful in letting us know where he could be the most helpful.

At no time did Jody Richards assist in the fall campaign. He did not even respond to requests from us for assistance.

Former Governor Edward T. Breathitt was extremely helpful in the early part of the campaign. Ben needed his advice and counsel. Normally, Ned and

I talked by telephone and discussed the important topics of the moment—we didn't chit chat. Neither of us had time for that. On October 10, the day Governor Breathitt collapsed at the University of Kentucky, I called him late in the afternoon and we talked for about forty-five minutes about a variety of subjects. He seemed to want our conversation to continue, which was not like him. That final telephone conversation will always be one of my most outstanding memories of Gov. Edward T. Breathitt.

Prior to the campaign, Charles Owen and I did not know each other. Each of us knew who the other was, but that was about all. We both seemed to take it slowly in becoming better acquainted. But by the November election, we trusted each other and had developed an excellent relationship. I believe that Charles Owen has tremendous ability and I know he has a very strong desire to serve the people of Kentucky. He is deeply concerned about all the many problems facing state government. In my opinion, Owen would tackle most of them, if not all, successfully. He simply needs an opportunity to serve.

I truly believe Charles Owen would be a second Bert Combs because, like Combs, he recognizes and understands problems quickly and is very creative in solving difficulties. With the many financial problems facing our state government, particularly in education and health care, Kentucky would be very fortunate to have him leading state government as governor.

Ironically, Ernie Fletcher's victory over Ben Chandler in the 2003 election for governor left a vacancy in Fletcher's congressional seat. Feeling that he had a good organization in place now and knowing his approval ratings remained high even after a crushing defeat, and realizing he could not be known any better than after the governor's race, Ben decided to try for Fletcher's old seat. Ben was the favorite against state Republican Senator Alice Forgy Kerr, in the special election to fill the open Sixth District seat. Ben won handily and has since been reelected. He now has a very safe seat in Congress and is happy as Central Kentucky's congressman. In my opinion, Ben's future political career lies in Congress, not in the governor's office. I have advised him to stay in his seat, so to speak, and then—when U.S. Senator Jim Bunning—retires, run for the U.S. Senate.

Congressman Ben Chandler Sixth District

Well, in the final analysis, after all was said and done, Ernie Fletcher ended up with the job Ben Chandler had always wanted. Ironically, Fletcher had not been so sure that he wanted the job of governor. Meanwhile, Ben Chandler ended up with Ernie Fletcher's old job. With all the problems facing state government, I think Ben Chandler got the better deal.

As for me, I felt that I had fulfilled my promise to Ben's grandfather, Happy Chandler. He had asked me to help make Ben governor and I had promised to do everything within my power to do so. I had done everything I could to elect Ben; it just simply wasn't within my power.

39 Steve Beshear & the 2007 Gubernatorial Campaign

My participation in Steve Beshear's successful run for governor marked my fifteenth gubernatorial campaign. I am not sure anyone else in Kentucky has actively participated in that many. If so, I don't know who!

In 1974, I met Steve Beshear for the first time while he was serving his first term in the Kentucky House of Representatives. I was very impressed with him. He was personable, honest and straight-forward. Steve was representing the 76th District, a Lexington district, to which he was elected three times serving in the House from 1974 through 1979. In the House, he established a reputation for independence and hard work. His priorities included education, welfare reform, consumer protection and governmental efficiency.

Steve was named the Outstanding Freshman Representative by the Capital Press Corps. Perhaps his greatest achievement during his service in the Kentucky House was winning approval for the $10 million expansion and improvement of the much needed Neonatal Unit at the University of Kentucky Medical Center.

But I am getting ahead of myself here. Steve Beshear was born in 1944, in the western Kentucky town of Dawson Springs in Hopkins County, about twelve miles southwest of Madisonville. Dawson Springs is a strip mining area and a small industrial and commercial city. Steve grew up one of five children. His father, Russell, a funeral director, also was a Baptist minister, just like his father before him. His mother, Mary Elizabeth, dedicated herself to many community endeavors—making life easier for others. Steve attended the University of Kentucky where he received a bachelor's degree and a law degree. He was a member of the U. S. Army Reserves from 1969 to 1975.

Following his three terms in the general assembly, Steve was elected attorney general serving in that capacity from 1980 to 1984. He was an outstanding attorney general. As attorney general he was best known for investigating and prosecuting welfare fraud, Medicare provider fraud, and food stamp trafficking. He also received much praise for his intervention in utility rate increase cases, his assistance to senior citizens and his strong record of drug law enforcement.

Elected lieutenant governor in 1984, once again Steve performed admirably. He is most remembered as lieutenant governor for his active participation and assistance to Gov. Martha Layne Collins in the successful effort to bring a Toyota manufacturing plant to Kentucky.

In 1987, Steve ran for governor and lost in a crowded Democratic primary field. He finished third behind former Governor John Y. Brown, Jr. and the winner, Wallace Wilkinson, who went on to win the general election in the fall.

After his defeat in 1987, Steve practiced law in Lexington. He was the Democratic nominee for the U.S. Senate in 1996, but was defeated by incumbent Senator Mitch McConnell. After the senate race loss, he returned to private law practice not planning to run for public office again. His political career certainly seemed at an end. But when circumstances change, sometimes plans change. Lazarus rose from the political graveyard!

On December 16, 2006, Steve formally announced his candidacy for governor in 2007 with State Senator Daniel Mongiardo as his running mate for lieutenant governor.

After a big win in the Democratic primary, in the general election Steve faced incumbent governor, Ernie Fletcher, who was mired in a hiring scandal. Steve's platform included expanded gambling, which Fletcher opposed. His platform also included achieving sustainable economic growth, life long learning opportunities—beginning with pre-kindergarten—affordable health care and ethics reform. On November 6, 2007, Steve defeated Fletcher by a 59 percent to 41 percent margin and became Kentucky's sixty-first governor.

As Steve begins his leadership of Kentucky, he has at his side his wife of thirty-eight years, Jane, the commonwealth's First Lady. The Beshears have two grown sons, one practicing veterinary medicine and the other, following in his father's footsteps, is an attorney.

The following is the story of my role in the Beshear campaign. My involvement proved to be both important and interesting. Before Steve made his public announcement that he was running for governor, Joe Graviss and I met with Steve and Daniel Mongiardo in Joe's Versailles office. At that late afternoon meeting on the day Steve and Daniel shook hands to become a ticket, we discussed what our role would be in a Beshear campaign and our role in the Beshear administration should Steve be victorious.

I was insistent that I wanted to continue working as a team with Joe. At my age, I was not looking for a career-building position. I told Steve that I would serve wherever my background would be of help. At the end of the meeting, Joe and I pledged our support for the Beshear-Mongiardo ticket.

During the meeting, I informed Steve that Joe and I had traveled the entire state over the past two years introducing Joe to county officials and influential citizens and we had never mentioned Steve as a possible candidate for governor nor had anyone mentioned his name to us. Therefore, I told Steve, it was important for him to spread the word of our support for his candidacy. Thus, on the day he formally announced his candidacy, Steve mentioned the names of only three of his supporters—Tracy Farmer, Joe Graviss and me.

Now that I have stated that Joe Graviss was my "teammate" in the Beshear campaign, I need to mention how that came about. I met Joe Graviss in 2004. He is a very successful young businessman who lives in Versailles. He is the owner-operator of Graviss Restaurants which operates several McDonalds' restaurants in Lexington, Versailles and Frankfort.

Joe had run an excellent, but unsuccessful campaign, against former governor, Julian Carroll, for a vacant state senate seat. Although not nearly as well known as the former governor, Joe gave Carroll a tough time before finally losing the primary by a much closer margin than had been expected by the political experts. After his narrow defeat, Joe decided he needed to learn more about Kentucky politics. So he turned to an old-hand in the political arena and we became friends.

Joe is honest and hard-working, a willing and eager learner, a man of unquestioned integrity and, very importantly, a man who wants to give something back to this state which has been so good to him. I am proud to work with him and to call him my friend.

Before our meeting on the eve of Steve's announcement, I had not seen Steve for several years. During our meeting, it quickly became apparent to me that Steve had a vast knowledge of Kentucky politics, had a very sharp and quick mind, was a good decision maker, and had plenty of energy to run a hard race. He even looked like a governor. Joe and I were both impressed.

Thus Joe and I were in on the campaign from the very beginning. We participated in many meetings as the campaign was being planned. Steve quickly accepted us into the fold and seemed to truly appreciate our advice, suggestions and opinions. Steve's door was always open to us—We felt welcome and right at home. We had been accepted as important advisors, and we were in a position to make a difference.

Fontaine Banks with Gov. Steve Beshear

From the beginning, it was obvious to Joe and me that Steve's wife, Jane, was a very valuable campaign asset. She is a beautiful lady who dresses well and looks the part of a First Lady. She is very intelligent, speaks well and is totally dedicated to and proud of Steve. She meets the public easily and is charming and friendly. Jane says all the right things never making an incorrect or damaging statement. She was a real bonus. We knew immediately that Jane would make a tremendous positive contribution to her husband's campaign for governor. In fact, Jane may have been Steve's greatest political asset.

Another tremendous asset for Steve was his very wise choice of Daniel Mongiardo to be his running mate. Mongiardo is a physician who has served the health needs of eastern Kentuckians for many years. At the time of his choice to run for lieutenant governor with Steve, he was a state senator representing the Hazard area. He had run a fabulous campaign for the U.S. Senate seat held by Hall of Fame baseball pitcher, Jim Bunning. Daniel came very close to upsetting Bunning. Tall and very personable, he was a major factor in Steve's winning the governor's race.

The Beshear campaign marked a rarity for me. I had participated in fundraising on only one other occasion—a fundraiser I held for Brereton Jones. Back in 1955, when I supported Bert Combs for governor in my first gubernatorial campaign, all campaign contributions were made in cash. I did not want to be involved with handling cash. I refused to take any part in fundraising and continued my stand on that issue for many years and through many campaigns. But, during the Beshear campaign, my position changed.

Contributions were no longer made in cash, except rarely. Campaigns had to account for contributions and thus the opportunities for illegal activities were severely limited. Another reason was that I very much wanted Steve to win and I knew I could be of great assistance in the fundraising area.

Thus, as a team, Joe Graviss and I worked to raise funds for the campaign. As I had thought and hoped, we were very successful. We held three very successful fundraisers and raised a substantial amount for the campaign. The final fundraiser was held in a tent erected at my home. We had a great time meeting old friends and dipping into their pocketbooks. Fundraising, which I had so strongly avoided in the past, turned out to be a major contribution by the Banks-Graviss team to the campaign.

During the course of both the primary and general election campaigns, I worked very closely with many prominent Beshear supporters. For example, I worked closely with former Governors Brereton Jones and Martha Layne Collins. In addition, I worked closely with ResCare CEO, Ron Geary, former State Senator Joe Prather, State Senator Bob Jackson, Congressman Ben Chandler, retired Franklin Circuit Judge Bill Graham, Jerry Lunsford and Larry Arnett.

All during the campaign, Joe was my student and I was the old professor. We began with Politics 101, but, by the end of the campaign, Joe had earned an A+ in Politics 501. Joe is now ready for graduate school. He will earn his master's and doctoral degrees while playing an important role in the Beshear administration. He is a wonderful student and a very special friend.

Steve Beshear won the Democratic nomination for governor handily in the primary. He won for several reasons. Two things he absolutely had to do and he did them both. First, he had to raise adequate funds and secondly, he had to run a smooth campaign with no mistakes. The other candidates generally failed at both of these necessary elements. They failed to raise enough money, except for Bruce Lunsford, and they all made major mistakes and miscalculations. The other candidates simply imploded while Steve, who had hired excellent fundraising and polling firms, just sailed smoothly along without any gaffs. Things went so well that Steve was able to get through the primary without having made any promises to anybody.

Most of the campaign decisions were made by Steve and Jim Cauley in concert with the Washington, D.C. firm the campaign had hired. Dick Prelopski, one of Steve's oldest friends and who had been involved in all of Steve's previous campaigns, also played a key role. Dick had the patience of Job, a characteristic not often found in political campaign workers. He organized all 120 counties masterfully.

At the beginning of the primary campaign, the Beshear-Mongiardo Headquarters was established in Frankfort in a two-story brick building near Interstate 64. Joe and I moved in and began our activity on behalf of the Beshear-Mongiardo ticket. Primary campaign strategy called for Dick Prelopski and me to work together organizing all 120 of Kentucky's counties. But after discussing this approach for several days, I decided that it was in the campaign's best interest to do this critical job of organizing the counties in a different way. I decided to let Dick proceed with organizing a county and then, when he was finished, I would add my contacts into Dick's organization. To our delight and the campaign's great benefit, this approach worked very successfully and made Steve's victory in the primary much easier. The difficult aspect of the organization of the counties was that we had only six weeks in which to complete this very large task. But our efforts went smoothly and we completed the organization of the counties in the allotted time.

Steve put together an extremely competent, well-experienced staff. The campaign manager, Jim Cauley, had successfully managed several campaigns. Jim is from Pike County, my home county, where his family is actively engaged in local politics. Some family members have held public office in Pike County. Of course, I was very experienced, this being my fifteenth gubernatorial campaign, and altogether I had spent fifty-two years, more than half a century, in state politics. Some of the other campaign staff at headquarters included:

Larry Arnett .... Congressional Contact
Susan Bryant.................................... Finance
Chuck Geveden .... Security
Mae Girkey .... Finance
Bill Graham...................................... Franklin County Contact
Joe Graviss....................................... Senior Advisor
Eddie Jacobs .... Labor Contact
Bob McWilliams .... Finance
Dick Prelopski .... County Organizer
Tommy Preston............................... Public Affairs
Floyd Seals .... Assistant to Dick Prelopski
Susan Turner .... Volunteer Coordinator

The finance team, led by Scott Gale, did an incredibly fine job changing old fund raising paradigms from holding huge fund raisers loaded up with $1,000 hosts to holding multiple, smaller fund raisers in order to maximize candidate contact. This new strategy worked brilliantly.

One of the key aspects of the primary campaign was the candidacy of State Treasurer Jonathan Miller. Miller was serving in his second term as state treasurer when he decided to make the governor's race. He and Jack Conway, an unsuccessful candidate for the Congressional seat of Republican Ann Northrup, had discussed forming a ticket, but neither could overcome his ambition for the governor's post. Thus neither Miller nor Conway was willing to take the lieutenant governor spot on the ticket. A Miller-Conway or Conway-Miller ticket would have been a formidable one. The Beshear campaign benefited from the two would-be-governors' inability to get together.

In the end, Conway ran successfully for attorney general and Miller ran for governor with Jefferson County Attorney Irv Maze as his running mate. Miller's campaign, however, never got off the ground. In my opinion, Miller should have taken the second spot on a ticket with Conway and run for lieutenant governor. After all, he's young and has many years ahead of him in which to run for governor.

Late in the primary campaign, Miller began to realize that he had no chance of defeating Beshear or even Bruce Lunsford. So, about two weeks before the election, Miller withdrew as a candidate for governor and publicly endorsed Steve Beshear. This gave the Beshear campaign a definite boost. Steve would have won the primary anyway, but he probably would not have received enough votes to avoid a runoff. Following Miller's withdrawal, there was a rush of supporters to the Beshear campaign and they were not just Miller supporters. Voters began to see the handwriting on the wall and Steve began quickly picking up voters from all the other Democratic candidates.

Meanwhile Steve and Daniel were running a near flawless campaign. Both did well in televised debates. Steve, especially, looked and sounded like a governor. Things were going well. We had the best candidates, we raised sufficient funds, the counties were well organized, we made no major mistakes, the opposition made gaff after gaff, the public was desperate for change and our campaign was peaking at just the right time. All these factors added up to a solid victory for the Beshear-Mongiardo ticket.

Six weeks prior to the primary election, I predicted that Steve would receive from 41 to 43 percent of the vote, 40 percent being just enough to avoid a runoff. Almost everyone scoffed and laughed at my prediction. They thought I was off my rocker. But a few days before the election, several began to think that the ol' campaigner just might be correct. On election night, the Beshear ticket received 40.9 percent of the vote, not only winning handily, but also avoiding a runoff. I also predicted that Steve's vote in the November election would be 60 percent—he received 58.7 percent.

All during the primary campaign, Steve had been an outstanding candidate. He is an excellent speaker and his talks were well received. He was always calm and collected during the several KET-sponsored debates. Steve was always well prepared and conducted himself like a governor should. He was also something most candidates are not. He was a master of the telephone. He was the main reason the campaign raised more than $2 million during the primary.

Let's look at the opposition for a moment. Several leading potential candidates decided not to make the race. Among these were former Governor Brereton Jones, State Auditor Crit Luallen, Congressman Ben Chandler and Charles Owen. In the previous governor's race, Chandler, who was serving as attorney general at the time, was soundly defeated by incumbent Governor Ernie Fletcher. As I have previously mentioned, subsequent to his defeat, Chandler had won election to Fletcher's former congressional seat. Chandler had lost the governor's race largely because the public wanted a change of party in the governor's office due to former Governor Paul Patton's scandalous love affair.

During Fletcher's term as governor, his administration became mired in a hiring scandal, which virtually assured his defeat in his bid for reelection. For Ben Chandler it was a clear opportunity to reverse his earlier defeat. But, happy with his Congressional seat, he decided not to run thus clearing the way for other candidates including Steve Beshear.

Those opposing Steve in the primary were former gubernatorial candidate and millionaire, Bruce Lunsford; former lieutenant governor, Dr. Steve Henry; and Speaker of the House Jody Richards. Gatewood Galbraith and perennial candidate, Hensley, were also in the field, but had no chance of winning. Attorney General Greg Stumbo, who prosecuted the Fletcher administration scandal, ran for lieutenant governor on the ticket with Bruce Lunsford.

As the campaign began in January 2007, Lunsford was the favorite to win. I was one of the few who did not think the Lunsford ticket would do well. I felt that way because I knew that many Democrats deeply resented Lunsford's efforts to defeat Ben Chandler in his governor's race against Fletcher. Lunsford had been a sore loser in the primary in 2003. At the end of the campaign, seeing that he could not defeat Chandler, he withdrew and threw his support to Jody Richards who, as a result, almost defeated Chandler. Then in the general election, Lunsford supported Fletcher instead of fellow Democrat, Ben Chandler. I knew how we Democrats dislike a turncoat and thus I was convinced that all of Lunsford's millions would not bring him close to a victory over Steve. Not even his selection of Attorney General Greg Stumbo as his running mate, was helpful. In fact, joining the Lunsford ticket was a huge mistake for Greg Stumbo as thousands of his supporters deserted him because of Lunsford's previous party disloyalty. Primary election night proved me right.

As for Jody Richards, his campaign got off to a late start due to a legislative session and it never gathered any momentum. As for Dr. Henry, he stayed high in the polls for awhile due primarily to the favorable public image of his wife, a former Miss America, but, as in the past, he made several big mistakes and quietly faded from contention. Steve's path to victory was now clear and smooth.

I was involved with one other candidate in the primary. There was a period of about two months when, as a friend, I attempted to help Jody Richards understand his position and chances in the race for the Democratic nomination for governor. We talked on several occasions. Evidently, Jody interpreted my position as an endorsement of his candidacy, which it was not. Jody was very upset with me when I told him I was supporting Steve. But Jody never had a chance in the governor's race. He got started late and he experienced early staff difficulties. His candidacy was weak from the beginning. Jody and I have been friends for a quarter of a century and I still call him my trusted friend. I hope, now that the political war is over, that he feels the same about me. Sometimes politics can cost you a friend or two, but I try to avoid that situation at all costs.

Primary election day was spectacularly beautiful—we had the best weather possible. Nice weather is always a good sign for Democrats who sometimes fail to turn out and vote in bad weather. This is to be contrasted with the Republicans who turn out come hell or high water. As a result of the good weather a larger turnout occurred than had been expected. The Beshear-Mongiardo ticket won handily.

Immediately after the Beshear campaign won the primary election so convincingly, we began planning the fall general election campaign. We had two main concerns. First, we had to raise a large amount of money in order to wage a strong campaign against what we expected would be a well-heeled Fletcher campaign. Secondly, we had to smoothly accept into the Beshear campaign members of the primary opposition forces who now wished to help elect Beshear to the governor's chair.

Fortunately, things went well and by early July the campaign had raised more than $1.7 million of our goal of $4 million. We had more folks wanting to hold fundraisers than we could accommodate. Everything went well and Joe and I continued our efforts at fundraising, which ultimately resulted in our being number two in fundraising for the entire campaign. We also spent a great deal of time helping others raise much needed funds, as well as calling hundreds and hundreds of people ourselves.

In the general election, the campaign concentrated on the many televised debates between Steve and Governor Fletcher. Steve handled himself very well in each of these debates being careful not to make any mistakes and keeping Fletcher on the defensive. Each debate seemed like a repeat of the previous one. This was good for us because Steve was doing so well in each confrontation. It was obvious during each debate that Fletcher was nervous, unsure of himself, lacking in confidence and not well prepared. Fletcher contrasted badly with the calm, self-assured, confident and well prepared Steve Beshear.

Fletcher kicked off the general election campaign with a series of deceitful and unfair attack ads. Throughout the campaign, Fletcher continued his untruthful attack ads. One particularly unfair and misleading ad pictured Steve and his law firm as the reason for the Kentucky Central bankruptcy. The ad accused Steve and his firm of stealing millions of dollars from the bankrupt company's shareholders. This was a complicated issue to explain and many voters were misled by these false claims made in Fletcher's TV attack ads.

Fletcher's big mistake was falsely attacking Steve instead of touting his own administration's accomplishments. As Fletcher's attacks worsened, however, Steve continued to move further ahead in the polls. By early fall, Steve had the election won barring any major mistake made on his part. As one supporter put it, "Steve, you've got your heel on Fletcher's neck. Now break it."

And break it he did. The people, Republicans and Independents, as well as Democrats, sick of Fletcher's hiring scandal and his pardoning of his administration's offenders, turned out in droves to turn Ernie out. The Beshear-Mongiardo ticket won easily carrying 92 of Kentucky's 120 counties.

I had thoroughly enjoyed my role in the campaign as senior advisor. I had worked hard and long hours. I opened campaign headquarters every day and made a pot of coffee. For an old campaigner like me, the hours were especially long, but the result was well worth the effort. As senior advisors, Joe Graviss and I did everything from cleaning the office to raising substantial amounts of funds, from calling more than 2,000 friends all over the state and asking for their support to attending rallies, from meeting with county officials, to convincing Republicans to support Beshear. I learned early in my career that in political campaigns you do whatever is necessary to be done. You must do a little bit of everything. Nothing can be beneath you.

What now? Well, during the campaign, Steve asked me to prepare a day-by-day outline of what he must do after being elected. I completed that project and advised our new governor as he proceeded toward Inauguration Day and then his first legislative session in January 2008. I thank Steve and Daniel for affording me the opportunity to play a major role in their campaign—my fifteenth governor's race. I also want to thank Joe Graviss who proved to be far more than just my student. During the campaign, he proved to be my very good friend and my strong right arm. Someday soon I hope he gets his wish to be an unselfish servant of the people. God knows in leadership roles we desperately need public servants of Joe's character and integrity.

Will I participate in a sixteenth governor's campaign? Only God knows the answer to that question. But I must say that I would certainly enjoy helping my friend, Steve Beshear, win what I think will surely be a well-deserved second term. We will just have to wait and see. But if the 2007 Beshear campaign proves to be my last, it feels great to go out a winner.

40 A Few Anecdotes from a Life in Kentucky Politics

People from eastern Kentucky had a habit of coming down early on Sunday morning and attempting to have breakfast with Governor Combs at the Governor's Mansion. My new bride did not understand why this happened—so often causing me to have to rise early and head for the Governor's Mansion. I told her that it was a security matter, but that didn't appease her. She wanted her new husband home with her on Sunday morning and I can understand that. I just couldn't do anything about it.

One of the main concerns I had was security for the governor. The state police had codes for us; the governor was X1, I was X2, and Lieutenant Governor Wyatt was X3.

We had already been warned once that someone was going to try to harm Governor Combs when he made an upcoming trip to Paducah. I didn't tell the governor about the threat or what we were doing about it, but I had several the State Troopers dressed in civilian clothes and several members of the city police also dressed in civilian clothes. I had these officers surround Governor Combs when he got off the airplane in Paducah. Fortunately, nothing happened on the trip. Later, the governor said he had noticed a lot of men that day and wondered what was going on. It was then that I told him about the threat on his life.

Later, he began receiving razor blades in the mail. The envelopes had a Winchester postmark. The Kentucky State Police began an investigation and in a few weeks they caught the man. He turned out to have some mental problems, but the state police kept very close tabs on him. The state police performed admirably in regard to the security of the governor.

The first time the U.S. Secret Service had reason to check out the governor's staff they found that I had a top secret security clearance. After that, whenever members of the secret service or the President of the United States or someone of great national importance was coming to Kentucky,

Pres. Lyndon B. Johnson and
Gov. Edward T. "Ned" Breathitt
Source: Kentucky Department of Libraries & Archives

I always got a phone call alerting me to what was going to take place. In other words, I became the contact man in Kentucky for the secret service.

One day we had a breakfast meeting with Pres. Lyndon Johnson at the Seelbach Hotel in Louisville. This occurred during the presidential campaign of 1964, and Johnson was going to be the speaker at a Louisville campaign event. As I started into the room, secret service personnel stopped me and said, "Fontaine, please help us, we don't know the people here." So, in helping the secret service officers identify folks attending the breakfast, I was standing on one side of the doorway with the secret service personnel stationed on the other side. As I leaned over to look into the dining room, all of a sudden somebody slapped me on the back very hard and said, "Hi ya' pardner," as I saw stars. I looked over at the secret service agent braced against the other side of the door. He just smiled and said, "Fontaine, he's so big he doesn't know he hurts people." I kept seeing stars as President Johnson entered the room.

During the 1960 presidential campaign when Sen. Lyndon Johnson was running for vice president on the ticket with John F. Kennedy, I received a call from a secret service agent traveling on an airplane headed for Kentucky. Senator Johnson was scheduled to speak at the Capitol in Frankfort at 5:30 p.m. The agent said, "Fontaine, the senator says he's related to a former Kentucky governor. Could you check it out and let me know, he might like to make some comment about it when he speaks this evening." He gave me the name of the former governor and I checked with Colonel Chin at the Kentucky Historical Society and he said, "Oh my God, Fontaine, he's the biggest crook we've ever had. Don't let him mention his name." So I called the secret service agent and told him what Colonel Chin had said. Johnson didn't mention the former governor's name and I'm not going to either.

The Combs administration employed a fellow from central Kentucky who always carried a pistol. What made the situation even worse was that he worked for the commissioner of Public Safety. Two or three times he got mad at the commissioner and said he was going to shoot him. Well, we couldn't have the employees threatening to shoot their bosses so I decided to nip this situation in the bud.

I called the man to come to my office one day and, as he entered the office, I patted him on the hip pocket and, sure enough, he was carrying his pistol in there. I reached in his hip pocket and took his pistol out. He said, "Oh, Fontaine, don't do this to me, I feel naked without my pistol."

I said, "You're not going to shoot my commissioner of Public Safety."

He said, "I'm not going to shoot him, I'm just joking with him." We sat down and talked for a few minutes and finally he said, "Fontaine, I promise you I won't shoot anybody or do anything wrong."

It was obvious to me that the fellow was harmless so I gave his pistol back to him and said, "Here's your pistol, but if I hear just one more story about you threatening anybody or pulling out that weapon, you're out of a job." I heard nothing further and, as far as I know, he was a good employee for the rest of his state government career. Of course, if this incident occurred today, I would have no choice but to handle the situation much differently.

One morning as Governor Combs and I were flying to Hazard, I noticed a huge line of cars near the airport. It looked like there was going to be a large crowd at the airport to greet the governor when we landed. Sure enough there were thousands of roving pickets waiting for the governor. When we landed, I got off the airplane and told the governor to remain on board until I checked things out. As I got off of the airplane, I spotted a big man who appeared to be the crowd's leader. I walked straight toward him. As I neared the apparent leader, he began to walk toward me. Just as we reached each other, he said, "Fontaine, we're just here to tell the governor that we love him." I turned around and motioned for Governor Combs to get off the plane. As the governor came off the plane, at least 5,000 voices roared a cheer that echoed down the whole valley. It could be heard for miles. These eastern Kentucky boys just wanted to tell Bert Combs how much they appreciated him.

When Governor Combs dedicated Jenny Wiley State Park, a state trooper came into the lodge and said, "Fontaine, there's 500 pickets out here scattered all over the mountainside."

The trooper and the others were concerned so I went outside to check things out like I had done at Hazard. To my surprise, the same man that had led the crowd in Hazard came down the hill and said, "Fontaine, we're here for the same reason we were in Hazard. We just want to let Governor Combs know we love him."

So, once again, when Bert Combs came out hundreds of voices could be heard throughout the mountain valley, all cheering loudly for their governor—Bert Combs.

During one of western Kentucky trips to take "State Government to the People," a delegation asked to meet with Governor Combs. When he met with them, he found out that they wanted him to change the name of the community which is called Monkey's Eyebrow to something else. As soon as I heard that this was their request, I went to the back of the crowd where the governor could see me and shook my head, "No." So Governor Combs listened to them politely and then said, "I'll let Banksie handle this."

Then he turned around, looked at me, and said, "Banksie, will let you know what we can do."

I said, "I'll let you know, but there will be a revolt if we change the name of Monkey's Eyebrow." Today, the name "Monkey's Eyebrow" still exists as the name of that community.

One day Governor Combs rang for me and, when I walked into the governor's office, there sat about thirty people from Magoffin County. The governor said, "Banksie, these people want to make a deal with me, but they want you as a witness." The deal concerned an election Kentucky was having for a seat in the U.S. Senate. Both Keen Johnson and John Y. Brown, Sr. were running in the Democratic Primary. Governor Combs was supporting Keen Johnson. Ray Holbrook, the county judge of Magoffin County, said, "We want to make a deal with you. We're going to carry the county for John Y. Brown against your candidate unless you turn the county patronage over to us and take it away from the ones who have it now."

Governor Combs looked at me and said, "What do you think Banksie?"

I said, "Well, it sounds like a good deal if they carry the county for Keen. You need the strength."

So we shook hands on it and promptly forgot all about it. The day after the election I walked into the governor's office and there sat the thirty Magoffin County citizens. Ray Holbrook said, "Fontaine, we came to claim."

So I walked over to the Governor's Mansion and said to the governor, "Magoffin County is over there waiting for you."

The governor said, "What do they want?"

I said, "Governor, they came to claim."

He said, "Oh my, I forgot all about them."

So Governor Combs turned the county patronage over to the Holbrook family which was a better, stronger group than the folks we had been using.

On several occasions, former Governor Lawrence Wetherby, who was then a state senator, and I walked the senate floor attempting to gather enough votes to pass or defeat some particular piece of legislation. One morning we needed just one more vote to pass an important education bill, but we were having a difficult time finding that single vote. I just happened to glance down the hallway and there I saw a senator who had been nipping at the bottle. So I said to Wetherby, "Governor, I'm going down the hall to talk to the senator. When I do, if I turn around and smile at you, call the bill immediately." So I went and collared the senator and said, "Senator, how are you doing this fine day?"

He said, "Fontaine, my good friend, what can I do for you?"

I said, "Senator, all you need to do for me is to vote 'Aye' on the education bill.

The senator said, "Okay I will," and he marked it down in a little notebook he was carrying. I turned and smiled at Wetherby and he had Lieutenant Governor Wyatt, president of the Senate, call the bill immediately. When the roll call reached the nipping senator's name, he voted "Aye," which was the one additional vote we needed for passage.

The senators in opposition to the bill all ran over to him for an explanation. They were in an angry mood. Over all the commotion, I could hear the senator say over and over again, "I promised my friend, Fontaine, I would vote for the bill; I promised Fontaine I would vote for the bill."

Thus, a very crucial education bill passed the Senate by one vote.

On another occasion, the galleries were filled with college presidents and their entourage. They were there because they thought a bill was going to be passed that day upgrading their colleges to universities. Former Governor Wetherby came to me and said, "Fontaine, let's have a little fun."

I said, "Governor, what do you mean?"

Wetherby said, "Let's delay that bill so they'll remember us."

So we arranged to adjourn the senate early and the bill didn't get called for a vote. Wetherby looked at me and said, "Fontaine, in about two minutes the Governor is going to send somebody up to get you and me to come downstairs to his office."

Sure enough, in about two minutes, here came one of the secretarial staff saying, "Fontaine, the governor wants you and Governor Wetherby in his office right now."

Wetherby winked at me and we went downstairs to the Governor's Office and there sat all the college presidents. When we walked in, by the expression on our faces, Governor Breathitt knew exactly what we'd done. He grinned at us and said, "What happened?"

I said, "Well governor, it just didn't get passed today. Maybe we'll do it tomorrow."

He said, "Fontaine, is that a promise?"

I laughed and said, "It's a promise."

So all the soon to be university presidents came back the next day and we passed the bill making each of their schools universities.

We had an important bill that needed to be passed by the senate. Senator Turner of Breathitt County had promised me that he would vote for it. It was going to be a close vote. The morning we scheduled the vote, I checked and found that Senator Turner wasn't in. I knew he was trying to hide from me because he didn't want to live up to his commitment and vote for the bill. I thought for awhile about where I might find him. Finally I decided that the Phoenix Hotel in Lexington was the best bet. I called the Phoenix Hotel and talked to the Bell Captain and asked, "Is John Raymond there?"

The bell captain said, "Now, Fontaine, you're going to get me in trouble."

I said, "If you think you're in trouble now, you don't know what trouble is. If you don't tell me whether he's there, I'm going to send the state police after you."

He laughed and said, "Okay, Fontaine, you might be able to find John Raymond in room 340."

I immediately called and had a state police trooper pick him up and bring him to my office. He walked in and said, "Fontaine, you're the only SOB I know who would do something like this; I need a drink."

Another senator was present and had a bottle so we gave John Raymond a drink. He downed the drink, steadied himself at a table, and went upstairs and voted for the bill.

When I was assigned to the governor's office on a permanent basis, Dick Stewart came to see me and said that Lieutenant Governor Wyatt was having a problem trying to work out a proper salary for his assistant Bob Bell. I asked what exactly did he mean and he said, "Fontaine, those boys in the governor's office don't want Bob to make any money, can you take care of it?"

I said I'd look into it. I went up and talked to some friends in Personnel and they had approved a salary of $5,000. I asked Wyatt what he wanted to pay Bell and he told me. I got the paperwork done, walked it through, and went over and told Wyatt that it had been done. I still remember how surprised he was that I could do that.

Governor Combs was looking for a way to show his appreciation for those who worked for him and for certain folks who had supported him. He came up with the idea of having "varmint dinners." On these special occasions, all sorts of varmints were cooked and served. I'm not so sure how much was actually eaten. I know I could never get enough to eat. I just couldn't eat some of those critters, but the varmint dinners were very enjoyable events and we had more and more of them.

Most of the dinners were held at the Old Stag Distillery clubhouse in Frankfort. The clubhouse could accommodate 300 to 400 people. That many people require a lot of varmints. Virtually every type of critter was cooked. We served possum, squirrel, rabbit, venison, bear, wild boar, elk, antelope and who knows what else. Over a period of time, we served everything imaginable.

Governor Combs invited many state government people and members of various groups from around the state. It came to be a great honor to be invited to one of the governor's varmint dinners. He often acted as emcee for the event. He would get up and tell a few jokes and some humorous stories. Everyone had a good time. The atmosphere at the dinners was very relaxed. On the occasions of the varmint dinners, Governor Combs was very approachable. He made an effort to greet and speak to everyone who was in attendance. This was a big task, but, there's no question in my mind, that, at almost all of the varmint dinners, he spoke to everyone.

There's one very important matter that a lot of Kentuckians may not remember: until the Kentucky Constitution was changed in 1992, the lieutenant governor became acting governor assuming all of the powers of the governor whenever the governor went out of state. In 1978, when Julian Carroll was governor, Thelma Stovall was lieutenant governor. One morning she called and asked me to come have breakfast with her. So I went to the Old Governor's Mansion and had breakfast with Thelma Stovall. And we talked, and talked, and talked at the breakfast table. Finally, she said, "Fontaine, are you in a hurry?" I said, "No." She said, "Come, let's go talk some more." So we spent another two hours talking about various topics—I spent probably four hours with her that day not knowing that she was having a call issued for a special legislative session. The governor was out of town—out of the state as I recall. And, of course, she had all the powers of the governor. That afternoon, to my surprise and shock, Thelma Stovall called a special session of the legislature to cut property taxes, which ended up being a death blow for Kentucky's economy.

Looking back, it's hard to say what was the most thrilling thing that ever happened to me in my years in Frankfort. But, I guess it was when Brereton Jones called me to come to his office, and said "You're now the secretary of Human Resources," which I didn't know was going to happen, and I was not expecting it to happen. But also, Governor Combs—I had no plans to be in his administration and he literally forced me, which meant he really wanted me.

Things happened in every administration that I am proud of, but I guess the merit system is what I'm most proud of. I was the one who pushed Governor Combs to include it on his platform in '59. I had researched it all one summer—when he became governor, I handed him the written plan for the merit system and the regulations and they got that passed. The Republicans referred to me as the backbone of the state merit system. I'm glad Governor Combs liked it and very happy that it's still around today.

41 A Few Friends from My Life in Politics

My intention in this chapter is to briefly describe a few of my friendships, accumulated over a lifetime in Kentucky politics. I say "a few" because I have made so many friends through my involvement in Kentucky politics that it would be impossible to remember all of them here. With the exception of Wendell Ford, I will not discuss here those friends whom I have treated extensively in previous chapters.

Alben Barkley: "The Veep," as Alben Barkley was affectionately known, was a Congressman, U.S. Senator, and Vice-President of the United States serving in that office under Pres. Harry Truman. In 1877, Barkley was born in a log house near Lowes in Graves County in far Western Kentucky. He grew up poor with tenant farmer parents. They raised dark tobacco that was used mainly in cigars. After struggling financially he obtained a college degree and later clerked and studied law.

Alben Barkley, former U.S. vice president
Source: Wikipedia, Biographical Directory of the U.S .Congress

In 1901, he passed the bar and opened a law office in Paducah where his father had obtained regular employment. In 1903, he married and later had three children. In 1905, he ran for county attorney and won. He was a tireless campaigner making hundreds of appearances. He loved to make speeches and to debate. In a vicious campaign in 1909, he was elected county judge. Barkley then nearly bankrupted McCracken County by repaying his supporters with a massive program of road improvements. In 1912, Barkley continued to climb the political ladder by running for and being elected to the U.S. Congress. He proceeded to serve seven consecutive terms as a congressman.

In 1922, Barkley announced his candidacy for governor. He faced strong opposition from the horse-racing and coal-mining interests and narrowly lost in the Democratic primary. Undaunted by his defeat in the 1923 gubernatorial race, in 1926, he ran for the U.S. Senate. Unopposed in the primary, Barkley defeated incumbent, Richard P. Ernst, in the general election. He made an outstanding impression in the senate almost immediately and, just two years later in 1928, was considered for the vice-presidential nomination.

During the Great Depression, Barkley played a national role as spokesman and policy-shaper during Franklin Roosevelt's terms as president. Alben Barkley of Kentucky became senate majority leader in 1937. Roosevelt's necessary concentration on foreign affairs during World War II gave Barkley extraordinary power in domestic programs. In 1944, Roosevelt chose Harry Truman over Barkley as his vice-presidential running mate, possibly in retribution for some legislative defeats at Barkley's hands. Barkley through these years in congress was extremely popular with Americans. He was ranked as the most popular Democrat in the late forties and early fifties and vied with General and President Dwight Eisenhower as *Look Magazine*'s "most fascinating" American.

In 1948, Pres. Harry Truman asked Barkley to be his running mate. In a major upset, Truman and Barkley upset Dewey. On January 20, 1949, Barkley took the oath as the nation's thirty-fifth vice president. Barkley was the oldest man to ever be elected vice-president. Being a widower, Barkley became the only vice-president to wed in office when he married Jane Rucker Hadley in 1949.

Barkley was the first "working" vice-president in the history of the United States. Because of his vast legislative experience, Truman insisted on Barkley's inclusion in all cabinet-level meetings and placed him on the National Security Council. Another reason for Barkley's inclusion in these meetings was because Truman did not want Barkley to be "in the dark" as Truman had been in case he had to take over as president.

Barkley's extraordinary speaking abilities made him the principal spokesman for the Truman administration. Barkley would have been a likely candidate for the Democratic presidential nomination in 1952, except for his advanced age. Thus, at the end of his term, Barkley retired and hosted a national political television show and began to write his memoirs. Finding retirement unsatisfactory, he entered the senate race in 1954, easily defeating Republican incumbent, John Sherman Cooper.

On April 30, 1956, Barkley traveled to Lexington, Virginia, to give a keynote speech before a mock convention conducted by students of Washington and Lee University. There he said he "would rather be a servant in the house of the lord than to sit in the seats of the mighty." At the conclusion of his address, he collapsed with a fatal heart attack. He was buried at Paducah.

In the early 1950s, when I first met Alben Barkley, he was still actively involved in Kentucky politics. He had been an extremely important person in Kentucky politics, indeed in national politics for more than a quarter of a century, culminating in his election to Vice President of the United States under Harry Truman. He was an extremely close confidant of both Franklin Roosevelt and Harry Truman. The last time I was with "The Veep" was in Berea when he stopped for a meal at Boone Tavern.

Alben Barkley's great grandson, Clay Barkley, who works for the Legislative Research Commission, is also a friend of mine. I admired Barkley greatly as a speaker. He was one of the last of the old-time stump speakers and debaters. His speeches were filled with good-natured humor and good common-sense philosophy. Whether you were a Barkley supporter or a Barkley opponent, you couldn't help but enjoy his speeches. He spoke with strong emotion, flourishing phrases, and with great enthusiasm. "Colorful" is the first word that comes to mind when I am reminded of "The Veep."

While after his death his estate had major difficulties with the Internal Revenue Service, the Alben Barkley I knew was a man of honor and integrity. He was among the greatest of twentieth century Kentuckians.

Flem D. Sampson: Flem D. Sampson was governor of Kentucky from 1927 through 1931. He was born in 1875 near London. He received his law degree from Valparaiso University in 1894. He opened a law practice in Barbourville and, in 1906, was elected county judge of Knox County. In 1911 and again in 1916, he was elected circuit judge. His reputation for strict law enforcement helped send him to the Court of Appeals in 1916 and got him reelected in 1924. He was chief justice in 1923-1924.

Sampson and John M. Robsion built a powerful Republican faction in eastern Kentucky. This faction gained him his party's nomination for governor in 1927. The Democrats were badly divided over such issues as parimutual gambling on horse races, the liquor industry and a proposed severance tax on coal. When the antigambling faction of the Democrats managed to nominate J. C. W. Beckham for governor, many supporters of the racing and liquor interests switched sides and supported Sampson. After a campaign even more bitter than usual and one in which Sampson was labeled "Flem-Flam," he defeated Beckham in a close race. All other Republicans on the ticket lost. When Sampson left office in 1931, he returned to Barbourville and resumed his legal practice. He died in 1967.

Sampson had a rough term as governor. The Democratic General Assembly killed most of his proposals. "Ripper" bills stripped him of many of his statutory powers and gave them to a three-man commission on which he was outvoted by the Democratic lieutenant governor and attorney general.

Governor Sampson was even indicted during his term for accepting gifts from textbook companies, but the grand jury's indictment was dismissed. The indictment resulted from the passage of Sampson's proposal for free textbooks in the public schools, but the plan was not funded by the legislature. To make Sampson's term as governor even worse, the Great Depression began in 1929, with devastating effect on the state. After his four years as governor, Sampson, who had served as the top official in two branches of state government (governor and chief justice) quietly disappeared from the public eye.

I had never met Flem Sampson, when one afternoon, late in the day after we had closed the governor's office, there came a loud knock on the main door to the governor's office. I opened the door to find a very short, elderly gentleman dressed with the finest attention to every detail, standing there. He said, "Young man, I'm Flem Sampson. Is your governor in?"

I introduced myself and took him in and introduced him to Governor Breathitt. The three of us had talked for a long time when the former governor stood up and said he had another appointment. He quickly disappeared almost as suddenly as he had appeared.

I had known little about Sampson except that I knew he had been governor and had been stuck with the nickname, "Flem-Flam." Our discussion of the "old days" of rough and tumble politics in Kentucky had been very enjoyable. This entirely unexpected incident was a wonderful experience for me and for Governor Breathitt. Even though Sampson was a member of a different party and from a different era, there is a kind of a bond between those who have served the Commonwealth as its chief executive. Sampson and Breathitt shared that bond and I was fortunate to be there when they met.

John Y. Brown, Sr.: John Y. Brown, Sr. was an energetic, enthusiastic and optimistic attorney who was a political maverick at least twenty-five years ahead of his time. Being ahead of his time, he lost almost all of the many races he entered. His son, John Y. Brown, Jr., governor from 1979 through 1983, once said that he was determined to win to vindicate the seven U.S. Senate races his father had lost. John Y., Sr. had managed to have a few winning races having spent one term as a congressman back in the 1930s and having won election to the general assembly on several occasions.

John Y., Sr. was a farm boy who also worked in the coal mines of western Kentucky. After graduating from law school, he became one of the state's most outstanding criminal lawyers. He built his reputation as an excellent attorney in the criminal cases that received wide publicity and, of course, his notoriety as a criminal attorney brought him many much more lucrative civil cases. He was a wonderful raconteur who could spellbind a jury or any audience for that matter.

John Y., as he was known, attended Centre College in Danville in those amazing years of the "Centre College Praying Colonels," a football team from a tiny school that ascended the pinnacle of success with its monumental upset of the great Harvard team of 1921. John Y. was a scrub on the team with such football immortals as Bo McMillan, Red Roberts, Red Weaver, Uncle Charley Moran, Chief Myers, and Matty Bell. The great Western Kentucky University basketball coach, Ed Diddle, was also on the team. John Y. always said that the Centre College football teams were great because of the players' intense loyalty to each other, there devotion and dedication to the game of college football, their desire to accept any challenge, their talent and ability and their teamwork. Those attributes of the immortal Praying Colonels were also the attributes of John Y. himself.

Many stories illustrate the character and philosophy of John Y. One occurred when the University of Kentucky was involved in the basketball scandals shortly after World War II. Brown, an enthusiastic Wildcat supporter, went to the defense of seven-foot UK center, Bill Spivey. His defense of Spivey involved striding into the lion's den because the trial was held in New York City. John Y. accepted the challenge even though he knew the odds were stacked against his client. The trial resulted in a hung jury and Bill Spivey was freed.

It was my pleasure and honor to have been a friend of John Y. Brown, Sr. for more than a quarter of a century. During the Breathitt administration, I wanted John Y. to be the majority floor leader in the Kentucky House. Governor Breathitt was a little wary of John Y., but I finally convinced him and he approved. The governor, however, agreed only if I watched John Y. closely and worked with him during the session. This was alright with both John Y. and me and we had a successful session

In 1961, John Y. ran against John Sherman Cooper for a seat in the U.S. Senate. I was drafted by Governor Breathitt, and former governors Wetherby and Clements to manage his campaign.

Of course, no one was ever able to really manage John Y. and that included me. We had no money for the campaign. He wanted to have a picnic for state employees so I contacted John Y., Jr. of Kentucky Fried Chicken (KFC) fame and he told me to go ahead and schedule the picnic and he would furnish 3,000 KFC chicken boxes for the event, which he did.

During the senate campaign, John Y. decided he wanted to go on a whistle-stop tour by train much like President Truman's famous whistle-stop campaign in 1948. Once again, Johnny paid the bill. I told the railway staff at a stop that, when I blew my whistle, the engineer would then blow his whistle and start moving the train for we had a tight schedule to keep. At the first stop John Y. continued talking well over the time limit. So I blew my whistle and the engineer started the train while John Y. was still talking. The public address system was still live and over came John Y's voice yelling, "I can't believe it! The SOB went and did it!"

John Y. wanted Colonel Harlan Sanders to be chairman of the finance committee for his senate campaign. I was ardently opposed to his choice of the Colonel. I knew the Colonel knew nothing of election laws or properly accounting for funds received by the campaign, but, most of all, I opposed the selection of the Colonel for this role because I knew he was unpredictable. The Colonel was famous for his great chicken recipe and infamous for his unpredictability. After several long discussions and debates, I caved in, but warned John Y. that he would be sorry. In just a few weeks the *Courier Journal* carried a front page story that Colonel Sanders, the finance committee chairman of Democrat John Y. Brown, Sr.'s campaign, had made several contributions to Republican candidates. I didn't say a word to John Y., Sr.; I simply called Johnny. The next thing I knew, Colonel Sanders was in Canada and remained there for the duration of the campaign. Of course, as I expected, John Y. Brown, Sr. went down to defeat at the hands of the popular John Sherman Cooper. However, John Y. didn't get down on himself over the loss. He just said to me, "Fontaine, don't worry about it, we had some fun, didn't we?"

U.S. Sen. John Sherman Cooper
Source: Wikipedia, Biographical Directory of the U.S. Congress

John Sherman Cooper: John Sherman Cooper, U.S. Senator and diplomat, was born in 1901 at Somerset. His father, a prominent lawyer, farmer and businessman, served as Pulaski County Judge, a position also held by Cooper's maternal grandfather. Politics was in the Cooper genes. Cooper attended Centre College, Yale and Harvard Law School. Cooper began a law practice in Somerset and was elected to the General Assembly's House of Representatives in 1928. He served two terms as Pulaski County Judge and then ran for governor in 1939, but was defeated in the Republican primary by King Swope.

In World War II, Cooper enlisted in the army as a private, but was commissioned a second lieutenant in 1943. He served with General George Patton's Third Army in France, Luxembourg and Germany. After the war, now Captain Cooper headed the reorganization of the German judicial system in Bavaria and served as legal adviser for the repatriation of displaced persons in the Third Army occupation zone. While still in Germany, Cooper was elected circuit judge back home in Pulaski County.

In 1946, Cooper was elected to the U.S. Senate to fill the unexpired term of Happy Chandler, who had resigned to become commissioner of baseball. He won by 42,000 votes over John Y. Brown, Sr. Cooper's bid for reelection was thwarted by Democrat Virgil Chapman. In 1949, Cooper became affiliated with a Washington law firm. Democratic President Harry Truman appointed him a delegate to the general assembly of the UN. He served either as a delegate or alternate delegate on several additional occasions.

Cooper decided to run for the senate once more and, in 1952, he defeated Tom Underwood to fill the vacancy created by the death of Virgil Chapman. In 1954, however, his bid for reelection was defeated by his good friend, Alben Barkley, and thus Cooper left the senate in early 1955. In that same year, President Dwight Eisenhower appointed him ambassador to India and Nepal.

U.S.-Indian relations improved greatly during Cooper's tenure there. Once again the death of an incumbent senator led to Cooper running to fill an unexpired term. This time the death of Alben Barkley created the vacancy. He was elected over former governor, Lawrence Wetherby. Cooper won his first full term by defeating Democrat Keen Johnson. In 1966, he won reelection by defeating John Y. Brown, Sr. once again. This was the campaign I managed for John Y. Cooper, who did not seek reelection in 1972, served in the U.S. Senate from November 1956 to January 1973.

As a U.S. Senator, Cooper cosponsored, along with another friend of mine, Jennings Randolph of West Virginia, the Appalachian Regional Development Act. He vigorously defended the Tennessee Valley Authority against all attempts to weaken it. He was also one of the earliest, most persistent and most influential critics of the Vietnam War. A 1960 *Newsweek* poll of fifty Washington news correspondents named Cooper the ablest Republican in the Senate. In 1963, President Lyndon Johnson, a Democrat, appointed him to the Warren Commission which investigated the assassination of President John F. Kennedy.

From 1973 to 1989, Cooper practiced law in Washington. He took leave of the firm in 1974 to accept Pres. Gerald Ford's appointment as the first U.S. Ambassador to the German Democratic Republic, serving in that post until late in 1976. John Sherman Cooper died in 1985 and is buried in Arlington National Cemetery.

Out of the 1966 senatorial campaign of John Y. Brown, Sr., of which I chairman, I became a friend of John Sherman Cooper. Becoming a friend of someone on the opposing side in an election has always been difficult, but to become a friend of the opposing candidate, himself, is especially rare. But this happened to me and I have always been grateful that it did because Cooper was not only a loyal friend, but also an excellent example of what a politician should be. He was honest and took firm, clear stands on issues such as U.S. participation in the Vietnam War. He was the consummate diplomat and a statesman of the world. He was just as at home talking to a world leader as he was talking to the president of the Somerset Garden Club. He was not a great speaker, but he was a great thinker. He studied issues and you knew that his opinion was based on thoughtful study, not just "off the cuff."

Several times Cooper invited me to come to Washington for a visit with him. His wife, Lorraine Shevlin, became a member of my Board of Directors at the Appalachian Regional Hospitals. In my opinion, John Sherman Cooper was the greatest Kentucky Republican politician of the twentieth century. It was a privilege to be his friend. It was a privilege to have him as a foe.

LAWRENCE WETHERBY: Lawrence Winchester Wetherby, governor from 1950 to 1955, was born in Middletown in 1908 and, ironically, is the only governor who was born in Jefferson County, the state's most populous county. He received a law degree from the University of Louisville in 1929. In 1947, Wetherby was elected lieutenant governor. When Gov. Earl Clements was elected to the U.S. Senate in 1950, Wetherby took his place. In 1951, Wetherby was elected to a full term as governor defeating Republican Eugene Siler by almost 50,000 votes. After leaving office in 1955, Wetherby went into private law practice. Then, in 1956, he ran for the U.S. Senate, but Republican John Sherman Cooper defeated him by about 75,000 votes. He served in the state senate in 1966 and 1968 and was its president pro tempore during the first term.

In retirement, Wetherby served as a consultant to Brighton Engineering. He passed away in 1994. In my opinion, his proudest moments came in 1954 and 1955 when, as chairman of the Southern Governors' Conference, Wetherby supported the U.S. Supreme Court's school desegregation order and urged its peaceful implementation as the law of the land.

In 1955, in the last six months of the term of Governor Wetherby, he requested that I be loaned from the Department of Education to the Legislative Research Commission (LRC) for a special project. Dr. A. Y. Lloyd was the director of LRC at that time. When I took the assignment, Governor Wetherby told me to come to him any time that I needed him. When I gave A. Y. Lloyd the final draft of the study, he said, "I can't accept this."

I said, "Dr. Lloyd, please discuss this with Governor Wetherby."

He did and the final draft was published. As a result of the study, the 1956 legislature enacted a new law on rehabilitation which was adopted by several other states as well. Governor Wetherby and I remained friends until his death in 1994. He lived in Frankfort and I saw him frequently. When he was elected to the state senate in 1966, we worked very closely together. Governor Wetherby made many innovative changes when he was governor for which he has never been given credit.

In many ways, Wetherby was a politician ahead of his time. He was a strong progressive leader and was very effective. In governmental reform, he worked for a governor's right to succession, something that would have to wait for a number of years before becoming a reality. Lawrence Wetherby was an excellent governor and history will record him as such.

Henry Ward: If you could appoint a governor, Henry Ward would have been a natural choice, but he just wasn't electable. He would have made an outstanding governor.

Henry Thomas Ward was born in 1909 near Paducah. He became a journalist for the *Paducah Sun-Democrat* (now the *Paducah Sun*) holding the position of city editor and editorial writer. In 1934, he was elected to the state House of Representatives and served five consecutive terms to 1943. In 1942, he served as majority leader. In 1945, he was elected to the state senate and served until 1948, when he became commissioner of conservation. He held that position until 1956 and was instrumental in expanding the state park system as well as implementing new forestry programs.

In 1956, Ward became the top aide to U.S. Senator Earle Clements, and in 1957 began working as a lobbyist for the National Real Estate Association. He returned to Kentucky in 1957 becoming general manager of the Louisville Chamber of Commerce. In 1960, he returned to state government as commissioner of the Highway Department under governors Bert Combs and Ned Breathitt (1959-1967). It was during these years that Henry Ward and I worked closely together. Then, in 1967, Ward ran for governor on the Democratic ticket against Louie B. Nunn. In a close race, Ward, the favorite, lost to Nunn by about 29,000 votes. After his defeat, Henry Ward returned to the *Paducah Sun-Democrat* as publisher. Ward retired from public life in 1974 and moved to Florida, but he returned to Kentucky in 1987 and settled in Lexington.

During the eight years when I was chief of staff to Governors Combs and Breathitt and Henry Ward was commissioner of the Highway Department, Henry and I talked on the telephone every morning at 7:00 a.m. and discussed any problems until 7:30. This was very helpful to both Henry and the governor because it meant that neither had to be tied up in another meeting each day. I would relay Henry's information to the governor and any reply back to him. This system improved the efficiency of both the governor's office and the Highway Department during these eight years. In all these years, Henry and I never had an ill word between us. We knew that neither of us would ever betray the other.

As I have said many times, Henry Ward would have been a great governor. He was highly intelligent and had good common sense judgment. He was especially efficient and businesslike. He stayed on top of the issues and could discuss almost anything intelligently. He was a decisive leader. A governor could virtually leave him alone to operate the Highway Department and never have a worry that something might not be going well. He was loyal and trustworthy.

In the 1967 race for governor, Henry had two handicaps. First, while he could do almost anything well, one thing he couldn't do well was campaign. He simply wasn't a good campaigner. He was not a charismatic leader. His manner on the campaign trail was not inspiring. Secondly, and more importantly, in 1967, the Democratic Party was in disarray after the Combs' and Breathitt administrations and the Republican Party candidate, the formidable Louie Nunn, took advantage of it. Nunn criticized Ward as a member of the inefficient and taxing Democratic "machine." Ironically, Nunn promised not to raise taxes. Of course, as governor, he did just that—raising the sales tax by two cents to five percent. Hence the phrase, "the Nunn nickel."

Nunn also closely allied himself to the national Republican Party's campaign against President Lyndon Johnson and he brought several nationally known and leading Republican figures into the state to campaign for him. Nunn ran an excellent campaign, which was simply too much for Henry Ward to overcome. Nunn made a good governor.

On the whole, his management of the state's finances was sound. He took a general fund facing a deficit when the Breathitt administration ended and restored it to solvency and kept it healthy during his term. No scandals scarred his record. He emphasized social service programs such as mental health and hospitals, child welfare, education, and state parks. I thought Louie Nunn did a good job as governor, but I will always believe that Henry Ward would have been one of the twentieth century's greatest Kentucky governors.

Jennings Randolph: U.S. Sen. Jennings Randolph (1902-1998) of West Virginia was a true friend to the Kentuckians living in the Appalachian region of eastern Kentucky and to all the people of Appalachia. I had reason to contact him on many occasions when I was employed by the Appalachian Regional Hospitals (ARH) as special assistant to the president. Our organization had two large hospital operations in West Virginia and there were times that I was able to do things for the senator that members of his staff simply were not in a position to accomplish. The reverse was also true—the senator could get things we needed accomplished in situations in which our organization was unable to act. Through these various needs and deeds, Jennings Randolph and I became friends. I grew to admire him greatly.

Randolph was a U.S. Senator from 1958 to 1985 and a six-term congressman before he became a senator. He was the last surviving member of the U.S. Congress to have served during the famous first one hundred days of Franklin Roosevelt's administration. He was born in Salem, West Virginia, where both his grandfather and father had been mayor. He was a descendant of colonist, William Randolph.

Jennings Randolph was named after William Jennings Bryan. Bryan was a close friend of Randolph's father. When he was told of the new arrival, Bryan said, "Have you named the boy?"

"No," the father replied.

"Then why don't you give him part of my name as a good Democrat?"

So Jennings Randolph received his name from the perennial presidential candidate, William Jennings Bryan.

Randolph sponsored many important bills in his years in the U.S. House Senate. He is best known for two of them. He is famous for sponsoring eleven times an amendment to the U.S. Constitution that granted citizens between the ages of eighteen and twenty-one the right to vote. He first introduced the amendment in 1942 arguing that young soldiers fighting in World War II should be able to vote. Of course, Randolph finally accomplished his goal and the amendment became the law of the land.

Secondly, Jennings Randolph, as a member and later as chairman of the Senate Public Works Committee, worked with President Lyndon Johnson to shepherd the original legislation through Congress creating the Appalachian Regional Commission (ARC). He was one of the chief architects of the original legislation creating the ARC and the chief sponsor and active champion of all succeeding ARC legislation until he retired in 1985.

Jennings Randolph had a profound love for his home state of West Virginia, for all of Appalachia, and for the nation. The people of Appalachia will long be indebted to him for his accomplishments on their behalf. His love for Appalachia and its people was unbounded. Highways and bridges, hospitals and clinics, schools and libraries are his lasting legacy to the people of the Appalachian region.

I recall another story that demonstrates the goal in life of Jennings Randolph. When he was a boy he told his father and mother that, "If I could just get a long pole and climb up our town water tower and hold out my pole, I believe I could touch the sky." This story clearly sets forth the theme of Randolph's life. He was a boy who wanted to touch the sky. And when that boy became a man, touch the sky he did. Not from the Salem water tower, however, but from the mountaintops of his beloved Appalachia. Jennings Randolph's goal in life was to help people and that's exactly what he did. He passed away in 1998. I will always miss this very special man. Like so many thousands of others, I can simply say of him, "Jennings Randolph helped me."

Barry Bingham, Sr.: Barry Bingham, Sr. (1906-1988) was a trustee of my old school, Berea College. On several occasions Mr. Bingham sent me a message that he would be in Berea on a certain day and at a certain time. This was my notice to get a group of Berea students together in one of the Boone Tavern lounges. We students would sit around on the floor and listen to Mr. Bingham discuss Kentucky, national and world events, past and present. He encouraged questions about Berea College and its most interesting history.

There is no question but that Barry Bingham Sr., owner of the *Courier Journal* media empire was a very influential person in all aspects of Kentucky life. He had great political influence especially in Democratic Party politics. He was a very kind and generous man who left his mark not only on us students at Berea College, but on all the people of Kentucky.

Barry Bingham, Sr. was born in Louisville in 1906 and was the patriarch of a family that dominated local media in Louisville and in much of the rest of the commonwealth for several decades of the twentieth century. Bingham's family owned a cluster of influential media properties—the *Courier Journal* and the *Louisville Times* newspapers, plus WHAS Radio and Television. The newspapers had been purchased by his father, Col. Robert Worth Bingham, using proceeds from an inheritance left by his second wife, May Lily Kenan Flagler, herself the widow of railroad magnate, Henry Flagler. The elder Bingham then used the profits from the newspapers to purchase the radio station.

Barry Bingham, Sr. attended Harvard then went into the family business in 1931. He took the reins of the company in 1937. At the time, the *Courier Journal* was little more than a local Democratic Party organ, but Bingham brought it into national prominence. The newspaper won six Pulitzer Prizes plus countless other awards during the Bingham years. The *Courier Journal* became the state's dominant newspaper, a position it still holds today.

He also founded WHAS-TV and the Louisville Crusade for Children, a telethon broadcast on both radio and TV that today collects more than $6 million each year for local children's charities. In World War II, Bingham served as an officer in the U.S. Navy and was twice awarded the Bronze Star.

While Bingham's media empire was very successful, his family life often was not. Both his youngest and oldest sons were killed in separate freak accidents. In 1971, Barry Bingham, Sr. stepped down from day to day operations, handing the companies over to his one remaining son, Barry Bingham, Jr. The younger Bingham's aptitude for the management of the companies was not what it should have been. The beginning of the end came when Barry, Jr., decided to bring his two sisters, Eleanor and Sallie, into the management of the properties in an effort to bring the family together. The result was just the opposite. Barry, Jr. sparred openly with sister, Sallie, and eventually, in 1984, had the two sisters and his mother thrown off the board. Sallie then announced her intention to sell her part of the business.

Finally, a weary Barry Bingham, Sr. had enough of the infighting and announced plans to divest the holdings. Gannett Corporation bought the newspapers, Clear Channel Communications got the radio stations and the parent company of the Providence Journal got WHAS-TV. Barry Bingham died in 1988. He had been a most influential Kentuckian, but, in many ways, he had experienced a difficult life. He lost two of his three sons and then saw the family's media empire, like all empires eventually do, go up in flames. The worst kind of flames—The flames of family dissension.

My memories of Barry Bingham, Sr. begin way back as a student at Berea College sitting on the floor at Boone Tavern with my classmates listening to the wisdom of this outstanding Kentuckian as he talked about politics, world affairs, and life in general. He was happy to share his wisdom and we were fortunate to be the beneficiaries of it.

Of course, I knew him later as an important consultant for the governors whom I served. He was always cordial and courteous to me. Barry Bingham, Sr.—a true gentleman.

Wendell Ford: I have already discussed my relationship with Wendell Ford in several chapters of these reminiscences. What I have said, however, is not enough. I feel the need to say more in an effort to make sense of what should have been a great friendship, but, unfortunately, was not.

I am sure Wendell had developed a well thought-out course of political action at a very early age. He was national president of the Jaycees. His career was moving along on schedule when, in my opinion, it was thrown off track when Wilson Wyatt ran for lieutenant governor on the ticket with Bert Combs in 1959. Had not Wyatt declared his intention to run for governor thus causing a split in the Democratic Party if nothing was done to prevent it, I believe Bert Combs would have chosen Wendell Ford to run for lieutenant governor as his unofficial running mate. When Combs and Wyatt got together and formed a ticket shutting out Wendell from running for lieutenant governor, Wendell's timetable was set back four years.

Gov. Wendell H. Ford
Source: Kentucky Department of Libraries & Archives

Thus, when Ford was finally ready to run for governor in 1971, his timetable was back on track and he wasn't about to allow anything to knock it off track again. So when Bert Combs was considering running against Wendell in the Democratic Primary and eventually did run against him, Wendell was determined not to suffer another four-year delay in his career by stepping aside for Combs. This determination not to even consider stepping aside, in my opinion, caused Wendell to refuse to even talk to me when I wwent to see him.

Here I was attempting to convince Combs not to run and ready to fully support my friend, Wendell Ford, for governor. For it not to have worked out was a major disappointment in my political life. Our resulting estrangement over the next two decades should never have occurred. Lieutenant Governor Ford should have seen me that fateful day I came to his office in an attempt to work something out with Bert Combs. My resulting support for Combs and opposition to Wendell was extremely unfortunate for me and, I think, for Wendell too. I will always be convinced that Bert Combs did not want to run, but was pressured into making the race by his second wife.

If those Ford supporters had not tried to get me dismissed from my position with ARH, there may have been enough time for Wendell and me to have solved our misunderstanding. I have always regretted what took place. I will always wonder if there wasn't more that I could have done to prevent the breach between us.

Wendell's term as governor was very successful and we still see the evidence of that today. His administration was honest and without scandal. He picked the very best people to head the different agencies. Two of the very best that come to mind were Charles Pryor and Jim Gray. One of Wendell's biggest problems was his own man, J. R. Miller, but I won't say anything else about that matter.

After his campaign for governor in which he defeated Combs in the primary, I always voted for Wendell. He made an outstanding U.S. Senator and achieved status on the national scene that was close to that achieved by Alben Barkley. In my opinion, historians will be very kind to Wendell Ford.

Carl Perkins: Carl Dexter Perkins (1912-1984), among the last of the New Deal liberals, served eastern Kentucky in the U.S. House of Representatives from 1949 to his death in 1984, a period of thirty-five years.

Perkins was born in Hindman, went through the Knott County schools and later taught in a remote Knott County school. He became an attorney and was elected to the Kentucky General Assembly in 1940. He was elected Knott County Attorney in 1941 and again in 1945, his tenure interrupted by combat service in the European theater during World War II.

A Democrat from Kentucky's mountainous Seventh District, Perkins was first elected to the U.S. Congress in 1948 and began his service in January, 1949. He was appointed to the House Education and Labor Committee and became chairman in 1967, just as it prepared to consider major antipoverty legislation. Many doubted whether the Kentucky country lawyer was up to the job, but Perkins' diligence, persistent commitment to liberal principles, mastery of Congressional procedure, and skills of personal persuasion soon gained him a reputation as one of the most influential politicians in Washington.

Perkins became a champion of the rights of labor, one of the nation's foremost advocates of federal social welfare programs for the disadvantaged and the father of virtually every postwar federal education program. Perkins's bill supporting vocational education became law in 1963. Perkins helped to formulate the Economic Opportunity Act, centerpiece of Lyndon Johnson's War on Poverty, and he became one of its strongest advocates. He was a champion of the Head Start program, the school lunch program, adult education, federal assistance to libraries, and federal aid for the construction of highways and hospitals in the depressed Appalachian region. He was an early supporter of civil rights. He also wrote federal legislation to improve safety standards in coal mines and to extend compensation to victims of Black Lung disease.

In his final years in congress, Perkins fought vigorously to protect federal education and social welfare programs from budget cuts and he emerged as a leading Democratic spokesman in opposition to the policies of the Reagan administration. Carl Perkins died of a massive heart attack on August 3, 1984, en route from Washington to his home in Hindman.

I really enjoyed knowing Carl Perkins. He was truly a politician of the old school. He was a master politician—the master politician of eastern Kentucky. Over his years in congress, Carl would work all day in Washington and then drive all night in order to be at home in his district by daylight. He knew almost everyone in his district by name. And, while talking to one citizen, if he saw another whose name he didn't remember, he would ask the first citizen the name of the second and, armed with the name, would run down the street after the second, while loudly calling his name. When talking to a constituent, he would put his arm tightly around him until the citizen had no choice but to surrender to Carl.

One day, Carl called me and asked me to come to Washington to meet with him. When I arrived at his office, I was escorted by one of his aides to a large committee room where Carl was holding an important hearing. I was taken behind the congressional seats to where Congressman Perkins was wielding his gavel as committee chairman seated in the middle of the members. He proceeded to tell me why he had called me to DC and to discuss the matter with me while, at the same time, he conducted the committee hearing. He whispered through his teeth to me as we discussed the matter which interested him. As we talked quietly, I looked up and down the committee and found that each member was doing the same thing. Each was involved in the hearing while, at the same time, conducting other business. It's very difficult for me to do something like that. I can usually do well only one thing at a time. Maybe this weird system of conducting other business while supposedly participating in a committee hearing is why we get so much incomprehensible legislation out of Congress.

Carl Perkins was simply a great congressman. He was of tremendous benefit to his constituents in eastern Kentucky. But not just the people of his district; he helped the poor and disadvantaged of all of Appalachia, indeed, of all America. He strove constantly for the enactment of legislation that was of direct, immediate assistance to those in need. To him, programs such as giving tax breaks to the rich and Reagan's "trickle down" economics were mere subterfuges to help the wealthiest of Americans—the people who needed governmental assistance the least. He favored and worked for programs that provided help to the people who needed it the most—the poor and disadvantaged of this nation. His work in enacting education programs and social welfare programs produced a brilliant record of bettering the lives of people in need.

In my opinion, Carl Perkins was one of this country's all-time greatest congressmen. He was the country boy from the mountains of hillbilly Kentucky that the Washington pundits said was doomed to failure as chairman of the House Education and Labor Committee. Were they ever wrong!

He became one of Washington's most powerful politicians. He became powerful by simply sticking to his good ol' eastern Kentucky values. Values that can be summarized simply by saying one should strive to help his neighbors. Carl Perkins had a whole nation of neighbors—neighbors who are better off today because he walked the halls of Congress working on their behalf. Ralph Waldo Emerson said that you were successful in life if just one person breathed easier because you were here. Millions of Americans of his generation and generations to come have breathed easier and will breathe easier because Carl Perkins was here. It was my privilege to call him my friend.

Smith Broadbent, Jr.: Smith Broadbent, Jr. was one of the most intelligent yet "down to earth" politicians I ever met. Smith was a farmer, but certainly not the ordinary farmer. He was what I would call an "agricultural developer." He was also a civic leader. He was born in 1914 in Trigg County in western Kentucky. He received a B.S. and a master's degree in agriculture in the mid 1930s from the University of Kentucky.

On his Trigg County farm, with the help of the University of Kentucky Experiment Station, Broadbent developed a hybrid seed corn, Kentucky 103, sold under the name Broadbent Hybrid. After completing work on a seed processing plant at Cadiz in 1946, he became a major supplier of corn seed throughout the south. Broadbent served as president of the Kentucky Farm Bureau in 1941-1942.

Smith Broadbent was appointed Trigg County Democratic Chairman in 1952 and held this position into the 1990s. He had absolute control of Trigg County politics. In Trigg County, Smith was king. In 1960, he was state manager for Keen Johnson's senatorial bid and John F. Kennedy's presidential campaign. During 1952-1968, he was a member of the Executive Committee of the University of Kentucky Board of Trustees. As chairman of the Kentucky State Fair Board (1947-1959), he supervised construction of the Kentucky Fair and Exposition Center in Louisville, which opened in 1956. A later addition, Broadbent Arena, built in 1977, was named in his honor. Broadbent turned over the family's farm operation to one of his four children, Robert, in 1983.

Smith was a very influential adviser to several governors. I got to know him during the Breathitt administration. During the summer he would telephone me to let me know when he was going to land his airplane at the Frankfort airport. I would meet him there and he always brought me a box of whatever vegetables were in season from his farm. He would use my car when he was in Frankfort. He and Governor Breathitt were the best of friends.

On one occasion, however, he thought that he had been lied to by Governor Breathitt and refused to come to Frankfort or to accept Breathitt's phone calls. Governor Breathitt knew something was wrong so he asked me to call Smith. Smith explained to me what was wrong, but told me not to tell the governor. This situation continued for several weeks with me attempting to resolve the matter. I talked to Smith on several occasions trying to smooth things over, but still Smith would not talk to Breathitt. Finally, Governor Breathitt told me to get Smith to Frankfort by whatever means necessary.

I was finally able to get Smith to come, but he still wouldn't talk to Governor Breathitt. After some lengthy negotiations with me, Smith agreed to meet with Governor Breathitt, but only if I was present as a witness. Smith told Governor Breathitt that he wanted me to act as "his" administrative assistant and all contact with the governor was to come through me. Breathitt reluctantly agreed. In a few weeks, however, I got the two together and their great friendship was renewed.

Smith Broadbent, Jr. was one of the best political advisers I have ever known. He had a combination of great common sense and great wisdom. Sometimes I think the two are the same thing. In any case, Smith was extremely intelligent yet his advice was always "down to earth" and practical. He was very energetic and enthusiastic. He was one of those folks who could get things done. Big things! Important things! Things like the State Fair and Exposition Center. Smith was no ordinary farmer. He was always an extraordinary farmer, but, in addition, he was also a top flight civic leader. He had a sense of responsibility and a feeling of civic-mindedness. He served his fellow citizens in so many different ways that it would be difficult to name them all. One thing was common to all his civic endeavors. They were voluntary and, in most cases non-paying. Smith felt an obligation to the commonwealth. Whatever that obligation may have been, Smith Broadbent, Jr. fulfilled his obligation to his state at least ten times over.

Edward Prichard: Edward Fretwell Prichard, Jr. was the most intelligent person I ever met. To listen to him talk about his life and Kentucky politics was an absolute joy. I regret not having recorded my conversations with "The Philosopher." Ed Prichard was both an outstanding attorney and an unparalleled political adviser.

He was born in 1915 in Paris, Kentucky. He was a brilliant student entering Princeton University at age fifteen. Graduating from college at the top of his class, he entered Harvard Law School and, upon graduation, became research assistant to Professor Felix Frankfurter. When President Franklin Roosevelt appointed Frankfurter to the U.S. Supreme Court, Prichard joined him in Washington as his law clerk. After a year, Prichard moved to the Immigration Service in the Justice Department and then served as assistant to the U.S. Attorney General and on the War Production Board.

In 1942, at the age of only twenty-seven, he became legal counsel and adviser to President Roosevelt. While in Washington he impressed political observers such as Katherine Graham, later publisher of the *Washington Post.*

In 1945, Prichard returned to Kentucky to practice law. Raised in a highly political Bourbon County family and touted in the press as a "boy wonder," Prichard at age thirty made it clear that his eye was on the governorship of Kentucky and he was considered a leading choice to succeed Earle Clements in that office. It was shocking, therefore, when Prichard was convicted of vote fraud conspiracy in a 1948 Bourbon County election and sentenced to two years in federal prison. He had served five months when President Truman pardoned him in 1950.

After his pardon, Prichard returned to his law practice, and, by the late 1950s, had begun his slow and difficult political rebirth as a campaign strategist for Bert Combs. This is the time when I first met Ed Prichard. In the ensuing years, he advised governors Clements, Wetherby, Combs, and Breathitt and, to a lesser degree, Carroll and Brown. Nicknamed "The Philosopher" by Bert Combs, Prichard came to be considered by many to be Kentucky's greatest intellect and sharpest legal mind. His voracious appetite for all forms of intellectual stimulation was legendary as were his gifts of wit and repartee. The stigma of his conviction remained, however, and he never sought political office, himself.

Prichard emerged as Kentucky's most visible political sage through the late 1960s and 1970s. In political philosophy he was a strong advocate of civil rights, strip mine regulation, constitutional reform, improved health care, and public education. In 1966, Governor Breathitt appointed Prichard to the Council on Higher Education, beginning the period of his full return to public life. Serving often as the council's vice chairman, he became a powerful advocate for Kentucky's universities. In 1980, the council appointed a citizens' committee to recommend improvements in Kentucky's universities and Prichard led the committee in preparing its 1981 report on higher education titled, "In Pursuit of Excellence." The committee afterward became an independent organization called, "The Prichard Committee for Academic Excellence." During the later years of his life, Prichard became almost blind, but continued on in his public service having volunteers read to him. Ed Prichard died in 1984 and is buried in the Paris Cemetery.

I remember one night when Governor Combs and I were working in his office on the upcoming general assembly election when there came a knock on the door. Governor Combs said, "That will be 'The Philosopher'; let him in."

I did, and shortly after, Combs told him that all of the legislative campaigns were in good shape except for the senate race in the Madison County area. Prichard proceeded to fold his arms across his chest, close his eyes for about five minutes and, opening his eyes, said, "Banksie, get me a pencil and a sheet of paper."

I did and he began to draw a picture, sort of a political cartoon, and, when he finished, he said, "Run this ad in the Richmond paper and you will win that senate race."

We ran the ad and won the race handily. That is a typical "Ed Prichard" story.

Ed Prichard was always my friend. We never had a quarrel or even a cross word between us. One reason was because I was somewhat reluctant to disagree with such a brilliant person. Especially when I knew that, even if I was right and "The Philosopher" was wrong, his position would prevail because he could defeat anybody or any argument in debate. But the truth is that I cannot remember disagreeing with him on any important matter.

His mind was not only brilliant and creative, it was also practical. His great common sense and wisdom always resulted in advice that was simple to understand and to implement. His advice was generally of the type that made you say to yourself, "Why didn't I think of that?"

In the final analysis, Ed Prichard was of great service to the Commonwealth of Kentucky. But for that one indiscretion, he could have been of even greater service to his state and, in all probability, to his country. But Ed Prichard made the most of a bad situation. He strived mightily to make a political comeback and finally succeeded. But he never served in public office. He never achieved his early ambition to be governor. In the end, Ed Prichard lived a life of missed opportunity.

Stan Cave: During both the Combs and Breathitt Administrations, George Richard Phillips was a strong supporter and close friend of both me and the two governors. On occasion, he would come to Frankfort and spend the day visiting with all three of us. I always made certain that he got to visit with both Governor Breathitt and former governor Combs. George Richard Phillips was the grandfather of my friend, Stan Cave, who has served as a member of the House of Representatives of the Kentucky General Assembly and later as chief of staff to Gov. Ernie Fletcher.

Stan Cave and I have a very strong friendship. During the ill-fated Fletcher administration (2003-2007), I talked frequently with Stan and did my best to assist him in any way that I could. I did this in spite of my having done everything I could to defeat Fletcher while fulfilling my promise to Happy Chandler to help his grandson, Ben Chandler, become governor. I want all Kentucky governors to succeed. The state has many problems and, after a governor's race has been decided, we all need to pitch in and help the governor battle these extremely difficult problems regardless of whether we voted for him.

I considered Stan Cave to have been the conscience of the Fletcher administration. He was a tremendous asset to Governor Fletcher who needed more people with governmental experience around him. I wish that I could have been of more assistance to Stan and Governor Fletcher. The difficulties the governor experienced over the administration's handling of personnel under the merit system could have been addressed in much better manner had the governor received good advice from his advisers.

After the merit system difficulties arose, Stan contacted me about my willingness to serve on the governor's newly-created Merit System Task

Force. I had a thirty-minute meeting with Governor Fletcher concerning my appointment to the task force. I found him to be very friendly and easy to talk with. He was cordial and seemed genuinely interested in having me serve on the task force.

The governor asked me if I was willing to help him. I said that it depended on what he wanted me to do. I did accept the appointment to the Merit System Task Force. After my work on the task force was completed, however, I had very little opportunity to help with the floundering Fletcher administration. I felt sorry for my friend, Stan Cave. I feel certain that Stan gave Governor Fletcher much good advice that the governor chose to ignore it to his detriment.

42 My Family

I HAVE SAVED THE most important two subjects for last. They are my family and my faith. My family has been so important to me that I do not have words to describe my love for them and their crucial importance to my life. Without my wife and two sons, all my work would have been for nothing. My mind and body were almost always at work, but my heart and soul was at home with my family.

Barbara and I began our married life in Frankfort in an apartment on Briar Cliff near the Governor's Mansion. She became a teacher at Bridgeport and taught for three years. We had a very busy life chiefly because of my position as senior aide to Governor Combs. Mrs. Combs was delighted with Barbara and we were invited to the Mansion on many occasions.

Our first son, Fontaine III, called Chip, was born on November 20, 1964. He immediately became the center of our lives. He was a very quiet youngster and a perfect gentleman. We traveled back to our home in eastern Kentucky for Christmas until I took over as Santa Claus. From that point on, our Christmases were celebrated in Frankfort. Both sets of grandparents came to Frankfort for Christmas.

Santa Claus gives Fontaine Banks III a Christmas gift in the Governor's Mansion

Our second son, Robert Presley, was born on April 29, 1970. He developed into an energetic youngster, always talking, always the center of attention. He was almost the exact opposite of Chip in personality.

When I drove to hospital to bring Barbara and baby Rob home, Chip wanted to go with me. As Barbara and Rob came out of the hospital, the baby was having a bottle. Chip was able to hold and feed his new brother all the way home.

Fontaine Banks and his wife Barbara on their 40th wedding anniversary

In 1963, we purchased a home at 136 Westover and lived there for ten years.

In 1973, we purchased two lots on Regents Park Lane and constructed the home that we have lived in for the past thirty-five years. Both boys grew up in this home. Both sons participated in normal youth activities such as baseball, bowling, soccer and dancing.

As our sons grew up they did not cause us any problems or concerns. They were told early that, if they completed high school with decent grades and no problems, I would purchase a new car for each at the end of their freshman year in college.

Our eldest son, Chip, decided to attend the University of Kentucky and graduated with a degree in Business Administration. Almost immediately, he went to work for Farmers Bank located in Frankfort. He is now the senior vice president for Investments there. Chip is married to Anne and has three children, Elizabeth Ann, Patrick Fontaine and Daniel Robert.

Banks family photo
(l-r) Robert Presley, Barbara, Fontaine and Fontaine "Chip" Banks, III

Robert Presley had a normal youth and wanted to attend Murray State University. He pressured me into attending a Parents' Day at Murray. A friend of Rob's was the director of Admissions at Murray. When we arrived we were told we were scheduled to have

Robert Presley and Stacey Banks and son Chase Forester

lunch at a certain time. When that time arrived, we were seated with the president of Murray State University. As you can imagine, he received our approval to attend Murray.

At the arrival of their appropriate ages, I took each boy to a large parking lot to teach him how to drive. For days they followed my instructions carefully. When I finally finished giving my driving lessons, I found out that their grandfather had taught them how to drive years before.

Rob majored in Business Administration and was employed by Fifth Third Bank in Cincinnati. Two years later, he moved to the Fifth Third Bank in Louisville. Rob is currently senior vice president and chief portfolio manager at Fifth Third Bank there. He is married to Stacie and they have one son, Chas.

The boys were very close to their grandparents. Their Grandfather Banks died in 1979, Grandmother Williamson died in February 1988, Grandmother Banks died in October 1991, and Grandfather Williamson died in December 1991. The boys were fortunate to have had them for as long as they did.

(l-r) Grandchildren Betsy, Fontaine holding Chase, wife Barbara holding Daniel, and Patrick standing

During the years that the boys were growing up to adulthood, I was always occupied with my career and the Marine Corps.

Barbara kept our family going. She was a fabulous mother. We raised the boys in a Christian life.

During my entire working career, Barbara has kept us together as a family. She made certain that we attended church every Sunday and that the boys were involved in all the church youth activities. When I decided, not long ago, to give my personal Christian testimony, both boys were in attendance at the worship service.

Barbara and I have been married for more than forty-seven years. During that time only one of our marriage group has passed away. Barbara and I have never had any marital problems. We have had a very deeply emotional marriage. With Barbara and our two sons and now our grandchildren, I have been greatly blessed by God.

Barbara and Fontaine Banks' sons and their families: front row (l-r) grandsons, Daniel Banks and Chase Forester; back row (l-r) grandson, Patrick Banks; granddaughter Elizabeth Ann; son, Fontaine Banks III and wife, Anne Banks; and Stacie and Robert Banks (son)

42 My Faith

My church and the teachings of our Lord and Savior, Jesus Christ, have been very important to me since I was a child. The members of my father's family were all Baptists. During the 1930s through the 1950s my great uncle, Elisa Banks, was a very famous and popular preacher in Floyd, Johnson and Magoffin counties. I had the privilege of listening to him preach on several occasions when I was a young man.

The members of my mother's family were all Methodists. My great grandfather, James Crager, was a soldier in the Confederate Cavalry during the Civil War and, when he returned home after the War, for the next thirty-five years he was a Methodist circuit rider.

When my parents married, they settled in the tiny community of Hardy, which is in eastern Pike County. There was only one church in Hardy, a Methodist church, so we became Methodists.

The church was of wood frame construction, had a pot-bellied stove for heat, and would seat about 200 people. This church was not only the spiritual center of the community, but was also the social center.

The preachers at our church in Hardy were local citizens who had received "the call to preach." The church was always full, even the standing room.

The weekly Wednesday night service always drew an overflow crowd. In the months that contained an "R" in their spelling, the women would serve an oyster stew. I have been eating oyster stew since I was three years of age.

Whenever the church doors were open, the Banks family was there. For several years I assisted the Sunday School Superintendent in collecting and counting the offering given that morning.

After I entered college, I continued to maintain contact with the Methodist Church through the Methodist Church in Berea and through Union Church located on the Berea College campus. Among my friends at Berea were three pre-ministerial students and a retired Episcopal Bishop who had served many years as a missionary in China.

During my senior year at Berea, I carefully considered becoming a minister and I applied for admission to two seminaries. To my surprise, I was accepted by both schools.

After my acceptance by both seminaries, I began the difficult task of deciding which school I would attend. After many weeks of walking around the campus day and night thinking about this decision I had to make, I was both mentally and physically exhausted. Yet I still had not reached a decision.

Then while walking on campus one evening while considering my options, I made the decision to choose that very night which school I would attend. I was under tremendous self-imposed pressure. While walking, suddenly I heard a beautiful voice in a very quiet tone say, "Fontaine, the ministry is not for you." I immediately felt a little warm and I seemed to be floating in mid-air. I do not know how long I was in this state, but it was the most beautiful moment of my life. I knew instantly that I had been touched by our Lord and Savior. The experience of those few moments and the warm glow I felt could only have been caused by contact with our Lord. Friends who saw me that evening said that my face had a glow that they had never seen before. They said I had an expression on my face of utter contentment.

After the decision had been made whether by me or by the Lord, I volunteered as a Marine recruit due to the fact that, at that time, the Korean War was going strong.

After my graduation from Berea College, I reported to the Marine Corps base at Parris Island for twelve weeks of intensive training. Following my training at Parris Island, I was assigned to Quantico for an additional six months of training. From Quantico, I was assigned to the Marine base at Cherry Point for even more training. After Cherry Point, I was sent to the West Coast. In June 1952, I embarked on a ship bound for Korea. During this whole period, I was undergoing special training and did not have time for personal thoughts about my future.

After my arrival in Korea, I had time, particularly at night, to re-think my decision not to enter the ministry. I thought about this every day for several months. I remembered the voice I heard that said, "Fontaine, the ministry is not for you." But, even so, I still had doubts about my decision not to enter the ministry. I began to once again think that maybe the ministry was the vocation for me.

Then one evening while I was posting the guard, out of the evening mist, a civilian approached. He saw my hand reach for my weapon and he quickly said he was a missionary and asked if he could he spend the night in our camp. This was very unusual since normally civilians are not permitted to enter a battle zone. Unusual or not, I agreed to allow him to stay the night in our camp.

I escorted the missionary to my bunker and then returned to finish my guard duties. When I returned to the bunker, we introduced ourselves. It was strange, but I could not remember the missionary's name even when we first introduced ourselves. We talked long into the night mostly about my decision not to attend a seminary and my lingering doubts about whether I made the right decision.

As our lengthy discussion wound down as the hour was very late, the missionary pointed a finger at me and said, "The Lord has plans for you and you will serve your church and your people, but not as a minister." When I awoke the next morning, the mysterious missionary was gone. No one in the camp mentioned seeing a civilian in our camp during the night. I asked around. No one knew who I was talking about. Nobody had seen a civilian in camp.

For many years I was convinced someone had been there. Now I wonder if the missionary may have been only a dream or a vision. I still am not certain. But whether the missionary who appeared from out of the night fog was real or only a vision, I believe on that night I was touched for a second time by God. My decision was made. My earlier decision not to become a minister was confirmed. I had been touched by the Lord twice. There would be no need for a third visit to this hard-headed Marine. I should have listened the first time.

Since returning home from Korea in 1953, in my Christian life I have done volunteer work at church especially in positions that help people directly and also in almost every administrative position in the church.

Although requested to do so many times over the years, I would not give my personal testimony in public. Then, when Reverend Jack Brewer became minister at our church and with the help of Paul Mauer and Kirk Hudson, I finally agreed to give my personal testimony one Sunday at the early church service.

My personal testimony must have been well received, for shortly after giving it at the early service, I was asked to present it at the second service.

From memory, I gave my Christian story beginning with my youth and explaining in detail what happened at Berea and in Korea. Once again, my testimony was well-received.

During the eight years I was working in the office of the governor, I was deeply involved in every program funded by the commonwealth and, in many cases, I guided legislation through the House and Senate that was designed to better the lives of our neediest citizens. The bills I guided through the legislative process that were aimed at helping our less fortunate fellow citizens were based upon Christian principles. That is why I supported them. That is why I worked especially hard to see that they became law. I know in my heart that I could not have performed well in the various positions I have held in my career without my Christian principles to guide me.

In my personal testimony, I stated that I believe in the power of prayer —prayer brought me home safely from Korea. I prayed that the woman I fell in love with would say "yes" when I asked her to marry me and she did forty-seven years ago. I prayed for the Lord to give me a friend that would be like a brother and He did.

I prayed that I would live to see my sons reach adulthood and He granted my request. The Lord has been so good to me. He has been overly generous to this old sinner. I do believe, however, that He has used me and I pray that I have responded in ways pleasing to Him.

As I finish writing my memoirs, I feel I have had a wonderful life. I couldn't ask for better or for more. Today, I believe I am living on borrowed time. I am ready to go whenever my Lord and Savior, Jesus Christ calls me home. When that day comes I will be thankful for a full and useful life filled with opportunities to do the Lord's work. Yes, even in politics, there is room for Christian principles and Christ-like actions. Many such actions go unnoticed by the media, but not by God.

Today, I am still praying. My prayer for these memoirs is that future generations of the Banks' family will in some way profit by them.

Appendix A

There are two poems I hold close to my heart. The first is a hymn by C. Austin Miles: *I Come To The Garden Alone*

I come to the garden alone,
while the dew is still on the roses,
and the voice I hear falling on my ear,
the son of God discloses,
and he walks with me
and he talks with me,
and he tells me I am his own,
and the joy we share as we tarry there,
no other has ever known.

My other favorite is the Simple Prayer of Saint Francis of Assisi

Lord, make me an instrument of your peace
Where there is hatred—Let me sow Love
Where there is injury—pardon
Where there is doubt—faith
Where there is despair—hope
Where there is darkness—light
Where there is sadness—joy
O Divine Master, Grant that I may not so much seek
To be consoled—as to console
To be understood—as to understand
To be loved—as to love
For it is in giving—that we receive
It is in pardoning—that we are pardoned
It is in dying – that we are born to eternal life.

Appendix B: A collection of Poems by Alex Rose

Fontaine Banks: The Political Legend

By *Alex Rose*

What is a "political legend," you ask.
Well, in the case of Fontaine Banks,
Explaining it is an easy task.

A political legend is a traditional, historical story
About an outstanding person who is deserving
Of fame and glory.

But, you say, for all his success, Fontaine has received little notoriety;
The governor gets all the credit in Kentucky society.
Right you are, but that's not the end of this allegory.

You see, Fontaine never sought any fame–
He made sure that others received all the acclaim.
He just did his job; he never played to the mob.

His humility and self-sacrifice only add to the legend he's made.
No, there is no doubt—Fontaine Banks has made the grade.
He's a Kentucky political legend whose story will never fade.

Fontaine Banks: The Soldier

By *Alex Rose*

From the mountains of Belfry
To college at Berea,
Then into the Marine Corps
And off to Korea.

America was in a distant war
With many soldiers not even knowing
What they were fighting for.
But Fontaine Banks had no doubt–
He knew what the fighting was all about.

"It's about freedom and the flag," Fontaine said,
"And halting Communism's deadly spread."
To Democracy and the red, white and blue
He had given his heart.
Fontaine was ready to do his part–
He wasn't about to stand by idly and watch freedom fall apart.

This was a shooting war—nobody was firing blanks–
When Fontaine Banks joined the ranks.
While far, far, from home,
From his faith in God, he didn't roam.
The Marine Hymn and Amazing Grace–
Helped Fontaine the enemy to face.

Many times he fell to his knees;
He was a Marine warrior,
But spirituality was one of his keys.
After surviving many a close call,
Fontaine returned home safely–
He did not fall.

While fighting for America in that far away land,
God had held him in the palm of His hand.

Even though he had served his time,
He couldn't get the Marine Corps off his mind.
His country, his honor, his duty
He could not ignore.
If his country needed his service again,
He wanted to be ready once more.

So, Fontaine remained in the Corps,
Ready for whatever was in store.
He loves this land of the free
And home of the brave
And to it many years of service he gave.

Throughout all his years of service
And, indeed, all his life,
Fontaine has been strong, caring and free–
The kind of man a Marine Officer ought to be.

He was a high-ranking Colonel
In his beloved Marine Corps,
When on his military career he finally closed the door.
A Marine Colonel true and tried–
A much different kind of Colonel
than Kentucky Fried.

Throughout his life,
Fontaine has served his country well
As we have seen;
Colonel Fontaine Banks–
Soldier, patriot,
United States Marine.

Fontaine Banks: The Statesman

By *Alex Rose*

From the mountains of Belfry
To college at Berea,
Then into the Marine Corps
And off to Korea.

Then back home and to IBM
With its computing machines,
Then from Big Blue to state government–
As a key member
Of Governor Combs' political team.

To be in politics had never been his intent,
But that's where most of his years have been spent.
The governor was at a loss–
He ordered things done,
After all, he was the boss,
But when he checked,
He found nothing complete;
He saw failure lying at his feet.

The Governor could think of only one way
To prevent his administration's fall–
So he picked up the phone and gave Fontaine a call.
His loss caused IBM much anguish and pain,
But the Governor and Kentuckians made a huge Capitol gain.

With "Banksie" as Chief of Staff, the Combs program
Was implemented just right.
Fontaine single-handedly defeated the bureaucracy
With all its might.
So many victories - we can cite only a few–
The sales tax, education, the floral clock and the Mountain Parkway
With its breathtaking views.

Well, that's how Fontaine's political career

Got its start,
Ole Bert Combs was plenty smart.
Next, Governor Breathitt saw Fontaine's merit
So he asked him to continue to carry the load–
For four more years to grin and bear it.
And so much was accomplished especially in civil rights -
All because Fontaine held onto those reins real tight.

Thus Fontaine Banks became the only person
To serve two consecutive governors as Chief of Staff–
It was all hard work, there weren't many laughs.
History records those administrations as two of the best–
Both owe much to Fontaine's meeting every test.

Fontaine continued on to serve almost every Governor–
It seems each saw the need for a loyal brother.
They each needed someone they could trust–
Someone who would get the big things done or bust.

Now a little older and a little bent,
Sometimes he wonders what it's all meant.
Never out front,
Slow to confront,
He wasn't out for glory.
No, that's not the Fontaine Banks story.

He left the glory for other men–
A great governor he would have been.
But it wasn't in his make-up to run–
He was the man to get things done.
So, though he worked behind the scenes,
His accomplishments are not diminished by any means.
They say for one person to make a real difference
Is something very difficult to do,
But, if you want a perfect example of such a one,
Fontaine Banks is the man for you.
He is a statesman tried and true,
A man to whom we owe a heartfelt thank-you.
All Kentuckians are better off today
Because Fontaine Banks, Jr. passed this way.

Fontaine Banks: The Campaigner

By *Alex Rose*

From the mountains of Belfry
To college at Berea
Then on to the Marine Corps
And the war in Korea.

Then back home and on to IBM
With its computing machines.
Then from Big Blue
To the political scene.

In campaign after campaign,
From election to election,
Fontaine Banks learned
The political ropes to perfection.

Nobody can organize and run a campaign
Like Mr. Fontaine Banks.
For their election,
Many governors have Fontaine to thank.

The best campaign organizer in the state,
Fontaine's work has decided many a candidate's fate.
His advice is to start early—don't be late;
Organize each county at an early date.

While he's lost a few, he's won most–
More often by far, he's drunk the winner's toast.
But win or lose in each campaign
He's given his all, just the same.

From opposing Happy Chandler
With all his might,
To organizing the campaign of his grandson, Ben,
In his gubernatorial fight.

Among candidates, with Fontaine
It's never been just "who,"
The candidates' principles matter too.
It's not enough to just win,
Fontaine wants to know where his man has been.

He doesn't expect his candidate to be without sin,
But neither does he want too many fences to mend.
He knows the issues his candidate must face,
If he's going to win the governor's race.

So if you have hopes of filling
That ol' governor' chair,
Go see Fontaine, he'll tell you
If you have a chance of ever sitting there.

But one thing is for sure–
You'll never join the gubernatorial ranks
Unless, on your side, you have Fontaine Banks.
He knows what the candidate must do each day,
He's the perfect guide all the way.
As an advisor, he's the best;
As an organizer, he meets every test;
As a fund raiser, he'll fill your war-chest;
To run a campaign,
He's simply better than the rest.

So let's give the Ol' Campaigner his due,
Like so many before him,
The next governor will be indebted to Fontaine too.

For him, 2007 is gubernatorial campaign number eleven–
He'll be running campaigns for the Perfect Candidate
When he gets to Heaven.

As always, he says this campaign is his last,
But he's had at least five of those in the past.
Four years from today,
Fontaine will be campaigning again–
Making certain his candidate gets in.

As a campaigner, Mr. Banks has no equal,
In 2111, we will see another edition
Of his "last campaign"–
The 2111 Fontaine sequel.

Fontaine Banks: The Family Man

By *Alex Rose*

While laboring all these many years
For corporations such as ResCare and Big Blue;
While working in state government for me and you;

While campaigning long into many a night,
Fontaine Banks has still managed to keep his priorities right.
First and foremost, he has been a family man

Through all the years—quite a span.
Always deeply devoted to Barbara, his wife,
He knows without her he could not have achieved so much in his life.

He loved his sons with their cheeks of tan–
They were more important than how state government ran.
Now that he's a grandfather, he still feels the same way;
"Forget the campaign today I'm going to the game
To watch my grandson play."

In politics and the corporate world,
Fontaine has wanted others to get the applause and glory.
With family members through the years,
It has been the same old story.

As a husband, a father, and a granddad now,
He did the best he could;
As he tried to be there for the family when he should.
If you ask Fontaine what his family means to him,
He says, "I cannot put such love in words except to say,
Without my family, my life would have been grim."

He worked hard and bought a beautiful house;
He's been a good-provider for his children and spouse.

But today, as Fontaine looks back over the years,
He wishes he could have been there more
To lend them his strength and calm their fears.

But Fontaine need never look back;
Nothing ever did his family lack.
To Barbara and the kids, he gave his all,
Winter, spring, summer and fall,
He always tried to meet their call.

When speaking of family,
We must remember this too–
Fontaine has accomplished so much for all of us–
Even me and you.
You see, Fontaine's family includes Kentuckians all–
Rich and poor, short and tall.
He's been a quiet, behind-the-scenes father to the whole state–
His work is helping to make our Commonwealth great.

Fontaine knows a public servant is one who helps others.
To him, all Kentuckians are his brothers.
Yes, four million Kentuckians compose the family
Of Fontaine Banks.
Through his long years of service,
He's watched them march by in seemingly endless ranks.

From the Appalachian mountains from whence he came,
To Central Kentucky where he won his fame,
From the Golden Triangle to the Western lakes
Even from Kentuckians now living in other states;
We all rise to salute–
All of us, with grateful thanks,
Kentucky's finest family man–
Mr. Fontaine Banks.

Fontaine Banks: The Christian

By *Alex Rose*

Politics isn't always the fairest game;
Some politicians are honest only in name,
Their ethics are often amiss;
Some would betray you with a kiss.

But I know a man of political fame
Who is a true Christian all the same.
To most politicians, Voter Registration
Is the most important book.
To him, the Holy Bible is where to look.

The man I speak of is Fontaine Banks;
A dedicated Christian marching in the Lord's ranks.
In an election, he goes all out to win,
But he runs the campaign free of sin.

He keeps the campaign ethical, legal, honest and fair.
God only knows how it would be run if he weren't there.
He always practices the tenets of the Christian life;
The Ten Commandments and the Golden Rule–
These are his everyday tools.

In his church, he's given his testimony–
It's clear that here is no phony.
He's held every lay position in his church–
He won't say, "No," and leave his pastor in a lurch.
All these many years, he played the political game,
But on his reputation, there's not a single stain.

He's experienced unexplainable incidents—very spiritual;
His visits with our Lord have become his ritual.

He has served his country,
He has served his state,
He has served the Lord,
He stands ready to accept his fate.

He's experienced God's love and grace;
With the Lord's many assignments for him, He's kept pace.
A great Christian role model is Fontaine Banks,
He looks toward Heaven as he gives thanks,
A dedicated Christian marching in the Lord's ranks.

Fontaine Banks: The Mentor

By *Alex Rose*

Fontaine has been a mentor to many;
All his knowledge comes free of charge–
It costs not a penny.
Joe and Eric,
Alex and Jim,
Countless numbers have learned from him.

How to organize each county,
How to get folks to contribute their bounty,
Campaign strategy—how to plan,
How to turn fence-sitters into fans,
How to make a little-known candidate a person of note,
And, of course, how to get out the vote.

On an issue, how and when to take a position,
How to get the crowd to listen,
When to let the campaign workers have a little fun,
How to defeat the likes of Louie B. Nunn;
How to avoid the cardinal sin,
In short, Fontaine simply knows how to win.

Then, when your candidate wins in the end
That's when the really hard work is about to begin.
That's when the legislature comes in.
The governor has a program to be put through,
And to get it enacted may be up to you.
But you'll be able to get it passed by the legislative ranks
So long as you listen to Fontaine Banks.

He can even teach you how to manage large numbers of people,
A job tougher than climbing a steeple.
He's managed agencies with a lot of class,

But when necessary, he's kicked a few people in the ass.
I use this questionable language because government is tough;
Sometimes it gets pretty rough.
But if you've listened to Fontaine's advice,
The problems will get solved
And the troublemakers will follow like mice.

Yes, if you want to learn Kentucky politics first hand,
Fontaine Banks is the man.
His students learn at his side,
Then scatter far and wide.
Each works to make Kentucky a better place.
Each learns to conquer the problems we face.
All over the state, Fontaine's graduates roam
All working to make the Commonwealth a better home.

The true worth of Fontaine's mentoring may never be known,
But with each passing year, it has grown and grown.
His experience and knowledge are boundless,
Fears that he'll slow down are groundless.
He'll keep mentoring all of us as long as he lives,
You see, this is one of the many ways Fontaine gives.
Yes, Fontaine is a giver,
But he gives more than just wisdom and light,
He gives of himself every day and night;
He gives of himself with all his might.
So, Fontaine, from all whom you've mentored,
We come giving our thanks.
Thanks to a great man–
Thanks to Fontaine Banks.

Fontaine Banks: The Friend

By *Alex Rose*

If you're in need of a great friend,
Fontaine Banks is the man I recommend.
I have been extremely blessed to have a friend like Fontaine Banks;
I and hundreds of others in seemingly endless ranks.
Oh, there may be a few folks who call him an old blankety-blank,
A few that would like to see him walk the plank.
But these are few and far between,
Just some sore campaign losers, I mean.

Fontaine is everything a good friend should be,
Loyal, forgiving, trustworthy, supportive and caring–
All these and more to the ultimate degree.
If you can call Fontaine a friend, you're home free,
He fits the picture of a perfect friend to a tee.
Fontaine, I want to thank you for befriending me
And Charlie Owen, Joe Graviss and Jim—another three.
You are the kind of person who makes a difference in a friend's life–
The kind who is there to help you through life's stress and strife.

Fontaine has wisdom and knowledge–
The kind you won't find at a university or college.
He loves his Creator, his family and wife;
His family bonds couldn't be cut with a knife.
He's made a difference in the lives of his friends,
A helping hand he's always ready to lend.
He's never out for revenge nor holds a grudge;
He believes that only Our Father should judge.

To know Fontaine has been one of my greatest joys;
To watch a man who handles himself with such poise.
He has sought not glory; he played his role behind the scenes,
He's made governors successes by using all his means.
If, in your life, you have just one friend who meets every test,
Thank the Lord, for you have been blessed.
People like me, all friends of Fontaine, thank Our Father each day
That in our lives, we met Fontaine Banks along the way.

Fontaine Banks: The Man You Want To See

By *Alex Rose*

In state government, the governor is at the top of the family tree,
But Banksie is the man you want to see.

Yes, the governor is number one and sits where he wants to be,
But, to get anything done, Banksie is the man you want to see.

Of course, you need the governor to say, "Yes,"
But to get it done, go see Banksie; he'll do the rest.

To get a bill passed, you need the governor's okay
And the General Assembly's too,
But it takes Banksie to get it through.

Some bills make the governor happy, some make him mad,
But, in either case, it's Banksie who takes care of them–
Good or bad.

During a campaign, the team talks about election strategy,
But, in the end, it's Banksie that they come to see.

Yes, in Kentucky, the governor is number one,
But Banksie is the man who gets things done.
So, no matter what the project or the bill may be,
Fontaine Banks is the man you want to see.

The Long, Long Road

By *Alex Rose*

Fontaine Banks has traveled a long, long road;
On his life journey, he's shouldered many a heavy load.

He's been the right hand of the CEOs and governors who passed by;
He's helped them all with many a smile and many a sigh.

He's traveled a long, long way;
He's worked seven days a week – night and day.

In summer bright and winter gray,
In the hot sun of the business world
And in the political fray.

He's never lived in a sheltered way,
But neither has he sought to shine
In the spotlight of the sun's ray.

No, Fontaine just toiled up the rugged hill–
To get things accomplished was his thrill.

He says, "Wherever I chanced to be,
There was always a need for me.

I wanted to lend a helping hand;
Politics and government I wanted to understand.

I wanted to comfort those who weep,
I wanted to help folks out of the rough and steep.
I wanted to work for the benefit of the common man;
I wanted to make his life better–
That was my plan."

Over the long, long road, Fontaine has accomplished much
And had his say,
And, most importantly, he did it all his way.

If he had his life to live over again,
He wouldn't change much;
Maybe the outcome of a few elections and such.

Today, Fontaine Banks is still traveling that long, long road;
On his life's journey he's still carrying a heavy load.

But he wouldn't have it any other way,
He's making Kentucky a better place day by day.

Fontaine Banks: The Beshear Campaign

By *Alex Rose*

When Steve Beshear decided to run for governor this year,
The first thing he said was, "I must call Fontaine, I need him here."
So he called Fontaine Banks,
The finest campaigner in the Democratic ranks,
"Old Lazarus needs your experience and knowledge,
I can't win using these kids just out of college.
I need someone to mentor them,
I'm throwing them in, you must teach them to swim.
I know you said Ben's campaign was your last,
But without you, I can't start campaigning nearly as fast.
So come on Fontaine for one final time,
Help me make the governor's office mine."

Fontaine listened politely, but in his heart he already knew,
He couldn't refuse, there was too much to do.
So the Ole Warhorse gathered himself once again,
Ready as always to help a friend.
He said, "Barbara, the number of campaigns I've run,
I can't remember!"
Barbara said, "Fontaine, forget it, I'll see you in November."
Beshear started out in last place,
But in a couple of months,
Fontaine had him leading the primary race.
On election day, Democrats turned out for Beshear,
He won by more than 30% - no runoff here.
Now it's October and Steve's 20 points ahead in each poll,
With Fontaine's support, he'll make his goal.
The Ole Warhorse has done it all;
He's worked the phones;

He's called everybody he's ever known.
He held a fundraiser and collected a lot of "green;"
He's constructed the Beshear political machine.

He opens campaign headquarters every morn;
In the side of Ernie Fletcher, he's been a thorn.
He's prepared a scheduling book so the new governor
Will know what to do each day;
He's advised him on key appointments
And the role each should play.

In the Lazarus Campaign of Steve Beshear,
Fontaine's done enough to turn a man gray,
But, what the heck, he was already that way.
Just like each time before,
Fontaine has again met the challenge he found laid at his door.
Being Governor of the Commonwealth
Is a tremendous task;
But when questions arise, Steve will have Fontaine to ask.
I wonder if the Beshear Campaign is truly his last?
We know that's what he's said in the past.

We'll just have to wait and see,
But I must admit that it wouldn't surprise me
To see Fontaine campaigning again in 2011,
And even someday electioneering in Heaven.
I can see him sitting around talking politics with the old band.
There's Happy, The Veep, and Clements too.
There's Combs and Breathitt and Wendell Ford, all up there in the blue.
There's John Sherman Cooper and Louie B. Nunn
Reliving old battles they all think they won.
All these old adversaries and friends can agree on only one man in their ranks.
They all know that the best of them was the Ol' Campaigner–
Fontaine Banks.

The Beshear Campaign: The Final Weeks

By *Alex Rose*

Each morning Fontaine Banks
Unlocks the Beshear Headquarters door–
He's always the first to arrive
On the floor.

Always ready for battle;
Always thirsting for more–
With the Fletcher campaign,
He's settling the score.

On the governor's reelection campaign
Fontaine has poured burning gasoline;
Soon the electorate will send Ole Ernie
To the guillotine.

He's continuing to douse the Fletcher folks
With gallons of flaming kerosene–
Ernie's administration has been
Placed on permanent quarantine.

Fontaine has Beshear's campaign running
Like a well-oiled machine.
Fletcher's campaigners look
Confused, bewildered and green.

Desperate, Fletcher has placed false TV ads
That attempt to demean
While the governor poses
As the Nazarene.

But the public is becoming smarter
Concerning the political scene,
In the eyes of voters, Ernie acts as if he's on codeine–
Whatever he says, you know he's not clean.

With less than a month to go,
The election is looking great–
A twenty point lead in the polls
As of this date.

But Fontaine's not feeling
All that well,
He says you can't afford to be over confident–
You've got to keep fighting until the final bell.

Fontaine knows "it's not over 'til it's over"
As the pundits say;
He counsels hard work
Right on through election day.

He knows he must keep oiling
His political machine;
Here and there he applies
A little Vaseline.

From this date to election day
And all the days in between,
He'll keep the campaigners working–
Sticking to their daily routine.

Soon Fontaine will be able to savor
A victory won fair and clean,
But not just yet is he ready
For the victory party to convene.

This election may result in the largest victory
A governor's race has ever seen,
But wary Fontaine keeps tinkering
With his Beshear machine.

Every morning out at headquarters he can be seen
Walking the floor with his cup of caffeine.
He's still thinking up new strategies
From his office on the mezzanine.

You'll find him there – a bit worried,
Not at all feeling serene.
He's always worried about
The unexpected and the unforeseen.

He's still attacking
Like an angry wolverine,
But that's what you'd expect
From that ol' Marine.
Yes, soon Steve Beshear will be governor
And owe many people his thanks,
But no one will he owe more to
Than Fontaine Banks.

Oh! By the way, there's a PS to this poem too!
It goes like this and is certainly true:

When the campaign is over and victory won,
Fontaine's work will not be through;
He will still have to explain to the new governor
Day by day exactly what he is supposed to do.

First Class

By *Alex Rose*

Most of the sand in the hour glass
Of Fontaine's life
Has passed through to the bottom
Where it lies in a mass.

But until the last grain
Has slipped through from the top,
Fontaine will keep on working–
He's impossible to stop.

He just keeps going—he lasts and lasts;
He's simply never out of gas.
He outworks young campaigners half his age;
They line up to learn from the political sage.

Great successes Fontaine continues to amass;
And everything he's done has been
First Class, First Class.

In Kentucky politics, his accomplishments
No one will ever surpass
And, after all this, he can still look at himself
In his looking-glass.

No, he's never done things with sounding brass;
Never has he been mean or crass.
With the dishonesty and deception of many,
Fontaine's flawless character has been an exemplary contrast.

Everything he's done in his life
Has been First Class, First Class.
Check it out—go to anyone and just ask.

Yes, Fontaine's honor-roll of achievements for Kentucky
Will last and last;
And he did it all the only way he knew how–
First Class, First Class.

Fontaine
(From the Chandler Campaign)

By *Alex Rose*

When Ben Chandler decided to run for Governor of this domain,
He had the foresight to call Fontaine.

Fontaine's services Ben had to obtain,
No one knows more about a gubernatorial campaign.

After working for years like a freight train,
From state government he had decided to refrain.

But he still had an itch he couldn't explain,
He missed the competitiveness of a governor's campaign.

When Ben called, he knew what he had to gain,
The ol' warhorse he had to unchain.

Yes, Ben's call was not in vain
Out of retirement came Fontaine.

His retirement activities went down the drain,
And his old touch he did quickly regain.

Long ago he promised Happy to help his grandson maintain
A winning effort in his gubernatorial campaign.

All offices, except governor, Happy did disdain,
He asked Fontaine, the governorship for Ben to obtain.

Ready for a fight was this ex-Marine,
A political legend he does remain.

Born in Eastern Kentucky amid the sugar cane,
He came to Frankfort to learn the political game.

The confidence of governors he quickly gained,

No governor could get along without Fontaine.

Governors always wanted him to retain,
This political genius from the Eastern Kentucky mountain range.

A place in Kentucky history Fontaine has already gained,
Behind many governors, he's been the brain.

Many a political opponent he has slain,
Many a would-be governor he's thrown for a sprain.

Fontaine knows the campaign work is not mundane,
"We're making history – it's that plain."

We listen to his wisdom
As he travels down memory lane.

Our young campaigners he has to potty-train,
How to win the election he does explain.

His many political stories do entertain;
He's a better storyteller than Mark Twain.

From the political wars he has some bloodstains;
But Fontaine says, "No pain, no gain."

Ben's early lack of organization caused Fontaine's shirt to be tearstained,
That the campaign needed organization he did quickly ascertain.

He operated on the organization using Novocain,
He wasn't about to let this campaign go down the drain.

He's traveled over the political terrain,
Organizing the counties and not allowing a single one to abstain.

He'll bring us as many votes as a silo full of grain,
He has 120 counties organized in a chain.

All the county organizers come to pay homage to Fontaine,
They're his army and this fall will raise Cain.
He went to Pike County, his home terrain,
To raise some money for Ben's campaign.

A quarter of a million the campaign did gain,
Thanks to the friends of Fontaine.

Through his efforts the momentum we did regain,
Now, all we have to do is maintain.

Fontaine can outwork a hurricane,
He works so hard he gives others a migraine.

There are some days when Fletcher is inhumane,
But Fontaine just calls him a featherbrain.

To Ernie he'll give much pain,
And lead Ben down victory lane.

If Ernie thinks he can win without a Fontaine,
Everyone will know he's insane.

With Fontaine at the helm, we'll be hard to contain,
We're coming on like a freight train.

Fontaine will wrap up Ernie in cellophane
And throw him through a windowpane.

Ernie Fletcher is mean and vain,
But Fontaine will send his candidacy down the drain.

On Ernie's parade Fontaine will rain,
He's making sure Ben will reign.

Fontaine will make Ernie look like a scatterbrain,
The voters will be calling Fletch a birdbrain.

The most brilliant political strategist he does remain,
Outfoxing Ernie is like taking, from a baby, a candy cane.

Ben's potential he helped to unchain,
And Ben's campaign he's helping to sustain.

Fontaine is a gentleman quite humane,
On the telephone he's never profane.

On Fontaine's record there is no stain,
His reputation will never wane.

No matter the problem and the pain,
In the end Fontaine will reign.

His spirit has lifted us like a crane,
He doesn't know how to complain.

His wit is as acerbic as acid rain,
He'll burn you so bad you'll need Solarcaine.

His political mind doesn't wander this way and that like a weathervane,
His thinking moves steadily like a wagon train.

Fontaine spends his day thinking in the main;
Thinking how to out-organize the Fletcher campaign.

Politics is Mr. Banks' domain,
Without Fontaine, Kentucky wouldn't be the same.

He's made history to the Commonwealth's gain,
In our political tradition, he's a vital link in the chain.

Fontaine's grassroots organization will Ben sustain,
For Ben, the Governor's chair he will obtain.

When we win in November we'll drink champagne,
And much of the credit will belong to Fontaine.

It's a blessing for each of us to know Fontaine,
A better friend we could never gain.

Turning Defeat Into Victory (From the Chandler Campaign)

By *Alex Rose*

It was election night 2003,
As we Chandler supporters
Watched the returns on TV.
But a gubernatorial victory
For Ben Chandler was not to be–
Change was coming–
The kind they call "sea."

Yes, election night for the Chandler folks
Was a sad occasion.
It was Ernie Fletcher who held the celebration.
He had won the election in a virtual landslide–
It would be Ernie who would serve
As the Commonwealth's new guide.

To Fontaine Banks the defeat came as no surprise,
But, just the same, it hurt him inside.
Such a big loss injured the Ole Warhorse's pride.
He had promised Happy he would help his grandson win,
But now any further political career seemed all over for Ben.

So Fontaine leaned back in his old leather chair and began to think–
Fletcher hadn't defeated Ben—it was the Patton stink.
The voters liked Ben, they simply wanted a change–
Just for awhile they wanted the Democrats to give up
State government's reins.

Fontaine knew that Ben had been running against two–
Ernie Fletcher and Paul Patton too.
Ben could have defeated either one,

But beating both couldn't be done.
Yes, Ben would have been elected to the governor's chair
Had it not been for the Patton affair.

It quickly dawned on Fontaine how to raise Ben
From the politically dead–
Change him from a Lazarus
Into a winner instead.
Sitting wide open was the perfect place for Ben–
It was the very place Ernie Fletcher had been.

Suddenly Fontaine jumped up from his chair on that sad election night;
"Ben, don't quit now we have yet another fight.
Ben, you've got a date,
You're going to be a Congressman from our state."
It's the perfect opportunity, thought Fontaine;
I've built the Chandler organization
And it's sitting right there, still in place.
Ben's all set to run in the Special Election Congressional race.

But Fontaine found Ben tired and demoralized–
Could he keep up the pace–
The speedy tempo of a ninety day race?
"Ben," said Fontaine, "you simply must make this run;
Give it your all, in ninety days it will be done."
Fontaine could detect a slight smile coming over Ben's face;
All it took was Fontaine getting on Ben's case.

Ben's opponent was Senator Alice Forgy Kerr,
But, from the beginning, it was "curtains" for her.
She ran hard and was tough,
A Forgy family member with money and means,
But it simply wasn't enough.

Well, to make a long story short,
Fontaine turned defeat into victory in only ninety days.
When the dust settled and you could see through the political haze,

Ben Chandler was a Congressman
And the Republicans were left in a daze.

They call Bill Clinton the "Comeback Kid,"
But you can call Ben that too
After what Fontaine did.

Fontaine's election-night idea had saved the career of Chandler, Ben;
Saved him from the fate of an irrelevant political "has-been."
Fontaine had been correct all along–
Even though they defeated him, the voters liked Ben
So they gave him the consolation prize
The Congressional win.
Yes, Fontaine had saved Ben from a watery political grave–
A badly beaten Ben Chandler he saved.

Today, Fontaine feels much better, his conscience is clear;
He's fulfilled the promise he held so dear.
Not exactly the way he expected,
But things turned out better than he had suspected.
Wherever he is, heaven or hell,
Ole Happy is glad that Ben quickly broke his one-election losing spell.
Happy feels that Fontaine his promise kept
When he persuaded his grandson his party's nomination for Congress to accept.

Today, Ben Chandler sits in a very safe Congressional seat.
There is no one on the horizon he couldn't defeat.
Half his time Ben spends in D.C. meeting the Congressional test;
The other half, he spends at home at rest.
Even while living the Washington political life,
He still has plenty of time for his children and wife.
With his future once again promising and bright,
He may someday run for the US Senate or even governor again
If the time is right.
For Ben, things turned out just swell
Because he listened to Fontaine's plan worked out on what seemed an election night death knell.

Meanwhile, Ernie Fletcher sits in the governor's chair–

The man who's going to clean up state government
After the Patton affair.
It won't be long now before the voters know that, in Ernie,
They elected a political hack.
In four years, they'll want a Democrat back.

For now, Fontaine sits in that same old leather chair and just smiles–
Sometimes he fiddles with the TV dials.
As usual, he says Ben's was his final governor's race,
"I'm just too old to keep up the pace."
But we all know Fontaine never leaves a job unfinished;
Ben's loss is no way for Fontaine to finish.
He will always see Ben's unsuccessful governor's campaign
As a blemish.
So, if I was a gambling man,
I'd bet Fontaine will campaign again.

Four years from now, in the governor's race,
Fontaine will back the winner – no more second place.
He'll be running the nominee's headquarters despite his age;
All the campaign workers will be taking direction from the old political sage.
And at the end of the 2007 gubernatorial campaign,

Fontaine will be drinking the winner's champagne.

The Straight Arrow

By *Alex Rose*

In this life you're doubly blessed
If you have just one true friend–
Someone on who you know you can always depend.

A friend whose opinions are always
True and wise;
Whose honesty and sincerity can be seen in his eyes.

A follower of Christ's teachings right down to his bone marrow;
A man who couldn't hurt a sparrow.
A man who always stays on the straight and narrow.

He keeps the laws of both God and man–
A man who does for others
All he can.

Many of us Kentuckians are blessed with such a friend;
Now, allow me to be frank–
That friend is Fontaine Banks.

To Fontaine growing old is just a bad habit
He's been too busy to form,
He's worked to improve people's lives almost from the day he was born.

He's learned much over his life's long range;
He knows nothing is lasting but change;
Fame for himself he's always disdained.

A political career usually brings out the basest qualities
In human nature,
But in Fontaine it only made him greater.

Oh, such men are so very few–
How blessed you are
If only one in your life you knew.

That friend who never strays from the straight and narrow–
Fontaine Banks–
A straight arrow.

God Gave Kentucky A Man

By *Alex Rose*

God gave Kentucky a man–
A man of the highest rank.
The times demanded a man of strong mind,
The kind of man that's hard to find.

A man with a great heart, great faith and willing hands;
The kind of man not found in many lands.
A man whom the lust for office would not kill;
A man who the political blood of his opponents, he would not spill.

A man whom the spoils of office could not buy;
A man whom for his reputation he was willing to die.
A man who possessed wisdom, good judgment and a strong will;
A man of unparalleled political skill.

A man possessed of high honor,
Fail him and you were a goner.
A man who would not lie,
Before being untruthful, he had rather die.

A man who would stand before a governor whom he held dear,
And tell him the truth he didn't want to hear.
A man who would defend his friend with assault and battery,
A man immune to political flattery.

A man concerned only with his public duty,
A man who could withstand the closest scrutiny.
A man never interested in worn-out creeds;
Or self-interested people who wanted favors and questionable deeds.

Yes, our state has been especially lucky,
For we have had a man interested in only what was good for Kentucky.
Yes, God gave us a man of highest rank;
A man for all seasons—Fontaine Banks.

A Tribute to My Friend Joe Graviss

ONE DAY IN 2002, after many weeks and months of sitting in my den thinking that my days were numbered and realizing that my past was much longer than my future, I heard a knock on my door. When I opened the door there stood a young man I had never seen before. There was something about him. I immediately felt that I wanted him to be my friend. That man was Joe Graviss.

I invited him and my good friend, Jerry Howard, who was walking the neighborhood with Joe, into my living room. Joe was campaigning for the Seventh District State Senate seat, which was open as a result of redistricting. His Democratic primary opponent was none other than former Governor Julian Carroll. Somehow, with my many years of experience I guess, I could sense his desire to serve honorably and make a positive difference. I also admired his courage to take on such a formidable and well-known old school politician.

Joe told me about his desire to be a truly dedicated public servant so that he could give back to the commonwealth which had so richly blessed him and his family. He said he was running to get Kentucky moving. I asked him what he meant. He replied that he was tired of Kentucky always ranking nearly at or at the very bottom of the fifty states in far too many meaningful measures of development. He then proceeded to rapidly rattle off many such measures.

He was passionate about bringing people together in order to solve many of the problems faced by Kentucky. Problems such as the low personal income of its citizens, the high drop out rate of Kentucky's students, low teacher's pay, the ever-increasing cost of higher education, the need for more college graduates and the companion need of keeping them home here in Kentucky, and the skyrocketing costs of health care. I was impressed when he told me about how well he treated the employees of his eight very successful McDonald's franchises. For example, his full-time employees all have the same health care insurance that Joe and his wife have. This is a first in the fast food industry.

Joe spoke of the need to greatly improve economic development in order to create greater opportunities for citizens of the commonwealth. He also saw the need for expanded gaming to help Kentucky's less than adequate budget, to assist the horse industry and help keep our beautiful horse farms here, and thus prevent them from fleeing to other states.

I asked Joe about his background and he told me that he graduated *summa cum laude* from Transylvania University with a double major in accounting and business administration and a double minor in political science and history. He is a Certified Public Accountant and a fifteen-year owner of eight McDonald's franchises.

Being an old Marine colonel and having dealt with thousands of people over more than half a century in politics and business, I know I am a good judge of people. With Joe Graviss, my experience told me that here was a person of honesty and integrity. Here was the type of person the state of Kentucky needs in public service. As Joe talked to me that day, I could not help thinking how shamefully many of Kentucky's political leaders had acted in the recent past and how ineffectively they had been in addressing the important issues affecting the lives of the people of this state.

My overall impression of Joe Graviss was that here is an aspiring public servant who, if he gets the chance, is going to really shake up things. I could tell that he would be more interested in accomplishing something for the people of Kentucky than merely seeking his own reelection. He said people have a right to aspire to a better life for themselves and their children. He said leaders were more worried about the next election than about helping folks to realize their hopes and dreams. He said that if this philosophy cost him reelection, then he could still sleep at night because he would have given his office everything he had without compromising his principles.

I believed him when he spoke of bringing people together, being open and honest about the issues and facts, and making progress on issues through collaboration and true problem-solving instead of the usual jockeying for the next campaign donation. It was clear to me that Joe and I think a lot alike and have virtually identical political philosophies. In his political philosophy and approach to public service, Joe Graviss reminds me of Governors Bert Combs and Ned Breathitt. They lived their philosophy uncompromisingly and the Commonwealth of Kentucky was much the better for it.

Right away, I knew I wanted to help this young man, if I could be of any service to him. Little did I know then, about five years ago, that I would take him under my wing and mentor him in the mine field of Kentucky politics and that he would also take me under his wing. Joe has been a true friend, especially in getting me out of my house and involved once again in meaningful activities. He works with me allowing me to set my own pace while, at the same time, allowing me the pleasure of mentoring him. Mentoring Joe has been an easy task because he is so eager to learn. I am extremely grateful to Joe and I sincerely believe that I might not be alive today without the benefit of our friendship and the important activities in which our friendship has allowed me to participate.

I didn't finish my story about the day Joe Graviss first knocked on my door hoping to get my vote in his race against former Governor Carroll for the open State Senate seat. After we talked for about ten minutes, he and Jerry Howard left to go knock on more doors. After a few minutes, I went outside, jumped in my car and began looking for them. Fortunately, I found them still canvassing my subdivision. I asked Joe to have lunch with me and he accepted my invitation. This began our friendship which has been for me a type of renewal of my youth.

I cannot emphasize the tremendous change in my life that Joe has made. Being a successful businessman, he has taught me many things about business dealings. I am certain that I am active today only because of Joe's friendship. Working as a team, we were the first volunteers in Steve Beshear's campaign for governor. Together, we raised the second largest amount of campaign funds for Steve's race.

Joe and I traveled the entire state for two years for the purpose of my introducing him to politically active citizens of the commonwealth. Joe is destined to once again be a candidate for public office sometime in the next few years. I have no doubt in my mind that he will make a truly outstanding public servant. Barbara and I plan on being there when he is sworn into office. In the meantime, I will continue to provide my advice and counsel as he requests it.

If ever I have been certain of anything in my long, more than half a century career in Kentucky politics, it is that Joe Graviss will make Kentucky a better place in which to live and call home.

Sources

Harrison, Lowell H., ed. *Kentucky's Governors: Updated Edition.* Lexington, Ky. The University Press of Kentucky, 2004.

Kleber, John E., ed. in chief. *The Kentucky Encyclopedia.* Lexington, Ky. The University Press of Kentucky, 1992.

Rennick, Robert M. *Kentucky Place Names.* Lexington, Ky. The University Press of Kentucky, 1984.

Robinson, George W., ed. *Bert Combs The Politician: An Oral History.* Lexington, Ky. The University Press of Kentucky, 1991.

Van Hook, J. O. *History of the Bert Combs Administration.* Unpublished manuscript.

LaVergne, TN USA
02 July 2010
188251LV00003BA/1/P

9 781883 589905